Sensuous Spirituality

———— ≈ ————

"*Sensuous Spirituality* is a courageous and intelligent book, full of theological freshness and wise insight! Out of her quest to teach the truths proven by her own
experience, Virginia Mollenkott offers a ringing challenge for women and men who
long to integrate authentic spirituality with a passion for justice. Mystics should
read it for practical instruction in bringing about a liberated human community;
and activists, for its confident assurance of the Christ within. *All* who read it will
find themselves enlivened by a new vision of cosmic wholeness."
—Gail Anderson Ricciuti
co-author of *Birthings and Blessings:*
Liberating Worship Services for the Inclusive Church

"I have always found Virginia one of the most irenic and spiritually reconciling
voices in the feminist movement. I was aware that Virginia sought prayerfully to
speak and write out of a spiritual center where she was deeply in harmony with
Wisdom, the Spirit of God. That peaceful and joyous spiritual voice has reached a
wonderful richness and maturity in this book. Virginia shares with us the deepest secrets of her striving to be one with the Spirit. The chapters dealing with
reconciliation and forgiving one's enemy will, I believe, become spiritual classics.

"Even where I find myself in disagreement with Virginia (as I do to some extent
in the discussion of abortion), I find her fairness and openness to dialogue and
obvious effort to put herself in the shoes of her adversary provide the ideal context
for mutual understanding and the real openness of mind necessary for the Spirit of
Wisdom to resolve antagonisms and open hearts."
—John J. McNeill
author of *Taking a Chance on God:*
Liberating Theology for Gays, Lesbians and
Their Lovers, Families and Friends

"For those whose concern with the Human takes precedence over gender, race, and creed, careful study of this immensely erudite and passionate plea for the full integration of our lesbian, gay, and bisexual fellow humans in our consistently 'hetero-patriarchal' culture is mandatory. It is indeed 'sensuous and passionate.'"

> —Frederick Franck
> author of *To Be Human Against All Odds*

"This wonderfully readable and challenging book reaches across the chasms that divide people of faith over issues that cluster around sexual matters. Always seeking to bridge passionate divisions so as to enable persons to be 'generous' to those who differ, Dr. Mollenkott models her teaching that 'people create social change by *being* the social change they are looking for.'

"Alive with fresh images (bridges and brakes, angels and dancing gazelles, needlepoint and moths), this book reads like a good conversation with a wise and deeply spiritual woman. Dr. Mollenkott is both! Her straightforward Christian convictions are based on the authority of Scripture, her wide-ranging literary background, and her own faith journey — all of which she shares in a very personal way.

"I know of no one else who can speak as persuasively and sensitively to evangelical persons about sexism, patriarchy, heterosexism, pro-choice decisions, sexual abuse, divorce, homosexuality, inclusive God language, and the host of other critical issues for Christians that cluster around sexual matters. But she is equally challenging to persons who share her point of view — but who may be without the grace-filled generosity of spirit and love for the Scriptures that are embodied in the author's faith expression."

> —Jeanne Audrey Powers
> General Commission on Christian Unity
> and Interreligious Concerns
> The United Methodist Church

Sensuous Spirituality

OUT
FROM
FUNDAMENTALISM

―――― ≈ ――――

Virginia Ramey Mollenkott

CROSSROAD • NEW YORK

1992

The Crossroad Publishing Company
370 Lexington Avenue, New York, NY 10017

Copyright © 1992 by Virginia Ramey Mollenkott

Printed in the United States of America

Library of Congress Cataloging-in-Publication Data

Mollenkott, Virginia R.
    Sensuous spirituality : out from fundamentalism / Virginia Ramey Mollenkott.
        p.   cm.
    Includes bibliographical references.
    ISBN 0-8245-1168-9
    1. Feminist theology.   2. Mollenkott, Virginia R.   3. Lesbian clergy — United States — Biography.   4. Homosexuality — Religious aspects — Christianity.   5. Feminism — Religious aspects — Christianity.   6. Fundamentalism.   7. Church work with gays.
I. Title.
BT83.55.M64   1992
230'.082—dc20   92-4943
                                                                      CIP

Dedicated to my darling Debra
for
thousands of reasons
and
in loving memory
of my dear mother
May Lotz Ramey
(1902–1989)

CONTENTS

— ≈ —

Preface
Some Essential Explanations and Acknowledgments   9

Chapter One
The Heart of the Matter   15

Chapter Two
A Tale of Two Handmaids   29

Chapter Three
Midwifing Justice as the Wisdom of God Herself   41

Chapter Four
Biblical Support for Honoring Human Diversity   56

Chapter Five
Femininity, Masculinity, and Human Fulfillment   72

Chapter Six
Gender Constructs and the Human Imaging of God   83

Chapter Seven
Eros Is a Spiritual Urge   96

Chapter Eight
The Sex-Love-Justice Connection
in the Hebrew and Christian Scriptures   109

Chapter Nine
Some Beatitudes for Today's Church:
Toward Becoming More Functional Church "Families"   125

Chapter Ten
Procreative Self-Direction and a More Just Society   139

Chapter Eleven
The Lesbian, Bisexual, and Gay Community
as Social Transformer   152

Chapter Twelve
Building Bridges between Interpretive Communities   167

Appendix A
Milton's Use of the Bible
to Defend Divorce for Incompatibility   189

Appendix B
Diverse Forms of Family Mentioned or Implied
in the Hebrew and Christian Scriptures   194

Works Cited   199

SOME ESSENTIAL EXPLANATIONS
AND ACKNOWLEDGMENTS

———— ≈ ————

Explanation One: Regarding Pronouns

In this book I am going to use the "generic feminine" pronouns *she* and *her,* a usage I hasten to acknowledge as a tongue-in-cheek feminist invention. Since it is men who usually consider language issues trivial and women who usually consider them important, a syndicated columnist once suggested, and I agree, that we "use a pronoun that pleases women. Men don't care what it is as long as it's not clumsy so, from now on, let's use 'she' to refer to the standard human being. The word 'she' includes 'he' so that would be fair. Anyway, we've used 'he' for the past several thousand years and we'll use 'she' for the next few thousand; we're just taking turns" (Gena Corea, as quoted in Miller and Swift, 33). Although I usually use genuinely inclusive language, I am so tired of grassroots resistance to it that I am trying the "generic she" as a refreshing alternative to traditional usage.

Why not? In the first place, we feminists are often accused of lacking a sense of humor. So by using the "generic she" in the midst of a heteropatriarchal society in which *man* is still considered both generic and normative, I am both proving that I have a sense of humor and providing my readers with an opportunity to exercise theirs. In the second place, anybody with their vision intact can see that not only does the word *she* visually include the word *he,* but the word *her* also visually includes the word *he*. Therefore, the "generic feminine" pronoun in English is inclusive in a way that the "generic masculine" never was. In the third place, that distinguished reference work called the *Oxford English Dictionary* has no entry for a generic use of *he,* but does explain that *they* is "often used in reference to a singular noun made universal by *every, any, no,* etc. or applicable to one of either sex." The closest the *Oxford English Dictionary* gets to a "generic he" is the use of *he* concerning "things not sexually distinguished"; and surely nobody would wish to argue that the two halves of the human race are "not sexually distinguished"! In the fourth place, to the best of my knowledge, rules about using *he* generically to mean both men and women were invented by a single male grammarian in the eighteenth century. If he could make up rules that had the effect of constituting maleness as the linguistic standard for being human, why can't women make up different rules that move femaleness into the linguistic center?

In the fifth and final place, if readers do not like my "generic feminine" pronouns, I will happily settle for genuinely inclusive language in the future. As Alma Graham has written, "If you have a group half of whose members are A's and half of whose members are B's and if you call the group C, then A's and B's may be equal members of group C. But if you call the group A, there is no way that B's can be equal to A's within it. The A's will always be the rule and the B's will always be the exception — the subgroup, the subspecies, the outsiders" (Miller and Swift, 32). Most publications now use inclusive language, which calls the human group C, except for God-language, which remains predominantly masculine and therefore perpetuates the normativeness of group A (the male group). But the language of most people's daily conversation has continued to refer to group A as *both* the name of the male half of the human group *and* the name of the whole group, making the female members (group B) into a subspecies of outsiders. In this book I am reversing the process, using B pronouns to refer both to the female half of the human group and to the human group as a whole. If anyone objects, wonderful — I'll be happy to settle for group C pronouns forever afterward. In the English language viewed historically, that would mean using *they* not only as a plural pronoun but also as a singular pronoun applicable to one of either sex. Is anybody ready to defy that eighteenth-century grammarian and switch their allegiance from "generic he and his" or "generic she and hers" to the genuinely generic precedent "generic they and theirs"? I hope that by the end of this book we'll *all* be ready for "group C" pronouns!

Explanation Two: Regarding God-Language

If my third-person singular pronouns are an attempt to give group A an opportunity to feel how it is to be subsumed under group B, and to give group B an opportunity to feel standard and normative at least for the duration of this book, in my God-language I am attempting balance of another sort. I believe that there is One Ultimate Interrelational Being who undergirds all personhood and relationships, One Consciousness that flows through all consciousness, One Love that is unconditional and embraces everything that lives (and everything *does* live). My name for this Cosmic Energy or Consciousness is God. I dislike the word *Goddess* because in our social context that word implies the presence of a second All-Encompassing Being — surely a contradiction in terms and logic. In a human race constituted of half males and half females, the term *God* ought to imply the presence of a *Goddess*-component just as strongly as the term *Goddess* implies the presence of a *God*-component: but after centuries of heteropatriarchal emphasis on male separateness, autonomy, and individualism, it doesn't.

However, I firmly believe (and will argue in Chapters Five and Six) that exclusively masculine God-language has created a serious imbalance in human society, causing ego-inflation in too many men and self-abnegation in too many women. Although the dictionary does not assign a gender to the term *God,* which is usually defined simply as "the supreme or ultimate reality," centuries of using exclusively masculine pronouns concerning God have established the word as masculine-gender in all but the most sophisticated theological minds. The predominance of masculine God-imagery such as King, Master, and Father has of course intensified the androcentric connotations of the term *God*.

Therefore, in order to restore a balance that will be healthier for human relationships, I have chosen to use capitalized feminine pronouns concerning God. It is my hope that by referring to God as *She,* the androcentricity of the term *God* will be offset and balanced by the gynocentricity of the capitalized feminine pronouns. To refer to *God Herself* seems to me a humanly just way of referring to the One who is neither male nor female nor neuter, and yet all-inclusively male and female and neuter.

Explanation Three:
Regarding My Sense of Primary Accountability

In her book *Speaking of Christ,* Carter Heyward explains her subtitle, which is *A Lesbian Feminist Voice:*

> At this moment in United Stated history, a largely reactionary church and state as well as progressive movements are attempting to keep lesbians and gay men in the closet and to mute the radical implications of genuinely feminist voices. In this context, it is critical that we who can (we who have access to publishers, for example) simply speak the words, "I am lesbian. I am feminist." The words I speak — whether about grocery shopping, Anglican spirituality, sex, or Christ — are lesbian feminist words because I speak them. (11)

Like Carter Heyward, I speak and always have spoken in a lesbian voice; the feminism came much later than the lesbianism, signs of which were apparent in me by age four. Although I have come to identify myself essentially as a spiritual being who is currently having embodied human experiences, those experiences have been authentically lesbian for as long as I can remember. (My heterosexual marriage was the attempt of a brainwashed fundamentalist to fit herself into the heteropatriarchal mold. I enjoyed motherhood, and I enjoyed respectability; but they were *all* I enjoyed.)

The first time I was empowered by Carter Heyward was when, inspired by her example, I added heterosexism to my list of sinful *-isms* when I was preaching. I half expected the church walls to crash in upon me when I pronounced the word, but I felt encouraged when they stood firm. Carter has inspired and empowered me many times since: it was her coinage *Godding* for instance that became the title of one of my books. It had become so integral to my own thinking when I wrote the book that I forgot where I had heard the word; but having re-read Carter's work, I gladly acknowledge that debt. And now Carter challenges me to "signal for the reader my sense of primary accountability" (10). So, Carter, I do just that: I am lesbian. I am feminist. And my special people are feminist lesbian women and gay men. My primary communities of accountability are the lesgay community and the feminist and womanist communities and, to one degree or another, liberation communities everywhere.

Explanation Four: Regarding the Current Social System

Throughout this book I refer to the structure of society as *heteropatriarchy*. That's a mouthful: but worth naming accurately, I think. Readers of feminist literature will be accustomed to the word *patriarchy*, referring to the hierarchical ways of organizing by which everyone and everyone is ranked and whatever is male and white tends to get the upper hand. People and things cannot simply be *different* from one another: one way of being, doing, and thinking must always be the norm, everything else being *abnormal*. So white skin is superior to skin of other colors, men are superior to women, the rich are superior to the poor, youth is better than age, thin is better than fat, straight is better than gay, reason is better than passion, and so forth. And of course the "superior" are often ready to use force to maintain their "superiority." Patriarchy is a profoundly mistaken social system that has caused misery to millions and could yet cause the destruction of humankind and the planet we share together.

But why *hetero*patriarchy? Because male supremacy is maintained by teaching young women that their destiny is to meet the needs of men and by teaching young men that their masculinity depends on gaining control over women. Compulsory heterosexuality is the very backbone that holds patriarchy together. And it seems to me important that the backbone be named prominently and repeatedly. If ever society is to turn from patriarchy to partnership, we must learn that lesbian, bisexual, and gay issues are not just private bedroom matters of "doing whatever turns you on." They are wedges driven into the superstructure of the heteropatriarchal system. That is the reason for the rage at the lesgay community's increasingly public presence. Most Americans will tolerate differences as long as they are kept shamefacedly secret. But the American right-wing senses that a widespread revolt against compulsory heterosexuality would bring abouᵗ the downfall of heteropatriarchy. I agree, at least to the degree that overcoming heterosexism would be a major step in the direction of pluralism and the acceptance of difference, and therefore of greater human health.

Explanation Five: Regarding Documentation

Instead of providing footnotes or endnotes for my quotations and citations of the works of others, I am following the recommendations of the Modern Language Association, which seem to me simpler and easier than traditional footnoting. That is, at the back of this book I have provided a list of all works quoted from or cited in my text. In the text itself, I have placed the last name of the author in a parenthesis immediately following any quotation or concept drawn from her work, usually with the relevant page number, but just the author's name if the reference is to a book or essay as a whole. All the interested reader needs to do to get full documentation is to flip to the alphabetical list of Works Cited. In those instances where I have utilized more than one work by a single author, the parenthesis will contain an abbreviated title as well as the author's surname: for example (Heyward, *Speaking*, 10). I have used footnotes only to give important information that would otherwise disturb the flow of my prose.

Acknowledgments

I feel profound gratitude to Debra Lynn Morrison, my dear life partner, for her loving and wise companionship during the years that this book has been gestated and delivered and for her kindness in word-processing the manuscript. I am grateful to my colleagues Dr. Carole Sheffield, Dr. Linda Hamalian, Arlene Holp Scala, and Dr. Janet Pollak for their special solidarity, and to my friends and former students Judy Baker Fronefield, Lynne Insley, Karen Booth, and Maria Wiseman for their ideas and their warm supportiveness. I thank John McNeill, a brother to my soul. I thank my mother for clinging to life until I could get to her deathbed, so that I could be present for the moment of her homegoing; and I deeply appreciate the several assurances she has since given me that she has "never felt better in her life." The strength of our ongoing relationship flows through this book.

I am grateful to my father and his wife for their expressions of love. I thank Linda and Jack Canning for supplying me with some books and tapes that have been most helpful, and for their friendship as well as the friendship of their wonderful children, Lanier and Ty Gardiner Canning. I thank the Rev. Dr. Gail Ricciuti, whose friendship, books, and correspondence are among my deepest delights; and Zoe White, whose articulation of ethical nuances repeatedly astonishes me. I thank Beverly Amorine Gibson, my college roommate, for keeping the vows of friendship we made forty years ago when we recognized each other instantly. Although we have lived separate and very different lives, our spiritual wavelength has always been similar.

I thank Wanda and Richard Lollar for proving to me by their very lives that it is possible for heterosexual fundamentalist people to become inclusive in response to new information and the love of God. And thanks to all the other dear people who light up my life, especially my son, Paul Mollenkott, and his partner, Barbara Yodice Mollenkott; my brother, Bob Ramey; the Morrison family; Nancy, Paul, and Joshua Bakelar; Ruth and George Canning; Letha Dawson Scanzoni; Dr. Rebecca Bowers; Ruth Tonkin; Dr. Marilyn Mollenkott; Karen Hughes; Inge Lederer; and Alice and Wally Howard. I also thank my editor at Crossroad Publishing Company, Frank Oveis, for his nonintrusive style.

Above all, I thank the angels who always hover near and the Depth that has called to my depths throughout this writing.

Chapter One

THE HEART OF THE MATTER

———— ≈ ————

When I was young, I memorized a lot of Scripture, all from the venerable King James Version of 1611. One of the passages I memorized was Jeremiah 17:9: "The heart is deceitful above all things, and desperately wicked: who can know it?" I now understand passages like that to be talking about the human ego-nature that imagines itself separate from God and separate from all other creatures, as opposed to the eternal and holy Self that is the human essence. In other words, I now understand that such passages refer to what the apostle Paul called "flesh," *sarx:* "the state of illusion in which the natural, fallen [human being] found [herself] believing that [she] had [her] life at [her] own disposal, that [she] could live out of [her] own resources, that [she] was not utterly and wholly dependent upon God" (Cole, 95). Paul contrasted "flesh" with "spirit," the sense of connectedness with God that is at the human core. But that is not what I was taught during my early years. Instead, I was given to understand that passages about the ego or "flesh" were descriptions of my deepest, most essential being, the very core of my personhood, which could be redeemed and controlled only by the installation of a totally-other Christ-nature (a pacemaker of the soul).

Consequently, I was suspicious of any psychologists or theologians who spoke of the goodness and beauty of the human core, "the dearest freshness deep down things" that Jesuit poet Gerard Manley Hopkins rejoiced in. No matter how much distortion has been produced in the personality because of its response to threats and traumas, several psychologists pointed out, underneath all the damage lies hidden a beautiful Self. I desperately wanted to believe them, but I was blocked by the interpretation of the Bible that I had been taught. And of course, at the time I was confusing a human interpretation with the absolute truth of what the Bible teaches.

So how does a fundamentalist who believes she is essentially and totally depraved become transformed into a person who knows she is an innocent spiritual being who is temporarily having human experiences? The answer is: through a long and gradual process involving the study of hermeneutics; a great deal of dreaming and learning to interpret those dreams; extensive journalling; psychological use of the *I Ching* and the Tarot to learn something about the movement of my unconscious mind; agonizing struggles with *A Course in Miracles;* studying the works of Paul Norman Tuttle; reading up on the hermetic tradition and on spiritual healing; much pondering of great theological poets like John Milton and Emily Dickinson; listening to and reading outstanding thinkers among my contemporaries; learning how to love and be loved; the experience of my mother's death and thereafter our continued closeness; here and there, some psychotherapy; and some mildly mystical experiences.

Inasmuch as I still sometimes revert to the judgmentalism and divisiveness of a human ego that is on its own in a hostile world, the process continues. But there was for me one distinct "holy instant" when my basic perception of myself flipped into a different mode. Prior to that "holy instant," I had inched my way from believing myself totally depraved (although redeemed by God's grace) to believing myself a basically decent human being who was having some lovely spiritual experiences. But one day while I was meditating, I experienced a reality that was even better than that: like my Elder Brother, Jesus, I am a sinless Self travelling through eternity and temporarily having human experiences in a body know as Virginia Ramey Mollenkott.

What is ultimately real about me, I realized, is the Consciousness that is currently within my body but even now is not limited to my body, since I can in my mind visit England or Japan in an instant. My body is not unimportant; it is in fact very important as the colleague of my soul. But its limitations are not my Self's limitations, for my Self is a consciousness within the all-embracing Consciousness I call by the name of God. Her consciousness is in mine, and mine in Hers, in a communion people sometimes feel when we are with a close friend and both of us get the same idea at the same moment.

Perhaps my Self has been on earth before in other bodies, perhaps not. That's not important to me. What is important is that my life, like all life, is eternal and is holy. During that first moment of feeling my oneness with God, I felt that at long last, I was home — home in the all-encompassing nature of a Loving God I had only imagined I had left. My loneliness was gone. I wept with the relief of knowing at last that I am and always have been home.

Never in my over fifty years of living had I really felt totally at home, except for little flashes of lightsome moments here and there. But since that first timeless "holy instant,"* I have been confident that wherever I am and whatever is happening, I am always and inevitably home.

The Ultimate, the Sacred, God Herself is everywhere at the core of everything and everyone (including me). If someone (including me) is acting nasty, it is because they are mistakenly identifying with their confused and superficial ego, trying to fend off guilt by projecting it onto somebody else. They are also using mechanisms they developed as children in an attempt to protect their precious and innocent core from the cruelties of a society that does not remember its Source. But because the nastiness stems from fear and error, the appropriate response to it is not judgment but a loving correction of perception. That is, if someone meets my nastiness with a good-humored and respectful response, their refusal to counterattack tends to jolt me into remembering my oneness with my sacred Source. It gives me hope that my ego-based fears about myself are unfounded, so that I can remember the One in whom I live and move and have my being (Acts 17:28). And when I remember my never-broken oneness with my divine Source, I am secure again and there is nothing to fear, hence no need to be snide or defensive. After all, everyone else at their core is exactly who I am: undivided from God Herself, ultimately secure in a love that can never be broken. Whether or not we are able to recognize each other's holiness during this little life, I believe that eventually we all will rejoice together in the bliss of universal at-one-ment.

Every Instant a Holy Instant?

Since that first conscious experience of heaven on earth, I have occasionally experienced timeless "holy instants" when it is easy to believe that eternal love will be the final word of the universe. (Are these moments what poet Henry Vaughan meant by "bright shootes [rays] of everlastingness"?) For instance, recently I was facing a weekend in which a former lover and I were planning to try to heal the unresolved grievances stemming from a break-up that had occurred over thirty years ago. As the date approached, I grew tense with the fear that reconciliation would fail, and that instead of developing a fiercely tender authentic friendship (Hunt), we might by speaking our painful perceptions destroy even the superficial friendship we had maintained through the years. I journalled; I prayed; I meditated; I asked that God's Self would manifest *through* and *in* and *as* my Self. And suddenly the still small voice of the Holy Spirit spoke in my heart: "Relax.

---

*The term *holy instant* comes from the three-volume set *A Course in Miracles* (see Works Cited for publishing information). References to "the holy instant" occur in the *Text Book*, 282, 288, 289, 290–93, 297–98, 300, 302, 305, 324–25, 335, 337, 340, 345, 354–55, 357–58, 362, 366, 369, 378, 419, 533–35.

I'm going to do this for you. Everything is going to be wonderful. Sit back and watch the miracles." And despite great frankness on both sides, the reconciliation did take place in an almost effortless fashion that was nothing like the ego-ridden struggles of former years. I came home feeling that in fact I had stood still and seen the salvation of the Sovereign Spirit, the one Person whose Personhood undergirds all personhood and can make even enemies (let alone alienated friends!) be at peace with one another.

My goal is to live in constant awareness of the heaven that is always there whether I am aware of it or not. I would like *every* instant to be a "holy instant." To that end, every day I pray this prayer: "Fill me today with all [that You are]. I don't want to continue trying to maintain this presence of a [separated ego] personality any longer. Fill me with the Light and reveal Me to me. Reveal Your Self to me, in me, as Me; and exalt my poor perception of myself into its primitive and natural state of divinity" (Tuttle, *Conversations*, Sept.–Oct. 1988, 19).

Because I am currently partaking of the human condition, I realize that the best I probably will be able to do is to lower the percentage of times that I react out of an alienated ego and raise the percentage of times that I invite the Holy Spirit to be channeled through my thoughts, words, and actions. I have learned that when I am centered in my Self and feeling loving, joyous, and peaceful, I am completely reliable and trustworthy. But when I am disturbed, fearful, anxious, or angry, I know that my ego is at the helm. At such times, I try never to make important decisions, and I urge my friends and students not to take any advice I might offer them in that frame of mind. Then, as soon as I possibly can, I bring myself back to the point of willingness to be filled with all that is loving. It isn't easy; the human ego dies *hard*. Dan Millman tells this story on himself: he said to the Holy Spirit "Please *fill me*. Why don't you fill me?" And the Holy Spirit responded, "I *do* fill you. But you keep *leaking!*"

All I have to contribute to bringing about the "holy instant" is my willingness to turn away from my ego and toward the Christ-nature (the sinless Self shared by every human being). I have discovered that the Holy Spirit and hosts of angels and spiritual beings eagerly await our willingness to be transformed and instantly spring into action when we ask for help.

I have discovered that if I need to know the answer to a question that is troubling my mind, I can ask that question when I am in a quiet, relaxed, and centered state of mind, and the answer will be given to me. Usually, for me, it works this way: I write the question in my journal, stating it as precisely as I possibly can. Then I write the words *"The Answer:"* — after which I close my eyes and listen expectantly for the Spirit's reply. A beginning concept occurs to me (sometimes something very surprising to me), and I begin to write. Usually the words pour onto the page very rapidly; but if I get stuck I simply close my eyes and listen once again. I never hear any external voice, but certainly concepts occur to me that did not come from my ego; and sometimes alternatives are offered that had never occurred to me before. Do they come from my unconscious mind? Or from a collective unconscious mind as postulated by psychologist Carl Jung? Do they come from my own wisdom, tapped because I am relaxed and focused? Do they come "supernaturally," from my guardian angel, a Spirit Guide, the Holy Spirit, or Jesus, or God's Self? It certainly seems to me as if they come from a "supernatural" Source. But since we human beings are *one* with our Sacred Source anyhow, does it matter? The important thing is that the answers *do come*.

How do I know that this process is not simply a masked form of egotism? This is how I know: in these answers, my personhood is never more central than everyone else's personhood, and my agenda is never more important than that of every other person involved in the question. There is no judgmentalism, only gentleness. It is the most wonderful, liberating sensation to witness my own identity displaced from the position of greatest importance and to see myself instead as part of a tender, gently interconnected web of relationships and realities that are entirely sacred and unstrained.

A Variety of Methods for "Hearing" the Spirit

I assume that not everybody would receive their answers through my method. Answers would probably be received very differently by people who are not comfortable with writing, or who are auditory or kinesthetic types rather than visual types. Despite the fact that other people's experience may be extremely different from my own, however, I will offer one example of how the process works for me, in the hope that others may be able to make their own application. I first tried this process after reading Paul Norman Tuttle's *You Are the Answer: A Journey of Awakening;* yet my process seems to be somewhat different from his. It seems to me wise to give the Holy Spirit plenty of elbow room so that we do not limit our experience to what we can imagine ahead of time.

Nevertheless, here's one example of my own question-answer process, drawn from my ninth journal (August 1990–January 1991, 168–71):

I have been feeling overwhelmed with work, . . . so I am going to ask for help from my Inner Guide concerning my work load. My question is, *what can I do to lower the pressure upon myself?* There are always letters to write, speeches to research and write, materials to sort and file, people to call or see, so that there never seems to be time to relax and be contented, just to enjoy being still. This isn't right. I *know* it isn't right — and yet it is human need I'm trying to respond to. What should be my attitude? . . . *What is the God's-eye view of my work load?*

The Answer: Virginia, you have correctly perceived that the problem lies in your attitude, not in the work load itself. You and I have
all eternity to get done whatever really needs to get done. While you
are in the human sphere, holding down a job, you must meet certain
expectations — but it is not really those that are wearing you out.
When you get a letter or card from someone, you should not automatically assume that you have to answer it. . . . If you want to finish
projects that come from your own center, you cannot drive yourself
to meet everybody's needs who asks you to do so. When you try to
do that, you are trying to love your neighbor *more* than yourself, and
are doing so because of your early training that your mother's needs
were more important than your own. Please ask me what needs to
be answered and what simply filed or discarded. I will help you to
discern. . . . Your work load will be transformed when you remember
to allow me to be your partner in it. You are an eternal being, as I
am. You have all the time in eternity (to coin a paradox). *Remember
that.* Work in a relaxed manner at all times. There are angels at your
elbow! Let's clean up the surface mess in your office now, as much as
is possible in these crowded conditions. Then you will feel more like
working on your [current research], which is going to come together
like magic. Be still and know that I am God!

I *did* proceed to clean up the surface mess in my office, and the research I
had been doing did come together with relative ease. Better yet, ever since
I received that answer I have felt more relaxed and unpressured and have
worked with increased efficiency.

What about Structural Injustice?

So I know from direct experience what it is like to recognize the holy instant and know heaven on a personal and relational level. But what about
structural evils, the injustices that assault human dignity by exploiting the
many in order to provide obscene luxuries for the few? Or that exclude
certain people from the respect, power, and privilege accorded to others?

I recently had a letter from a dear friend, who had just recognized that
she too is a spiritual being having human experiences. She wrote,

It seems to me that the pitfall of all this revelation would be to let
oneself become "otherworldly" and so of no *earthly* use. . . . I would
be suspicious of a spirituality that disconnected from this world —
because a foundational belief for me has always been that God(dess)
loves this world, delights in it even as she also suffers in it; but that in
any case she is *in* it, inhabits it (and us) and is *not* disconnected from
it.

And of course I agree. As for me and my house, we will actively try to share the good basics of life with everyone everywhere. In a sense, this book is my response to the widespread notion that spirituality always exists for the private comfort of the individual and has little or nothing to do with the needs of the world.

The thesis of this book is that spiritual beings who are having human experiences — at least those with activist temperaments — demonstrate love for their ultimate and eternal context by enacting tender concern for the penultimate and the apparently temporary. In other words, sensuous spirituality breeds concern for the well-being of the people and all the other creatures who are here on this planet at this time, and for the planet itself. By seeking direction from the Inner Guide at the center of her Self, a human being can glimpse the larger picture in which no person, group, or nation is more important than any other person, group, or nation. She will be helped to understand that in a righteous society (God's "kindom," emphatically different from God's king*dom*), we will all prosper together; but if we insist on maintaining the supremacy of alienated egos, we will all perish together. (Even a rationalist like Ben Franklin knew that if we refuse to hang together, we will all hang separately.)

Through the glimpses of the interconnectedness and spiritual unity of the larger picture, a sensuously spiritual being can receive instruction concerning her specific role for co-creating a more just human society. At the same time, she will be reassured by an outpouring of tenderness from the invisible spirit-world behind, beneath, and within that which is seen. And to the degree that she can keep herself centered, she will be enabled (by the angels at her elbow?) to do most of her designated social-justice work in confidence and joy, even in the midst of warring egos or warring nations. As multitudes of feminist and ecological writers have pointed out, concern for the body and the earth is concern for justice. So the chapters of this book will deal with aspects of justice as viewed from the quiet center of my Self.

Some Essential Definitions

It should by now be obvious that my title utilizes the word *spirituality* to refer to discovering and living out of the pure and eternal core of one's being, a very intentional willingness to respond to life out of the profound and sinless Self rather than out of the confused and superficial ego-nature. I am not using the word *spiritual* as opposed to *secular,* as if spirituality should concern itself only with ecclesiastical matters. (However, it is my opinion that ecclesiastical structures could use a good overhauling in a more spiritual direction.) Instead, I assume that to a genuinely centered Self everything that has life is sacred — and is either fulfilling itself in peaceful love or else is emitting distress calls because it is feeling alienated. Therefore, I assume that the attempt to establish justice on the earth is a sacred spiritual duty. But as long as a person is willing to remember that she is a spiritual being having human experiences, she can do her justice-work joyously, light-heartedly, and in good humor. She can *see through* the royal mess the ego has turned the world into — can see *into* a deeper place where not only will everything eventually be all right, but where everything already *is* all right, and salvation is complete.

It is in order to emphasize the embodied and justice-seeking nature of this kind of spirituality that I have used the modifier *sensuous*. I am using the word *sensuous* as the poet John Milton invented and used the word: to refer to sensations and sense-perceptions while avoiding the licentious connotations of the word *sensual*. In his tract *Of Reformation* (1641), Milton spoke of the body as the sensuous colleague of the soul; and in his pamphlet *Of Education* (1644), he described excellent poetry as "simple, sensuous, and passionate" (*Oxford English Dictionary*). In this book I use the word *sensuous* in both of these senses: to mean *embodied* or *physical,* as in the first usage; but also to mean linguistically concrete, direct, appealing to the senses, and concerned with beauty and justice, as in the second. From the perspective of the physical body, injustice is outrageous because it denies to certain bodies what it grants in superfluity to other bodies. Furthermore, the pleasure-hatred and erotophobia of most Western religion is unjust to the body itself, devaluing the means by which the spirit makes its impact in the world.

On the other hand, from the standpoint of aesthetics, injustice is simply *ugly,* an error to be corrected as rapidly as possible. From either perspective, sensuous spirituality demands a concern for justice in the here and now.

Seeing beyond the Physical "Facts"

Ralph Waldo Emerson wrote in his *Lectures on Transcendentalism* that idealists do not deny the sensuous fact, but neither do they see it *alone*. In my experience, it is possible to see a lovely reality beneath, beyond, and yet also within the physical facts of everyday reality. For instance, when I saw TV images of sea birds covered with oil in the Persian Gulf, I wept for them and for the cruelty spawned by human agendas at war with one another. But at the same time I perceived in the sea birds a patient quietness, a grace under pressure, a heads-up attempt to keep on living as normally as they could. It was heart-breaking in its beauty. So although I would do anything in my power to avert future catastrophes of this nature, and although I pray this one will be mitigated as much as possible, nevertheless I can perceive a glorious reality therein: "Yet for all this Nature is never spent/There lives the dearest freshness deep down things." I am less sure than Father Hopkins that Nature could *never* be spent by human foolishness; but I hope and pray nevertheless that he is right.

For another example, everyone has probably noticed the beautiful human solidarity that develops in the face of natural disasters, such as the devastation caused by earthquakes, hurricanes, cyclones, or major fires or floods. Of course there are some deeply alienated people who will take advantage of a tragedy to pillage and steal. But the remarkable thing is what happens to most people — the reaching out to help strangers, the willingness even to risk one's life to help someone else in dire need. Here, too, there is the "dearest freshness deep down." While no one would wish for natural disasters in order to witness this compassionate response, the person of sensuous spirituality will choose to be empowered by human caring rather than to rage angrily about "acts of God" — especially since some of these disasters may have been caused at least partially by acts of human egocentricity (overdevelopment of wetlands, nuclear experimentation, arson, pollution of air and water, and the like).

Everything Is Going as It Should — or Is It?

Admittedly, it is difficult to look at a world full of poverty, militarism, and all sorts of systems that favor the few at the expense of the many; it is difficult to work for social change in the direction of greater equity, and to perceive how slowly that change proceeds and how many are the setbacks; it is difficult to be realistic about all that and still to live in the quiet confidence that at some deeper level, everything is going as it should. That's why we need to spend some time each day in stillness, remembering who we are, practicing the presence of God Herself* within our Selves and within others, experiencing our oneness with the whole universe that is Selving itself in us all. To use a well-worn but effective illustration, most of the time while we spiritual beings are in the midst of the human condition, we are looking at the back of a huge piece of needlepoint, where there is chaotic ugly criss-crossing and knotting of the woolen strands. It is easy to assume that chaos is all there is. Several times each day, we would be wise to meditate, turning over the needlepoint, so to speak, to look at the design. We must carve out time to look underneath the chaos to assure ourselves that even if the design is very incomplete and we cannot *imagine* what the artist has in mind, nevertheless things are progressing with an order that is not discernible from the backside of the needlepoint.

---

* Please remember that whenever I use the word *God*, which has masculine connotations, I balance those connotations by using feminine pronouns or the word, "Herself." This is to witness to the fact that God's Spirit is *neither* male nor female and yet *both* male and female, and therefore inclusive of everyone.

Nature is replete with phenomena that seem disastrous to an untrained eye and yet turn out to work together for good if only human beings don't interfere. For instance, the emperor moth is encased in a flask-shaped cocoon with only a tiny opening through which the moth must emerge with tremendous, lengthy effort and difficulty. Apparently the pressure to which this emergence subjects the moth's body is necessary in order to force life's juices into the wings, which are much less developed than the body at the time of the great struggle to emerge. When a misguided person cuts the cocoon to ease the emergence of the moth, the result is disastrous for the moth, for its wings never grow and it never flies (Cowman, 9–10). Most of us hate those times in life that are equivalent to the moth's desperately painful struggle to emerge; yet after enough time has passed, we can look back and see that those struggles were the making of us. Might not the same thing be true of the corporate body of humankind? The sensuously spiritual person does not deny the grit and terror of the struggle, but neither does she fail to look toward the loving purpose that is working itself out *in* the struggle.

Thorns do not prick us unless we lean against them; and I have seen too many social-justice activists who think about the thorns of injustice night and day until their hearts are cinders and they drop out of the struggle because they are burnt out. This book is being written partly to say that the sacrifice of our peace and joy is *never* what the universe asks of us. Without peace and joy we become part of the problem rather than part of the solution. The secret of sensuous spirituality is to minimize life's thorns and maximize life's roses, not just for ourselves but for all of humankind. To do so, we must study social systems, conflict resolution, methods of reorganization, and so forth: and all of these can more readily be learned when our vision is not clouded by the hatred of the us-versus-them mentality. We are all losing together; the goal is to transform ourselves into a society in which we all win together. It is counterproductive to sleep on beds of thorn, never giving ourselves a minute's peace or joy because of our commitment to social change. As I have learned repeatedly, we work more efficiently when we work from the relaxed, humorous, gentle perceptions of the Self. We have a right to that relaxation, because we know that behind the scenes everything is working out as it should.

Then Why Bother to Work for Social Change?

On the other hand, it has occurred to me to wonder why anybody should lift a finger for social change. If everything is really working out as it should, why should I do anything other than eat, sleep, and be merry? Or perhaps read books on spirituality, meditate, and feel peaceful? When I asked that question of the Holy Spirit, I was told that asking that question reveals that I have forgotten that *I* am one aspect of the universal process that is working according to plan. The process will not be aborted if I fail to do my part in it, but in some infinitesimal way the process *will* be changed — and above all, I will miss out on the blessing of playing my position on a team in a universal game in which everybody wins.

Among other things, I was told,

Some people may be passive thoughts in my mind, and it is not your place to judge them or my way of being within them. But you are an active thought in my mind, and *it is your nature to work for the social change that is already in the process of happening.* (You can move mountains, as Jesus said [Matt. 17:20], precisely because the mountains are already on the move.) It is for this reason that you can work in a relaxed and joyous way. All you have to supply is the willingness to channel my energetic love and justice into the world, and I will work through you to bring about what I am already bringing about.

A great shift in consciousness is occurring in the world, and you are part of that shift. . . . I work in different people in different ways, and despite your passionate commitment to an activist way, you must allow other people to respond in ways that feel right to *their* natures, for thus the whole pattern is made perfect. . . .

To phrase all this another way, it is your privilege to be an agent of the social changes that are occurring. With you or without you, what should occur will occur. If you feel an impulse toward activism, you would be denying your own nature if you became privatistic and passive; so in that sense, it is essential for you to cooperate by being one of my activist channels into the world. On the other hand, it is impossible for you to make a mistake because even your apparent errors will be learning opportunities for yourself and others. Although Saddam Hussein means to be doing the non-Arab world harm because he is trapped in the ego's us-versus-them mentality, in reality his crazed actions are helping to expedite the shift that is occurring in world consciousness. Willingly or unwillingly, each person plays his or her position in the cosmic game!

But it is a special blessing to play your position *willingly,* because then your heart is able to feel the tenderness and supportiveness of my angels and Spirit Guides who surround the world in eagerness to help. "We know that all things [even your "errors"] work together for good for those who love God [i.e., who willingly open themselves to channel Her love into the world], who are called according to [Her] purpose" [Rom. 8:28, NRSV; that is, everyone is called to come home to a kindom of mutuality and peace-with-justice, but some remain alienated at this time and cannot sense or enjoy the benefits of loving God. They too will eventually come home; but those who offer God their willingness will become *awakened* and *consciously aware* that they are part of God's purpose — a truly beautiful and blessed state of mind!]. (*Journal* 10, 10–13)

In the chapters to come, I will explore some specific applications of the interaction between activism and wise passivity and their implications for people whose spirituality is of the sensuous kind. The ability to confront the sufferings and systems of this world with a tough-minded realism, and yet to remain willing to be shown some lovely possibilities beneath, beyond, and within those realities, possibilities that may not be apparent on the surface: this is what I mean by sensuous spirituality. And in my experience, it is the best antidote for burn-out.

What about Christian Doctrine?

I am aware that some of my readers may be thinking that I have deserted Christianity in favor of the new metaphysics. But I would ask them this: can you be certain that I am not being drawn back to the essence of what Jesus actually believed, lived, and taught? One of the reasons we may previously have misunderstood his teachings is that he spoke Aramaic, a multivalent Middle Eastern language that does not draw sharp distinctions between inner qualities and external actions, or means and ends. The Aramaic view of the cosmos is fluid and wholistic. Yet Jesus' words were filtered to us through Greek, a more rigid, less resonant language (Douglas-Klotz, 2–3).

Here, for instance, is the Lord's Prayer in one possible translation from the Aramaic:

> O Birther! Father-Mother of the Cosmos,
> focus your light within us — make it useful:
> Create your reign of unity now —
> Your one desire then acts with ours,
> as in all light, so in all forms.
> Grant what we need each day in bread and insight.
> Loose the cords of mistakes binding us,
> as we release the strands we hold
> of others' guilt.
> Don't let surface things delude us,
> but free us from what holds us back.
> From you is born all ruling will,
> the power and the life to do,
> the song that beautifies all,
> from age to age it renews.
> Truly — power to these statements —

> may they be the ground from which all
> my actions grow: Amen.

> (Douglas-Klotz, 41)

Gone are traditional Christianity's emphasis on sin, guilt, and retribution; instead, we are empowered toward co-creatorship, welcomed to continual renewal on a continuous Great Non-Judgment Day.

English translations from the Greek tell us "Be you perfect," but from the Aramaic the meaning emerges as "Be you all-embracing." "Blessed are the meek, for they shall inherit the earth" emerges as "soften what's rigid inside and you shall receive physical vigor and strength from the universe" (Douglas-Klotz, ix).

In Aramaic, "heaven" does not refer to an ethereal realm that is remote from what's going on but instead means that the word or vibration by which we can *recognize* that Oneness (God's name) *is* the universe; so that the word *heaven* actually refers to the universe (Douglas-Klotz, x and 14). In this context I can understand one of those mildly mystical experiences I sometimes have had. Many years ago I was asleep, but woke up because of a shimmering light in the bedroom. And a voice within me said, "Why this is heaven, nor am I out of it." I knew at the time that this was a take-off on what Mephistopheles says to Dr. Faustus in Christopher Marlowe's play. When Faustus disbelieves hell because Mephistopheles is obviously in Faustus's study and not in hell, Mephistopheles says, "Why this *is* hell, nor am I out of it." I knew at the time that I was being given a lesson in the fact that there is no impervious wall between time and eternity, that consciousness can easily overleap any wall our own egos have erected, and that our own state of mind may be either hellish in turmoil or heavenly in peaceful oneness with God. What I did *not* know at the time was that this experience was completely consonant with the prayer that Jesus taught us to pray.

Earlier in this chapter I mentioned that dreams were part of the process that transformed me from a sense of my own total depravity to a sense that I am a spiritual being working for justice in a universe in which ultimately everything is all right. Let me share with you one of the dreams that led to my transformation. I was riding in the back of a bus that was making its way on a bumpy narrow road through a pitch-black forest. Down the road stalked an enormous, lethal lion with a glorious mane; shortly thereafter, a Bengal tiger twitching its powerful tail. I knew there were plenty more of them in the area. Although I was fully aware of the danger posited by the presence of these wild animals, something forced me to get out of the bus and enter the dark woods. I was totally vulnerable and undefended, yet nothing attacked me. Down and down a long hill I walked through the woods, feeling my way through the vegetation because I could not see where I was going. But suddenly I glimpsed light far below — and moving toward it, at last I could see that at the heart of the forest was a pole lit up by a huge spotlight. Around the pole, moving clockwise, leaped and cavorted a circle of delicate, graceful gazelles.

Joseph Conrad wrote a famous novella called *The Heart of Darkness*. But my dream told me that beneath all the darkness and wildness in the world, deeper than any separated and defensive ego can ever penetrate, all the way down at the center of each person and of the universal process, there is unquenchable light and the sensuous spontaneity of dancing. And in this faith, I fly.

Chapter Two

A TALE OF TWO HANDMAIDS

———— ≈ ————

I have entitled this chapter "A Tale of Two Handmaids" because I have given much thought to the contrast between Offred, the narrator of Margaret Atwood's novel *The Handmaid's Tale,* and the Virgin Mary, mother of Jesus, who, according to the first chapter of Luke's Gospel, called herself the handmaid of God. These two handmaids, or servants, form an instructive contrast for sensuously spiritual persons. Offred is a handmaid entirely against her own will, whereas Mary the Virgin exemplifies the freedom and power that come from willingly co-creating with the God of the universe. Both of them demonstrate that the personal is political and that inner contact with God empowers us toward working for justice for ourselves and others in the "real world."

I realize there is much feminist skepticism about the free will involved in the Virgin Mary's servanthood, but I hope to show later in this chapter why I do not share it. My understanding of Luke's Gospel aligns Mary with the Righteous Servant of God as described by the prophet Isaiah, whereas Offred is a woman forcibly stripped of all her natural dignity and her moral agency by the iniquitous heteropatriarchal government in the Republic of Gilead.

Margaret Atwood's novel depicts a terrifyingly repressive right-wing takeover, in the near future, of the entire northeast section of the United States, centering at Cambridge, Massachusetts. The government represents a Nazification of society by people who legitimate everything they do with out-of-context phrases from the Bible. An elite corps of white men called Commanders holds all the real power in the Republic of Gilead, although their Wives hold a derivative status and have unquestioned control of in-house domestic discipline. Each Commander's house is staffed with several Marthas, women who wear dull green uniforms and do the domestic chores. If the Commander and his Wife have not been able to produce children of their own, the house is also staffed with a Handmaid, a woman who wears a red uniform and stiff white blinders, a womb on two legs whose sole purpose is to produce a baby for the couple by lying between the legs of the barren Wife while the Commander joylessly and impersonally attempts to impregnate her.

A Handmaid gets exactly two years to become pregnant by any one Commander, after which she is sent to a different post to try again with another man. After three posts, if she has not given birth to a healthy baby, she will be declared an Unwoman and sent to the Colonies to clean up toxic wastes or do other dangerous tasks along with rebels and old women who have outlived their usefulness for that society.

The average survival time in the Colonies is three years; so Handmaids try desperate measures to become pregnant after it seems obvious that the Commander they are with is not capable of fathering a child. Only by giving birth to a healthy baby is a Handmaid assured that she will never be sent to work herself to death in the Colonies. Because of widespread toxins in the air, water, and food, only one baby in four is born healthy. Deformed babies are designated Unbabies and are shredded immediately after birth. They do not count toward a Handmaid's status because all errors and problems are assumed to be the woman's fault. In fact, during the training period for Handmaids, the women are forced to testify concerning their experiences of being raped or otherwise abused by men before the founding of the Republic of Gilead. They are then forced to take full responsibility for what the men had done to them. Each must kneel alone in humiliation while everyone chants that God allowed this abuse to occur to teach her a lesson.

Wives of less powerful men than the Commanders are called Econowives. The Econowives wear cheap and skimpy striped uniforms and must perform all the combined tasks of the Wives, Marthas, and Handmaids on their own. The Widows must dress all in black. Incorrigible women are sent to Jezebel's, a sexy, secret Playboy club and brothel for the Commanders. Formerly professional women are sent to be prostitutes with the full knowledge that when they have lost their attractiveness they will be sent to the Colonies. In this way, women who were attorneys, clergy, or professors are reduced to playboy bunnies and prostitutes for elite ruling-class men. This is the secret underbelly of a society that has officially outlawed any sex except procreative sex.

There are no books or magazines in the Republic of Gilead, except for contraband stuff, because reading is too subversive. Even the Bible is kept chained within a locked box, from which it is removed only by the Commander, who reads to his household passages that (out of context) seem to legitimate the way things are done in Gilead.

Infractions of the rules are punished swiftly in the Republic of Gilead:

for being caught for the third time reading, a person has her hand cut off. For adultery, public hanging at the ceremonies known as Salvagings. For having performed abortions before the takeover, hanging. For making love with one's own sex, hanging. Gay love is called "Gender Treachery."

The bodies of executed people are hanged on hooks on the Wall of what used to be Harvard University, sometimes for days at a time, with placards around their necks depicting their crimes: placards with pictures, not words, because written words are too subversive.

We're talking about a white Protestant society in Gilead: the so-called "Children of Ham" and native Americans have all been shipped to farms in North Dakota and elsewhere — or so the propaganda says. At first, Jews had been permitted to emigrate to Israel; but the punishment for protesting Jews who remain, or for Catholics, or Jehovah's Witnesses, is hanging.

The Handmaids in Gilead have no names other than those of the Commander they serve: Offred, Ofwayne, Ofwarren, Ofglen. When they are sent to a new post, they take the name of their new Commander; so there will always be an *Offred* as long as Fred is trying to father a baby; but today she may be a different woman from the Offred of yesterday. Thus Handmaids have no identity that goes with them, no continuity, no individuality. Their name is the name of whatever man is using them.

Atwood as Social Prophet

How could things have come to such a pass — a society devoid of intimacy, so rigidly hierarchical that even within the household Marthas must stand, Handmaids must kneel, and only Wives may sit, although ultimately it is the male (the Commander) who rules? The Republic of Gilead is a caricature of today's right-wing attitudes and teachings, developed not only into a civil religion but into a heteropatriarchal theocracy. Does Margaret Atwood really believe that society could become this oppressive? I don't know. But as a person who lived for over thirty-five years in the context of Protestant fundamentalism and who currently believes that no action is too cruel for egos that see themselves as separate from others, I for one can believe that such a society is possible.

Margaret Atwood has imagined the hideous Republic of Gilead, and has delineated it for us, as a prophet preaches the destruction that will come if there is no repentance. She has provided a warning that the bridge is out only a mile ahead of us, so that we may apply the brakes. We ignore her warning at our own peril. It is particularly important to notice how the takeover was accomplished, the smooth, swift transition by which "normal heteropatriarchy" was transformed into the larger-than-life heteropatriarchy called the Republic of Gilead.

Before the takeover, all money transactions in the United States had already been delegated to a centralized Compubank, a computerized account in which every citizen had her own account number. Instead of portable cash, each citizen gave their number to whatever merchant they were dealing with, who then withdrew the amount of the purchase by punching in the customer's account number and transferring the purchase price into the merchant's account. The elite Commanders of Gilead established themselves in control by shooting the president, machine-gunning the members of Congress, blaming everything on Islamic terrorists, and declaring a military emergency in which they suspended the Constitution.

Their first official act was to freeze all the Compubank accounts that were in women's names and then to transfer the money in those accounts into the accounts of the women's husbands or nearest male relatives. The second move was to decree that no women could hold paying jobs and to enforce that decree by military presence. Instantly, all women are reduced to dependency upon male good will, and everybody becomes afraid to oppose the governmental decrees because now they are "the law." Roadblocks are built to keep people from escaping the area, and citizens are forced to carry Identipasses. People are so mystified, so in fear of the Islamic fanatics but with no enemy they can positively identify or confront, that the Commanders are able to establish the Republic of Gilead almost without objection. Those who do object are very soon hanging from hooks on The Wall of Harvard Yard.

In their restructuring of society, the Commanders are aided by the Aunts, dour older women with cattleprods who torture other women in order to break their wills and teach them subservience. One of their methods is familiar to anyone who ever read *Fascinating Womanhood, The Total Woman,* or other books teaching women how to manipulate men through sex and pretenses of inferiority in order to get what they want without frontal attacks on male supremacy. Here is Offred speaking:

> Men are sex machines, said Aunt Lydia, and not much more. They only want one thing. You must learn to manipulate them, for your own good. Lead them around by the nose; that is a metaphor. It's nature's way. It's God's device. It's the way things are.
>
> Aunt Lydia did not actually *say* this, but it was *implicit* in everything she did say. (186)

Margaret Atwood is surely demonstrating that the personal is political and that the maintenance of heteropatriarchal one-up, one-down dominance-and-submission relationships destroys all true intimacy by forcing the secondary people to learn the fine art of manipulation. Manipulation, in turn, leads to contempt for those who can be manipulated. So *everybody* suffers in the Republic of Gilead, even the Commanders, who miss intimacy as much as anyone else but who alone have the power to try to do something about it. They wind up deceiving their Wives and in secret meetings begging their Handmaids to "kiss them as if they really meant it." The Handmaids of course do their best to fake it because whatever tiny privilege they may enjoy is contingent on the Commander's good will. In short, everyone distrusts everyone else because everyone is expected to report the "disloyalty" of anyone to the Gilead regime. It is a world in which power-over is so brutally omnipresent that intimacy is impossible.

From the aesthetic standpoint, the best thing about *The Handmaid's Tale* is its verisimilitude, its plausibility. But from the standpoint of human life and human justice, that same plausibility is utterly horrifying.

At one point when Offred is remembering her relatively carefree life before the takeover, she muses,

> Is that how we lived, then? But we lived as usual. Everyone does, most of the time. Whatever is going on is as usual. Even this is as usual, now.
>
> We lived, as usual, by ignoring. Ignoring isn't the same thing as ignorance, you have to work at [ignoring].
>
> Nothing changes instantaneously — in a gradually heating bathtub you'd be boiled to death before you knew it. (74)

In her role of social prophet, Margaret Atwood is asking us to confront — to cease ignoring — those trends in society that might indicate a gradual heating up toward the boiling point of Gilead. When I first studied *A Course in Miracles,* I did not appreciate the pages that are devoted to describing the bloodthirsty brutality of the human ego when it imagines itself separate from God. In its fear the ego jockeys for prominence in a world where every other ego is perceived as competition for the scarce good things of life. Just as I recoiled from those descriptions, I know many readers would prefer neither to read nor hear about warnings like Margaret Atwood's. But as comfortable as it might be to float along in private good feelings, as surely as "God so loved the world" (John 3:16), we who are sensuously spiritual must give our energies to the expression of love. Otherwise, while we are withdrawn into our personal meditative heavens, society might careen into Gilead status — or worse.

A Women's Salvaging of Scripture

The Bible is used repressively in the Republic of Gilead — especially 1 Timothy 2:11–15, the strange passage blaming Eve for sin, advising the church to "let the women learn in silence with all subjection," and promising that "women shall be saved by childbearing." Nevertheless, the Bible is kept under lock and key because of its subversive possibilities. As Margaret Atwood comments through her protagonist Offred: "[The Bible] is an incendiary device: who knows what we'd make of it, if we ever got our hands on it?" (112).

And in fact there *is* an underground resistance movement in the Republic of Gilead. Offred herself keeps her resistance alive by reading and rereading the one word FAITH on a faded petit-point pillow in her room and reminding herself of HOPE and CHARITY to go with it. I strongly recommend "Margaret Atwood's Testaments," by Janet Karsten Larson, in which she explains Atwood's underlying themes and advises that a women's salvaging of Scripture is "a possible venture, crucial for our common future." As a fundamentalist woman who was eventually liberated and radicalized through the Bible, I suggest that we "get our hands on" Luke 1, where Mary describes herself as a handmaid, and see what we can make of it for ourselves.

Here is Luke 1:26–38, from *An Inclusive Language Lectionary*. I ask that however familiar this story may be to us, we try to read it this time as if we have never seen or heard it before — as if we had just risked our lives to unlock the Bible from the box where someone has denied it to us.

In the sixth month the angel Gabriel was sent from God to a city of Galilee named Nazareth, to a virgin betrothed to a man whose name was Joseph, of the house of David; and her name was Mary. And the angel came to her and said, "Hail, O favored one, God is with you!" But she was greatly troubled at the saying, and considered in her mind what sort of greeting this might be. And the angel said to her, "Do not be afraid, Mary, for you have found favor with God. You will conceive in your womb and bear a child, whose name you shall call Jesus.

This one will be great, and will be called the Child of the Most High;
and the Sovereign God will give to that Child the throne of David, the ancestor of the Child,
to reign over the house of Jacob forever;
and of that reign there will be no end."

And Mary said to the angel, "How shall this be, since I have no husband?" And the angel said to her,

The Holy Spirit will come upon you,
and the power of the Most High will overshadow you;
therefore the child to be born will be called holy,
the Child of God.

And your kinswoman Elizabeth in her old age has also conceived a child; and this is the sixth month with her who was called barren. For with God nothing will be impossible." And Mary said, "I am the

servant [handmaid] of God; let it be to me according to your word."
And the angel departed from her.

If we had grown up in the Republic of Gilead, how thrilled we would
be that an angel came to speak to an individual woman in such respectful
tones!

The Virgin Mary as Victim

Mary Daly has written extensively about the Virgin Mary as rape victim in
her book *Pure Lust*. She calls the story we have just read a "mythic Super-
Rape," and "the supremely sublimated male sexual fantasy" because "like
all rape victims in male myth, [Mary] submits joyously to this unspeakable
degradation" (74–75). Later in the same book, Daly says that in the story
we have read,

> The transsexed, broken *spirit* of the Goddess, [dis]guised as the
> holy ghost, raped the broken and dis-spirited *matter* of the God-
> dess (that is, Mary). Thus the myth-molding voyeurs have produced
> what could be designated the Purest Peep Show of the millennia,
> a male-identified counterfeit lesbian love scene, issuing in male off-
> spring. The product of this fantastic feat is Jesus.... The myth of
> the Incarnation, then, logically implies the usurpation of female
> power. Moreover, since the Virgin Mother symbolizes matter to the
> myth-masters, the myth legitimates the rape of all matter. (130–31)

Although I do not agree with Mary Daly's assessment of this story, I
have quoted it at length because I also do not think it should be ignored.
Nobody who knows anything about heteropatriarchal history could deny
that the story of the Virgin Birth has frequently functioned to legitimate the
usurping of a woman's power by keeping her barefoot, pregnant, and sub-
missive. Margaret Atwood implies an understanding of heteropatriarchy's
use of the Virgin by the greeting that Gilead's Handmaids must give each
other when they meet: "Blessed be the fruit," says the first Handmaid; and
the other gives the only acceptable response, "May the Lord open" (25).
Thus, even in their daily greetings, Handmaids must remind each other
that the only way for a woman to find favor with God and society is to
bear fruit. Unless the Lord will open their wombs, they will be declared
Unwomen and sent to the Colonies to work themselves to death.

So I would never deny that the scriptural story of the annunciation and
incarnation has indeed been used in ways that are deadly to the well-being
of women. But instead of discarding it, and in the spirit of Adrienne Rich's
great poem "Diving into the Wreck," I suggest that having acknowledged
the negative uses of this story, we then proceed to appropriate the treasure

that is nevertheless in it, as a means of subverting patriarchy by empowering ourselves.

In fact, Mary Daly herself suggests that sometimes feminists must hear old words in new ways, deliberately turning those old words into New Words for purposes of self-empowerment (262). That, I think, is what feminists should be doing with the Bible, and what I now want to do with several phrases from the story of the annunciation.

I find three particularly empowering phrases in Luke 1:26–38: first, the angel Gabriel's recognition that "God is with you"; second, Gabriel's promise that "the Holy Spirit will come upon you"; and third, the Virgin's identification of herself as "the handmaid of God." I propose to make "New Words" out of these familiar phrases, considering them one by one.

"God Is with You"

First, the recognition that "God is with you." In my own experience, God is no doubt with me at all times in the sense that I could not possibly survive for even one minute without Her energy. But there are times when I have gotten so lost in my separated ego that, for all practical purposes, God might as well not have been there. I am empowered by Her presence only when I am willing to be aware of it. If I refuse to make the time to pay attention to God's presence within me, I perceive myself as alone, vulnerable, and endangered — as someone who must put out a whole lot of effort just to break even. But when I take the time to remember that She is with me, I can do my work and live my life in confidence and joy.

Gabriel's greeting, "God is with you," indicates that God was always and habitually in Mary's consciousness. The fact that Mary was "troubled at that saying" may well mean that Mary's mind was so totally centered upon God's Presence that she was startled to hear the fact objectified by being named. (Sometimes we are surprised and even perhaps troubled when someone else names and thus lifts into conscious awareness some habitual attitude of ours that has been so pervasive we have never thought to give it a name.) I assume that the Virgin was constantly with God and God with her in the sense that children do not overtly *enjoy* Nature but are simply *one with* Nature. They would probably be disturbed if adults made a big thing out of their organic oneness with Nature; in that sense, perhaps, Mary is troubled at the angel's saying.

So I assume that Mary constantly experienced herself as keeping company with God, and liked it that way. In other words, according to Gabriel's greeting, Mary was chosen by God because Mary had already chosen God — had experienced life as continually walking with God and God with her. The angel could *announce* to Mary rather than *inquire* of her only because in her daily life Mary had already chosen a life of companionship with

God Herself. This is a far cry from rape, in which an external other person usurps and violates the being of the victim. Mary's being is already infused with God, full of God. Like Shange's "colored girls who had considered suicide when the rainbow was enuf," Mary had long ago found God in herself, and had "loved Her/had loved Her fiercely." So it was more a matter of reciprocation when God in turn chose Mary to co-create the holy Child.

There have been many people in history to whom it could truthfully be said, "God is with you!" In reality, God is with everyone, but there are many who at this time would feel outraged, embarrassed, or degraded at such a greeting; and their feelings should be respected. But the joyous condition of knowing God's empowering Presence with us is open to anybody who is willing to be open to it. God is with us, within us, already, but unless we train our minds to constantly *remember* that fact, we become unaware of our own legitimate power to make a difference in the world.

In fact, when the word *Virgin* is defined in a feminist way, Mary's designation as Virgin supports the meaning that "God is with you." I had always disliked my name Virginia when I thought it defined me in terms of a negative, with eventual completeness only through a connection with male sexuality (which in heteropatriarchy connotes *subordination to* male sexuality). Imagine my surprise when I discovered that in the ancient world, *Virgin* had nothing to do with physical virginity but meant "complete within herself," a woman's not needing marriage or anything outside herself to make her complete. Thus the Great Goddess of antiquity could simultaneously be Virgin, Mother, and Crone (old wise one). That's how it is for a person who has found God within herself; although she needs other people for community and relationships, she is no longer *needy* in the sense that she needs no one external to complete her or give her meaning. She is certainly *not* God in the sense that she is better than anyone else. Yet she *is* God because she feels her spiritual connection with everyone else and everything else, with the One-Who-Is-All. God is with her, and she with God.

"The Holy Spirit Will Come upon You"

The second phrase of importance to our purposes is Gabriel's promise that "the Holy Spirit will come upon you / and the power of the Most High will overshadow you." Far from being an image of a male overpowering a female, this is an image of human empowerment. I always know when the power of the Most High is *upon me* — those are the times I hear myself saying things I did not know I knew . . . the times I find myself feeling the most wonderful sweetness toward somebody who has apparently wronged me but whom for one reason or another it is useless to confront . . . the times when the knots smooth out in my brain (and muscles), when everything looks simple and safe and secure...the times I can do no wrong because I am so competent and "in the zone." We have all known such moments of doing something at a much more effective or loving level than we are capable of on our own. The Spirit of God is upon us.

The common word for this condition is *inspiration* — breathing in the *ruach,* the *pneuma,* the breath or wind or Spirit of God. Mary conceives of Jesus by the *inspiration* of God's Spirit, just as I pray, whenever I'm writing a chapter like this, that the words will not be only words, but *inspirated* or *inspired* words.

In fact the phrase "the Holy Spirit will come upon you" reminds me very much of the wonderful passage in Isaiah 61:1, which Jesus read one day in a Galilean temple and then applied to himself:

> The Spirit of the Sovereign [God] is on me, because [the Sovereign]
> has anointed me to preach good news to the poor. [God] has sent me
> to bind up the brokenhearted, to proclaim freedom for the captives
> and release for the prisoners. (NIV, inclusive language mine)

In the context of Isaiah 61, these words are spoken by the Righteous Servant of God; and I would argue that just as Jesus claimed them for himself, each of us is intended to claim them for ourselves.

It is only heteropatriarchal assumptions and language that have caused people to think that God's Righteous Servant is necessarily male. Even Isaiah 61 makes clear that the Righteous One is either male or female. Verse 10 quotes the Righteous Servant as saying, "I delight greatly in [the Sovereign]; / my soul rejoices in my God. / For [God] has clothed me with garments of salvation / and arrayed me in a robe of righteousness, / *as a bridegroom* adorns his head like a priest, / and *as a bride* adorns herself with her jewels" (NIV, inclusive language and emphasis mine). Male or female, those who seek justice are clothed in the garments of salvation and the robes of righteousness.

In fact, I think that Mary was consciously claiming her identification with the Righteous Servant of Isaiah 61, just as Jesus would later do, when she called herself the handmaid or servant of God and said in the Magnificat that "God has helped [God's] servant Israel" and that "God has filled the hungry with good things," has "put down the mighty from their thrones, and exalted those of low degree" (Luke 1:46–55). What is Mary doing there, if not preaching good news to poor people and proclaiming freedom for the captives?

Robert McAfee Brown has written, "If we were presented with the Magnificat without the God-language and were asked who had said this stuff about the overturning of the world's economy we might have answered Marx or Lenin. What the Magnificat does...is to put the mandate for radical change centrally within the Christian story. Change can no longer be a peripheral concern [because] in the Gospel account, Jesus' mother advocates change from the very start" (520–21).

Communism's failure (at least in Europe) does not alter the fact that runaway capitalism is also iniquitous, with the rich getting constantly richer at the expense of the poor. Surely there are compromise alternatives or wholly new structures — and surely in her Magnificat the Virgin has urged us toward the creation of economic justice.

Mary herself is a "Christed one," as is her son; she is part of the corporate Messiah or the New Humanity; she is the Righteous Servant of God. So is every other person who is concerned with making right relationship, doing justice and loving mercy in co-creatorship with God. It is up to us to empower ourselves as Mary did, as Jesus did, by claiming for ourselves the power of God's Spirit upon us. It is our birthright as the expressions of God's purposes.

We also should not overlook the fact that Mary's virginal conception involves the exclusion of male agency. By assuming that God is male and that Mary was raped as (say) Leda was raped by Jove in the form of a swan, Mary Daly has overlooked an important possibility for empowering Christian women. According to the Gospels, the redeemer came into the world by female agency in direct cooperation with the Spirit of God Herself. The poet W. H. Auden was clear about that point: in his Christmas oratorio *For the Time Being,* Auden has an angel tell Joseph: "Today the roles are altered; you must be the weaker sex...you must learn now that masculinity, to nature, is a non-essential luxury" (Coats and Coats, 5). Not that I (or most women) would want a world without men; but in heteropatriarchy, these facts are vital to the empowerment both of women and of men, who have a desperately undervalued "feminine" component.

"I Am the Handmaid of God"

Finally, the phrase Mary uses concerning herself, "Behold, I am the handmaid of God." To be God's servant is demeaning only if God is the Totally Other, totally abstracted, withdrawn, and controlling God of heteropatriarchal theology. But if God is *within* us as well as *above* us and *through* us, as Ephesians says — if God is Immanuel (God-with-us) — then to be God's servant is to co-create with a power that *is* our own and yet also is a power *beyond ourselves*. It is to "go with the flow" as the universe "selves itself" within our experience. Instead of resisting our own feelings and life circumstances, it means making things as right as we can and then trying to make creative use of the "negative" circumstances we can't change. We do so in the confidence that when we say "let it be to me according to your word," we are not speaking to an entity that is totally other from ourselves, but rather are aligning ourselves with that which already energizes us as well as the whole interconnected web of reality, all-that-is.

To be the handmaid of God is to serve no smaller cause than *the well-being of us all,* of the whole universe and all the creatures in it. Although our justice-building actions must be local and particular, to be God's handmaid means to honor God everywhere and always, in ourselves and in all creatures, but to confer ultimacy upon no Commander and no cause smaller than God's Very Self.

"Behold, I am the handmaid of God; let it be to me according to your word:" when spoken to the God whose name is "I am that I am," the God who is the structure and process of All-That-Is (including ourselves), these are the words of our liberation — and the world's.

Alexander Pope, the great eighteenth-century English satirist, once gave a dog to the British monarch, who was then living at Kew Gardens. The dog wore a collar bearing this inscription:

> I am his Majesty's dog at Kew
> Pray tell me, sir, whose dog are you?

I can't help wondering whether the monarch, when he bent to pet the dog, ever tried to answer that question. As Alexander Pope implies, all of us (even today's equivalents of kings and queens) serve somebody or something. I suggest that sensuously spiritual people regard ourselves as nobody's dog, nobody's handmaid, except for the service we willingly render to the well-being of the whole human race and the entire interconnected web of being and becoming. In this sense of showing our inward love for God by relating rightly to Her creatures, let us be the handmaids of God and God alone. For on this hangs all the law and the prophets.

Chapter Three

MIDWIFING JUSTICE
AS THE WISDOM OF GOD HERSELF

———— ≈ ————

It is by no means a foregone conclusion that people who are sensuously spiritual will also be interested in Bible studies. Many people who are spiritual assume that fundamentalists are right about the literal meaning of the Bible, which in turn would tend to make the Bible inimical to mystical experience. Hence they could care less about the book. Many body-loving feminists or gay people assume that the Bible is the enemy of women, pleasure, and justice in general, and certainly the condemner of lesbian women and gay men. For these reasons I have given in my earlier chapters brief discussions of why I consider the Bible important to human liberation. The following chapter will focus exclusively on biblical support for honoring human diversity. But even in this chapter, which will examine the Exodus story of the Hebrew midwives and the figure of Sophia, or Wisdom, I think it is important to explain why these biblical materials matter to me.

Sometimes the best way to find out about ourselves is to listen to someone from an entirely different culture, and then to ask ourselves how we are similar to her or different from her. Hence, in the context of interreligious dialogue and reading, I have been interested to learn that certain women of faith in the Jewish and Muslim traditions also understand the importance of doing justice-oriented theoretical studies of the basic texts in their traditions. This approach involves casting away heteropatriarchal assumptions and approaching the sacred text with the assumptions of feminism and human liberation.

For instance, Sartaz Asiz is an Islamic woman from Bangladesh. When the Pakistanis invaded Bangladesh in 1971, their goal was to degrade the people of Bangladesh as an act of religious cleansing, because the Bengali culture had become too tolerant and too civilized to satisfy the Pakistani leaders. Between one and three million Bengali citizens were murdered, and over two hundred thousand women were raped and sexually tortured, all in the name of Allah and the purity of Islam.

Sartaz Asiz narrowly escaped all of this, but was horrified that her beloved Islam "was being used to justify rape and murder as holy acts!" Nevertheless she did not repudiate Islam: instead, she writes, "For me, the answer was to turn in the most radical way to the roots of Muslim experience and to separate everything from it that was patriarchal. Patriarchy is the great enemy of everything that is good in spirituality and religion because it teaches that nations and individual persons can only define themselves by dominating others.... Patriarchy is international... and must be opposed by feminists in every religion." But it was Islam, Asiz says, that helped her understand herself as a social being *and as a feminist*. Hence, she says, "To repudiate Islam would be to repudiate the most important part of myself spiritually and morally." Therefore Asiz is now working to prove that "all the misogynist interpretations and practices were accretions added later, after Muhammad's time, by ambitious and sexist males." Similarly, a Pakistani friend of mine, Riffat Hassan, is preparing a book, *Equal before Allah,* that reveals the sexist *mis*interpretations of the Koran. Like other Muslim Women of Faith, Riffat Hassan and Sartaz Asiz are dedicated to proving that one *cannot* be a good Muslim without struggling against patriarchy, just as Muhammad did (Asiz, 53–55).

I resonate with the approaches of Asiz and Hassan because one of my identities is that of an evangelical lesbian feminist dedicated to proving that one cannot be a good Christian without struggling against heteropatriarchy, just as Jesus and (up to their respective lights) Paul and the other apostles did. But one does not have to be evangelical to see that it is not wise to let the errors of heteropatriarchy have a monopoly on the Bible. In that spirit, I turn again to the Scriptures to see what we "off-norm" people can make of them for ourselves.

The Public and Political Aspects of Sensuous Spirituality

Chapter Two utilized the stories of Offred and the Virgin Mary to demonstrate where personal justice-making power comes from: from the center or core of our being/becoming, where God Herself dwells within us. The lesbian musician Margie Adams has a song about entering into the center of our personhood and discovering, "It is so silent in here; it is not violent in here." To act out of that silent, healing, nonviolent sacred center on behalf of ourselves-in-community with all of creation is the essence of sensuous spirituality. In this chapter I want to focus specifically on the more public and political aspects of such a life.

The story of the Hebrew midwives occurs in Exodus 1:15–22. Its context is that while the children of Israel were in captivity in Egypt, they became so numerous that the pharaoh began to perceive them as a threat. Thus the Israelites form a marvelous symbol of oppressed people everywhere, who make normative power-groups nervous as soon as they begin to get in touch with their personal power and especially begin to network and realize their *power in community* and *in coalition,* which increases their numbers and their clout.* Here's the story of the midwives, Exodus 1:15–22 from the New International Version:

> The king of Egypt said to the Hebrew midwives, whose names were Shiprah and Puah, "When you help the Hebrew women in childbirth and observe them on the delivery stool, if it is a boy, kill him; but if it is a girl, let her live." The midwives, however, feared God and did not do what the king of Egypt had told them to do; they let the boys live. Then the king of Egypt summoned the midwives and asked them, "Why have you done this? Why have you let the boys live?"
>
> The midwives answered Pharaoh, "Hebrew women are not like Egyptian women; they are vigorous and give birth before the midwives arrive."
>
> So God was kind to the midwives and the people increased and became even more numerous. And because the midwives feared God, God gave them families of their own.
>
> Then Pharaoh gave this order to all his people: "Every boy that is born you must throw into the river, but let every girl live."

A few points of clarification are in order before we see what we can do for ourselves with this story. First of all, the reason the girl-babies were not targeted for destruction was not reverse sexism, nor was it entirely a matter of military potential. Rather the policy was related to the fact that when they were grown, the girls could be married to Egyptian men and thus would lose their national identity. It was because women would become Ofseth or Ofmoses or Oframses; it was because heteropatriarchal society had decreed that women derive their national and personal identity from the men in their lives, that the daughters would be spared but not the sons. Secondly, the fear the midwives felt for God was not terror and not timidity — these were tough women who were not easily frightened — but rather it was reverence. Because of their reverence for God, they naturally reverenced the human life that is the expression of God, refusing to destroy male infants, even at the command of their own ruler. Third, many of us would not consider it a reward to be given children as the midwives

---

*Mention of *clout* inspires me to invite any Christian lesbian readers to join me in C.L.O.U.T. (Christian Lesbians Out Together). For information, write to CLOUT, Box 460808, San Francisco, CA 94146-0808.

were. Presumably Shiprah and Puah were barren women who were midwifing because they had been unable to give birth themselves and yet wanted children. Within our diverse circumstances, some of us might prefer to interpret their being given children in a symbolic fashion, with the children symbolizing renewed or increased creative output. Certainly nothing tests our tolerance for diversity more than reproductive issues!

Living in Occupied Territory

I referred to the pharaoh as the midwives' ruler because many scholars think the midwives were Egyptian women who acted as chief midwives overseeing all those who aided in the delivery of the Hebrew babies. If Shiprah and Puah were indeed Egyptian women, they form wonderful illustrations of the way women are able to connect on human issues across the nationalistic and ideological barriers that mean so much to their fathers and husbands. In Israel today, Jewish and Palestinian women have together formed a beautiful peace movement even while their men continue to bruise, attack, and kill one another. (Israeli film director and producer Shuli Eschel has made a fine videotape about this movement; see Eschel in Works Cited.)

If only the men of the world would listen to the voices and values of women! But since they will not, we women must organize ourselves so that unco-opted women can be elected to decision-making posts in numbers large enough to affect policies. And in the meantime, because we are living in the enemy-occupied territory I am calling heteropatriarchy, we must learn to subvert the iniquitous systems as Shiprah and Puah did.

But whether these two chief midwives were Egyptian or Hebrew is actually unimportant to the point I am making. Because the Israelites had lived in Egypt for many years, the pharaoh was their ruler, representing what the apostle Paul would later refer to as "the powers that be" who are "ordained of God" and therefore ought to be obeyed except in highly unusual circumstances (Rom. 13:1–7). And like Paul himself, these midwives committed civil disobedience by refusing to obey an order that they felt would violate their commitment to life and to God Herself.

In this way Shiprah and Puah proved themselves to be the Handmaids of God rather than of Pharaoh. Although the king expected the midwives to identify themselves with Egyptian national interests, they in fact identified themselves with the best interests of humankind as a whole, refusing to engage in acts of infanticide against minority children. Like Shiprah and Puah, sensuously spiritual people need to bear in mind that when we act in solidarity with other oppressed people, we act in reverence for God and on behalf of the best interests of everyone, the oppressors as well as the oppressed, even though the oppressors probably would not be able to recognize that fact.

Shiprah vs. Puah

Shiprah's name, in Hebrew, means *beauty;* the name Puah derives from a Ugaritic word meaning *girl,* but is usually a male name in the Hebrew Scriptures (Gen. 16:13, Num. 26:23, 1 Chron. 7:1, and Judg. 10:1). Puah means *utterance* (see Young under "Shiprah" and "Puah"). *Utterance* is always an important word for oppressed people, because in a very real sense utterance (expression) is the exact opposite of depression. When we turn our rage at injustice inward, the result is depression; but when we focus our rage on the unjust systems that oppress us and express that rage creatively, the very act of expression transforms itself into new energy and increased creativity. In this way our rage can become our Pegasus, the winged horse on which we take flight.

Of the two names, Shiprah, or *beauty,* might be understood to represent the woman who looks and usually behaves in more stereotypically "feminine" ways; whereas Puah, or *utterance* (with her name that means *girl* yet was often given to men), might be taken to represent the more androgynous, assertive, outspoken woman, who cares more about ideas and communication than about being beautiful to the eyes of others. Heterosexual, bisexual, and lesbian women may individually fit into either the Shiprah or Puah category. But it is *together,* in *coalition,* that these two different types are empowered to do their civil disobedience as the Handmaids of God and the midwives of justice.

We women and gay people will get nowhere if we allow ourselves to divide our energies through internal judgmentalism. Sometimes that judgmentalism takes the form of lesbian feminists assuming that heterosexual women cannot possibly be *real* feminists because they have a tendency to "sleep with the enemy." Sometimes judgmentalism takes the form of heterosexual women's succumbing to heterosexism and rejecting their lesbian sisters for being lesbian. Sometimes it takes the form of post-Christian or post-Judaic feminists who see Christian and Jewish feminists as the arms of the Establishment, making it possible for people to stay in churches and synagogues rather than joining the Exodus out of traditional religion. Sometimes judgmentalism takes the form of Christian or Jewish feminists who reject the spiritualities and rituals of those who have left us to become nature-mystics or witches or Goddess-worshippers. Sometimes lesbian women reject one another because of lifestyle differences, as for instance the lesbian mothers of London tried to keep S/M (sado/masochistic) women and men out of the Lesbian and Gay Community Center there (Ardill and O'Sullivan, 277–304). Sometimes those who are socialist feminists treat nonsocialists as less than real feminists, or vice versa. Sometimes lesbians or gay men who "out" (are publicly identified as gay) have no tolerance for those whose life circumstances will not permit openness. Sometimes closeted gay people resent those who are "out" for fear that their high profiles might stimulate homophobic witch hunts. And sometimes judgmentalism takes the form of trashing female or gay leadership in a way that we would not trash men or heterosexuals in similar leadership positions.

Whatever form our judgmentalism may take, it is self-defeating. By failing to hang together, we assist heteropatriarchy by hanging each other separately. The fact is that we who are Shiprahs need the Puahs, and we who are Puahs need the Shiprahs. If we cannot accept diversity among ourselves, how can we hope to bring about a society that respects diversity and protects pluralism?

While it is vital that we express our different agendas and even our anger openly and directly, it is also important that we learn to do so as acts of loving and respectful sisterhood.* To attack one another is to dissipate our collective energy and impact. But to hide our differences in a false pretense of community is to bank down our passions, including our passion for justice. We can learn to negotiate fairly and even to fight fairly, as sisters must. The only argument worth having is an argument that is fought out of respect for right relationship, to restore the just conditions that are necessary for right-relationship to flourish. If we learn to speak to one another in ways that respect the Self or New Humanity in one another and constantly reassure ourselves that we are fighting to preserve the relationship as a whole, there is no reason for us to fear the expression of real differences. We can learn so very much just from listening to our various agendas!

One thing is sure: we cannot liberate ourselves in isolation, and certainly we cannot make a just society in isolation. Shiprahs and Puahs of the world, unite: we have nothing to lose but our chains!

Puah and Miriam

It is interesting to know that later Jewish legends identify Puah with Miriam, the sister of Moses and Aaron (*Interpreter's Dictionary*, 3: 967). If that is true — and who would know better than the Jews, with their careful preservation of oral tradition — Puah/Miriam not only took the great personal risk of disobeying the pharaoh's order, she also had the satisfaction of saving her little brother's life and bringing their own mother to nurse him — for wages! Notice the beautiful deviousness of women when confronted with an unjust and cruel order: having been ordered by the pharaoh to throw all Hebrew boy babies into the river, Puah/Miriam and her mother comply outwardly by in fact placing baby Moses into the river.

---

* I invite men to hear themselves included in this term *sisterhood*, just as Christian women were for centuries supposed to hear themselves included in descriptions of the Fatherhood of God and the brotherhood of man.

But they save his life by putting him into a basket that will float, *before* putting him into the river. And when Pharaoh's daughter finds the baby, Puah/Miriam pretends to be scouring Israel to hire a wetnurse for the baby, whereas in fact she goes straight home to tell her mother the good news that she will now be *paid* for nursing her own son. Later Puah/Miriam will gain distinction as a prophet when she sings her great song of victory after Israel has crossed the Red Sea (Exod. 15:20–21). And the prophet Micah will celebrate her as a liberator of her people on an equal basis with Moses and Aaron (Mic. 6:4).

In fact, although sexist assumptions frequently cause commentators to skip right over the heroic story of Shiprah and Puah, the truth is that without them, there would have been no Moses, and without Moses, there would have been no liberation from Egyptian slavery. History, being heteropatriarchal, has typically ignored the great achievements of our foresisters. We feminists and womanists (male or female) must be careful not to let ourselves be co-opted by heteropatriarchy, for it is up to us to tell women's stories now and in the future. We are called to act in solidarity with our foremothers in a Sisterhood of Saints that stretches across oceans and across centuries in unbroken continuity. God preserve us from failing each other by forgetting the feminist/womanist vision of human partnership.

The Necessity of Subversion

Getting back to the issue of deviousness and downright subversiveness: at a time when Elizabeth Bettenhausen and I were co-keynoters at a conference of Lutheran and Episcopal campus ministers, she mentioned her willingness to use subversion where unjust systems made that necessary. A white male, his voice quivering with anger, told her that he had a great deal of trouble with the duplicity involved in what she had said. When she tactfully but firmly pointed out to him that as a white, male, and presumably heterosexual person, he would not know what it was to feel the *need* of subverting an unjust but ironclad system, he refused to own his privileged status.

Because we were in an open discussion, I jumped into this by affirming from my own experience the illustration Elizabeth had used, that lesbian women and gay men who want to be ministers often have to subvert the heterosexist system by implicitly denying their homosexuality and pretending to be heterosexual. I also made an analogy to Martin Luther King's "Letter from Birmingham Jail," which responds to King's critics by distinguishing between the violence of the system (a violence many people seem willing to accept) and the counterpressures and demonstrations of the oppressed (which is what people usually mean when they express disapproval of violence). Although King was leading only nonviolent demonstrations and advocated creating legal pressures by nonviolent disobedience to unjust laws, he was accused by eight prominent Alabama clergymen of inciting hatred and violence by his direct actions.

Some of the white men at the conference refused to see any analogy between feminist or gay subversion and Dr. King's acts, arguing that because his actions were nonviolent and open whereas subversion is secretive and manipulative, there could be no analogy. But I think Dr. King would be amused to see how his reputation has laundered itself since his untimely death.

The truth is that King wrote the "Letter from Birmingham Jail" because Jewish, Catholic, and Protestant ministers and bishops had accused him of creating dissension and indeed violence by heading the demonstrations in Birmingham and by teaching people to disobey unjust laws either overtly or covertly. To quote King's critics precisely, "such actions as incite to hatred and violence, however technically peaceful those actions may be, have not contributed to the resolution of our local problems" (Axelrod and Cooper, 6). Only protected people can afford to speak so loftily! Well, as oppressed people have always known, sometimes they must confront and sometimes they must subvert. The issue is deciding which is more appropriate to the circumstances of the oppression that currently requires a response.

Subversion means a systematic attempt to overthrow or undermine a political system by persons who work secretly within the system involved. In the case of Shiprah and Puah, when the king decreed a political system of empowering Egypt by destroying Israelite boy-babies, they did not confront, they subverted. What would have happened had they said, "O Pharaoh, live forever, and all that, but you are wrong to order the killing of the Hebrew boys and we will not do it"? They would no doubt have been executed, and the next pair of midwives appointed by the pharaoh would no doubt have cooperated. Boy-babies would have died by the hundreds.

Knowing that open confrontation would wreak havoc on them and the people they wanted to help, Shiprah and Puah secretly subverted the king's unjust system. And when he asked them why the Hebrew boy-babies were flourishing, they told him an outright lie in order to cover up their civil disobedience. And the Scriptures tell us that God blessed them for their actions — subversion, lying, and all!

Years ago, a white male Lutheran theologian, Dietrich Bonhoeffer, defended certain kinds of lying in an excellent book called *Ethics*. Later, he gave his life for an attempt to subvert the Third Reich by assassinating Hitler. To my knowledge, he was not subjected to any vilification for his position on lying and subversion by his brethren in the theological establishment. But when a feminist and a woman speaks of subverting unjust systems for the sake of survival, that's a different story!

I confess that in my New Jersey state college classroom, which is part of the heteropatriarchal system as all state classrooms are, I regularly subvert heteropatriarchy by teaching mutual cooperation rather than one-upmanship, good human adult virtues rather than "masculine" and "feminine" virtues, and equal partnership rather than male primacy and female submission. I feel I have excellent precedent for this subversion: not only the acts of Shiprah and Puah and other righteous women, but also Jesus, who subverted heteropatriarchal understandings of power, insisting that power must always be used to benefit the people at the bottom of the social pecking order. And the apostles, who were accused of "turning the world upside down" by preaching the gospel (Acts 17:6). And the black people in South Africa, subverting and confronting a racist apartheid government that claims to be Christian and doing God's will. And the desperately endangered women who have killed in their sleep the men who have regularly abused them, and then have escaped to another country or lied to cover up what they have done, sensing that they could probably not get justice in misogynistic courts. And nurses who know that the doctor has given destructive orders for a patient's medication, and who quietly refuse to give the medication because they value the patient's survival more than obeying the doctor's orders and protecting their own careers.

We need to face the fact that there will never be equal rights or full civil rights for women (or those men who are treated like women) as long as the heteropatriarchal system is in place. As surely as the French lived in occupied territory while the Nazis controlled their country, we feminists and womanists and les-bi-gay people* are living in occupied territory. And a different set of ethics applies in occupied territory, as any study of the French Resistance groups (or those elsewhere) will reveal. Black people in America have been living in occupied territory for several centuries, and Katie G. Cannon explains that as a result they have developed an ethical method that can only be called situational. She writes, "Black women in their development, analysis and appraisal of various coping mechanisms against the white-oriented, male structured society do not appeal to fixed rules or absolute principles of what is right or wrong and good or bad, but instead they embrace values related to the causal conditions of their cultural circumstances" (75). Of course, so do lesbian women and gay men. So do heterosexual white feminists up against crushing odds in androcentric religious, educational, and corporate systems. Only people in the normative power group can afford to pontificate grandly about never lying and never deceiving and never subverting. All of that would change very quickly if they were rendered powerless and oppressed.

The best women and gay people can do under heteropatriarchal domination is seek some relief, some improvement, all the while we are subverting the system as rapidly as possible. At the Women's Rights Convention

---

* "Les-bi-gay people" is verbal shorthand for "lesbian women, bisexual people, and gay men," which gets a little weighty after a while. I refuse to say "lesbians, bisexuals, and gays," just as I refuse to speak of "cripples" or "Jews" or "the retarded" or "Mexicans" or any other label without adding the words that indicate that people are, first and foremost, *people*.

in 1852, Elizabeth Oakes Smith asked the delegates, "My friends, do we realize for what purpose we are convened? Do we fully understand that we aim at nothing less than an entire subversion of the present order of society, a dissolution of the whole existing social compact?" (Daly, 277). And now, almost a century and a half later, I am asking the same question. And I am suggesting that we toughen up mentally, calling subversion by its correct name and holding our heads high as we practice the situation ethics that are forced upon people in occupied or "enemy" territory.

Sophia and Inner Empowerment

To help us hold our heads up, I propose that we look now at the character-ization of Sophia, or Wisdom, in what scholars call the Wisdom literature of the Hebrew Scriptures. This literature is of special interest to femi-nists, womanists, and other liberationists, if for no other reason than that Wisdom literature has been attacked on grounds similar to the attacks on feminist and liberation theology. The Wisdom literature includes the canon-ical books of Proverbs, Ecclesiastes, and Job, and in a sense also the Epistle of James, as well as several books Protestants call apocryphal: particularly the books of Ecclesiasticus and the Wisdom of Solomon. Those who dislike this body of literature say that it is too utilitarian, pragmatic, and focused on human experience; it emphasizes human bodily life rather than theism in the abstract. It also tends to address individuals rather than nations and makes no use of the concept of any one people as exclusively God's chosen people. So its application is universally inclusive rather than narrowly na-tionalistic (Trawick, 337–38). Need I say more about parallels to feminist, womanist, and liberation theology?

Unfortunately, Wisdom literature contains some exceedingly misogy-nistic adages. But again, in the spirit of "Diving into the Wreck" to find the treasure within the debris, and in the spirit of turning old words into New Words, I would like to focus our attention on the personification of Wisdom, or Sophia, as a powerful agent who brings salvation to those who obey her voice. She describes herself in the book of Proverbs as being with God in the beginning and as making a feast to which she invites everybody who will listen. She says,

> [During the creation process] I was beside [God],
>   like a master worker;
> and I was daily [God's] delight
>   rejoicing before [God] always,
> rejoicing in [God's] inhabited world
>   and delighting in the human race....
> For whoever finds me finds life

and obtains favor from the [Sovereign];
but those who miss me injure themselves,
all who hate me love death.

(Proverbs 8:30–31 and 35–36, NRSV;
inclusive God-language mine)

Without a doubt, Sophia assumes the proportions of God Herself both in the canonical and apocryphal Scriptures. Although in the passage just quoted she is said to be *with* God, in other passages she seems to be conflated with God's Very Self: Wisdom of Solomon 7:10–11 or 8:1, or Proverbs 8:12–18, for instance. Some scholars think that Sophia represents a late Hebrew borrowing from nearby goddess-worshipping cultures, or perhaps a holdover from the ancient religion of the Great Mother. Whatever the origin of this characterization, as Susan Cady, Marian Ronan, and Hal Taussig point out in *Wisdom's Feast*, it is astounding that "the major spiritual figure of pre-Christian Judaism is female" (32).

In the Christian Scriptures, all one need do is stick to and capitalize the word *Sophia* wherever it appears, rather than translating it *wisdom*, in order to see that Jesus is identified with the Hebrew figure of Sophia in passage after passage. For instance, when we use this method, the apostle Paul refers to "Christ Jesus, who became for us Sophia from God." He also calls Christ "the power of God and the Sophia of God" (1 Cor. 1:30, 24). The first chapter of John's Gospel uses "the Word" (*Logos*) to identify Jesus with Lady Wisdom in the Hebrew Scriptures: "What John has done is give Sophia a new name [the Word], and then proclaim that this pre-existent co-creator is to be identified with Jesus. In short, Jesus is Sophia" (Cady, Ronan, and Taussig, 37). And according to Matthew 11:19, Jesus referred to himself as Sophia, claiming in defense of his own unconventional behavior that "Sophia is vindicated by her deeds."

Should Feminists Ritualize Sophia as Suffering and Dying?

The authors of *Wisdom's Feast* point out that "except insofar as she is identified with Jesus, the biblical Sophia does not suffer and die." They worry that "a Sophia who does not suffer is limited in her ability to function within a feminist spirituality." They comment that "the absence of suffering and death within the Sophia story . . . gives her a certain disembodied quality which is less than helpful in our attempt to express the connectedness of all things" (Cady, Ronan, and Taussig, 65). But what they have overlooked is that Sophia herself *is* the connectedness of all things; she is the eternal Self of God's infinite, omnipresent Consciousness that is extended and expressed in the existence of every human being born into the world. She is not disembodied because she is embodied in every body. She herself does not suffer and does not die, and yet she is identified not only with the essential Self of Jesus but with every other human being who has ever seemed to suffer and die. In fact, Sophia is able to remain peaceful, to laugh and play like a happy child, even in the midst of a suffering world — not because she is heartless, but because she knows that everyone is home-free the moment they relinquish their fatal attraction to the external appearances of things.

The Sophia of God says, "Come unto me, and I will give you *rest*." Restfulness requires peace of mind, not a morbid focus on fear and suffering. The phenomenon of physical death illustrates in an extreme form the suffering our ego causes us by clinging desperately to the judgment of our physical senses and past experiences as if they were the measure of all there is. The psychological suffering that attends death is not only saying goodbye to people and surroundings we have loved, but also is the ego's great final struggle to hold on to its body and its senses in the form in which it has always known them. When we finally let go, our suffering is over because at last we are able to see with senses that are still senses, but infinitely keener than the limited senses we currently use to find our way around in the world. Death is not the end of the body; it is the end of the ego's limited, distorted, and partial perception of the body.

At Jesus's transfiguration the veil was pulled back for a moment so that we could catch a glimpse at what bodies really look like ("his face shone like the sun and his clothes became dazzling white" — i.e., his body was so brilliant that even his clothes were shining, Matt. 17:11). But in our heteropatriarchal dualism, people have tended to come down on one side or the other of the human substance/spirit paradox, teaching either that we are essentially spirits or else that we are only physical, temporarily trapped in material bodies with a temporary consciousness — when the fact is that we are *both* embodied spirits *and* spiritual bodies. Like Jesus, we are eternal bodyselves, despite the evidence of our ego's limited sense perceptions that seem to put us at the mercy of our bodies as we currently misperceive them.

I think it would be a mistake for feminists to attempt to ritualize the suffering and death of Sophia, as the authors of *Wisdom's Feast* suggest we do. It is for good reason that the Bible depicts Sophia without suffering and without death: she is the calm eternal Self that is expressed in each of our bodyselves. She is the deep quiet *core* of us, never affected by our ego-nature's thrashings and sufferings and feelings of abandonment. Even Jesus went through those: but shortly after he had cried out about being abandoned on the cross, he committed his spirit (Self/Sophia) into the hands of God, an act that indicates that God Herself was still there and had never in fact abandoned Her Child, the embodiment of who She Is, the express image of Her person. Then after a couple of days Jesus was back on earth again, in a recognizable body, letting Thomas check out his death-wounds and cooking on the shore of the Sea of Tiberias (John 20 and 21). The apparently material body of Jesus did not return to the dust of earth as ours will do; but no less than Jesus, the rest of us will enjoy resurrected or astral or spiritual bodies rather than becoming disembodied spirit.

Sophia herself warned us in Proverbs 8:36 that she is the very opposite of injury and death; so wouldn't it be erroneous to ritualize her as suffering injury and dying? If we must ritualize suffering and death, it is enough to ritualize the apparent suffering and death of Jesus and all the others who have apparently suffered and died before and after him. But there is no virtue in worshipping suffering and death. As the Garden of Gethsemane illustrates, they should be avoided if at all possible. And as Easter weekend illustrates, they should be transmuted into a resurrected body and newness of life as soon as possible.

To ritualize the death of Sophia would be like celebrating the death of the spirit that kept those oil-soaked waterbirds calmly trying to live out their lives with dignity in the midst of disaster. It would be like celebrating the snuffing out of the revolutionary fire in the eyes of a member of a base community in Latin America who has known it is not *God's* will for peasants to be poor, but then slides back into apathy. It would be like glorifying the burnt-out bitterness and exhaustion of a feminist or womanist who has given up on the struggle. Or like celebrating the death of neighborliness in a person who came to the scene of a fire meaning to help, but overcome by greed, began instead to loot. These things happen, yes: but they are not the focus of ritual because they discourage or enervate rather than nourishing what is sensuously spiritual in us all. Sophia is a biblical symbol of the yearning for *shalom* in every creature, the divine "spark," the innate wisdom, the light that enlightens every human being born into the world. The darkness can never defeat that *logos*, that brightness, that Sophia. Accordingly, we should not build rituals around Sophia as suffering or dying.

The Apocrypha, the King James Version, and History

Those who know my earlier work are aware that I have for years drawn personal inspiration and empowerment from the descriptions of Wisdom, or Sophia, writing a chapter on "God as Dame Wisdom" in my 1983 book *The Divine Feminine: Biblical Imagery of God as Female,* and earlier than that, an article on Jesus and Lady Wisdom in *Daughters of Sarah*. In particular, I have loved the description in the apocryphal Wisdom of Solomon, a book that heavily influenced the writers of the Christian Scriptures (the New Testament).

Never have I forgotten my astonishment back in 1962 when I was studying, in the rare book room of the New York Public Library, a first edition of the King James Version. I was astonished because I was never told about the Apocrypha while I was being brought up on the King James Version, yet there it was in the first edition. And the margins of the KJV

New Testament were full of cross-references to the Wisdom of Solomon! But during the late seventeenth century, when the Puritan Synod of Dort decided to demote the prestige of the Apocrypha, it was silently removed from the King James Version and all the marginal references to its contents were quietly deleted. (That in itself is a lesson in how the losers and the minority perspectives get deleted from history as if they had never existed, so that history becomes a lopsided record of winners only, preserving exclusively the perspectives of the ruling class.)

Here then is a description of Sophia from a book the King James translators recognized as a very important influence on the Christian Scriptures. I hope that each of us will see in this passage a description of the eternal Self that expresses Herself *in* and *as* our Selves. Underneath our damage, despite our ego's perceptions of limitations and separation, *this is what our deepest core identity is like*.

> There is in her [Sophia, wisdom] a spirit that is intelligent, holy,
> unique, manifold, subtle,
> mobile, clear, unpolluted,
> distinct, invulnerable, loving the good, keen,
> irresistible, beneficent, humane,
> steadfast, sure, free from anxiety,
> all-powerful, overseeing all,
> and penetrating through all spirits
> that are intelligent, pure, and altogether subtle.
> For wisdom is more mobile than any motion;
> because of her pureness she pervades and penetrates all things.
> For she is a breath of the power of God,
> and a pure emanation of the glory of the Almighty;
> therefore nothing defiled gains entrance into her.
> For she is a reflection of eternal light,
> a spotless mirror of the working of God,
> and an image of [God's] goodness.
> Although she is but one, she can do all things,
> and while remaining in herself, she renews all things;
> in every generation she passes into holy souls
> and makes them friends of God, and prophets....
> She is more beautiful than the sun,
> and excels every constellation of the stars...
> against wisdom evil does not prevail.
> She reaches mightily from one end of the earth to the other,
> and she orders all things well....
> For she is an initiate in the knowledge of God,
> and an associate in [God's] works....
> Send her forth from the holy heavens,

and from the throne of your glory send her
that she may labor at my side,
and that I may learn what is pleasing to you.
For she knows and understands all things,
and she will guide me wisely in my actions
and guard me with her glory.
Then my works will be acceptable.

(Wisdom of Solomon 7:22–27, 29; 8:1; 9:10–12, NRSV;
inclusive God-language mine)

The Sophia-Nature within Us

After all these centuries of being associated with darkness-as-evil or as ignorance, and with heavy materiality, and with sinful Eve (as opposed to male
self-associations with brightness and the image of God) we feminists need
to take a good long look at this description of Sophia. We are not enticed
by Hellenistic ambitions to become pure spirit by transcending our bodyselves; but surely it is good news to learn that our bodyselves are infused
with the gorgeous eternal power of Sophia at the very core of us. (So are
male bodyselves.)

One final consideration: I am dismayed to notice how often men associate childbirthing with war and therefore with death. For instance, an
ancient Hindu proverb says, "What war is to man, childbirth is to woman."
And in 431 B.C.E., the Greek dramatist Euripides made a similar connection in the play *Medea,* claiming (with probable truth) that "three battles
are not equal to the pangs of one childbirth." An article by William Broyles,
Jr., in *Esquire* magazine made the same connection between birthing and
warfare, arguing that whereas women can plumb the depths of the human
soul in the birthing room, men can do so only on the field of battle. But
these are heteropatriarchal associations.

We women know that birthing and midwifing are not about death, not
about taking, but about life, about giving, about entering into a covenant
of caring with those who need our help. We know that all women and men
who will enter a covenant of caring express the nature of Sophia, of the
Logos, of the Christ Herself, the New Humanity. Some of us are Shiprahs,
some of us are Puahs, but all of us are sisters. In harmony but not sameness,
in a unity that embraces diversity, let us get on with the task of midwifing
justice into the world. We can do so in the confident power of the peaceful,
playful, creative, loving Sophia-Self that is our own most profound identity.

Chapter Four

BIBLICAL SUPPORT
FOR HONORING HUMAN DIVERSITY

———— ≈ ————

To receive maximum benefit from this chapter, it is important to do the following imaginative exercise before reading any further. The exercise will take only a very few minutes. Before you so much as glance at the choices, please be sure to imagine yourself in the situation suggested. No matter how obvious to you the "right" answers may appear to be, please jot down your responses and pay attention to your own reasoning process. This exercise will provide an experiential basis for much of the more theoretical material to follow.

An Imaginative Exercise on Biblical Interpretation

IMAGINE: You are appointed to a Futuristic Board of Planners to set forth the structure of a society into which you will later be born. Your charge now is to make the moral and ethical rules for that future society. Yet as you work on those rules, you are constantly aware that *you do not know whether you yourself will be born into that society as female or male; black, yellow, red, or white; homosexual, bisexual, or heterosexual; able-bodied or physically handicapped; mentally capable or incapable; poor or wealthy; nor do you know whether your nation will be powerful or weak.* The Bible has been specified as the basic foundation for the moral and ethical rules of the future society, and your Planning Board is committed to providing biblical justification for each of its rules. Which of the Bible passages on the following page — taken at face value and out of context as they are — would you be more likely to emphasize, knowing that in your own future life you will be forced to submit to the rules that are going to emerge from each choice?

ON RACE/CLASS RELATIONS

"Let all who are under the yoke of slavery regard their masters as worthy of all honor, so that the name of God and the teaching may not be blasphemed."

1 Timothy 6:1, NRSV

"Slaves who have escaped to you from their owners shall not be given back to them. They shall reside with you, in your midst, in any place they choose in any one of your towns, wherever they please; you shall not oppress them"

Deuteronomy 23:15–16, NRSV

ON MALE/FEMALE RELATIONS

"To the woman [God] said, 'I will greatly multiply your pangs in childbearing.... yet your desire shall be for your husband, and he shall rule over you."

Genesis 3:16, NRSV

"Be subject to one another out of reverence for Christ.... Each of you [men] should love his wife as himself, and a wife should respect her husband."

Ephesians 5:21,33, NRSV

ON PHYSICAL HANDICAPS

"No one whose testicles are crushed or whose penis is cut off shall be admitted to the assembly of the Lord."

Deuteronomy 23:1, NRSV

"But [Jesus] said to [the disciples] ... there are eunuchs [i.e., castrated men] who have been so from birth, ... and there are eunuchs who have made themselves eunuchs for the sake of the Kingdom of heaven."

Matthew 19:11–12, NRSV

ON SEXUAL ORIENTATION/BEHAVIOR

"Neither the sexually immoral nor idolaters nor adulterers nor male prostitutes nor homosexual offenders nor thieves nor the greedy nor drunkards nor slanderers nor swindlers will inherit the kingdom of God."

1 Corinthians 6:9, NIV

"For I am convinced that neither death nor life, neither angels nor demons, neither the present nor the future, nor any powers, neither height nor depth, nor anything else in all creation, will be able to separate us from the love of God that is in Christ Jesus our Lord."

Romans 8:38-39, NIV

ON INTERNATIONAL RELATIONSHIPS

"Now the woman was a Greek, a Syrophoenician by birth. And she begged [Jesus] to cast the demon out of her daughter. And he said to her, 'Let the children [of Israel] first be fed, for it is not right to take the children's bread and throw it to the dogs [of other nations]."

Mark 7:27, RSV

"From one ancestor [God] made all nations to inhabit the whole earth ...so they would search for God... though indeed [God] is not far from each one of us. For 'in [God] we live and move and have our being'; as even some of your own [Greek] poets have said, 'For we too are [God's] offspring.'"

Acts 17:26–27, NRSV

Because literary interpretation is a complex art, under ideal conditions we would have sat around informally, discussing all the implications and contexts of each passage before making the choices on which our future well-being would depend. However, because of the conditions under which writers write and readers read, I will have to hazard some generalizations about the choices involved in this exercise, based on my own experience and research and that of others.

Traditionalist vs. Liberationist Emphases

The choices in the left-hand column have been (and in some cases still would be) the preferred passages of those who utilize the Bible to block subordinated or marginalized people from access to opportunity, power, respect, and the good basics of life. Although no one with any credibility would attempt today to use the Bible to legitimate slavery, in fact 1 Timothy 6:1 was a key passage used in the defense of slavery by many people. Among them were John Henry Hopkins, Episcopal bishop of Vermont, who published a tract, "The Bible View of Slavery," in 1861 and a book defending slavery in 1864; Princeton Professor Charles B. Hodge, who published his essay "The Bible Argument on Slavery" in 1860; and Presbyterian pastor George D. Armstrong, whose book *The Christian Doctrine of Slavery* was published in 1857 (Swartley, 31–64). Despite the fact that no one in most societies would take such arguments seriously these days, nevertheless 1 Timothy 6:1 could be used to extrapolate a rigid class hierarchy in our futuristic society. Not knowing whether we ourselves would be rich or poor, masters or servants, as planners we would be wise to opt for Deuteronomy 23:15 as our guide.

By contrast to the issue of slavery, traditionalist arguments for perpetuating secondary roles for women in the home, church, and society are still very much utilized. Among those who hold that the male is intended by God to be the primary decision-maker while the female serves his purposes in a supporting role, one of the foremost is Stephen B. Clark, whose *Man and Woman in Christ: An Examination of the Roles of Men and Women in Light of Scripture and the Social Sciences* was published in 1980 by an outfit called Servant Books (really!). Others include Charles C. Ryrie, who in 1958 argued in *The Place of Women in the Church* that a woman's place is secondary, and George Knight III, who in 1977 published *The New Testament Teaching on the Role Relationship of Men and Women*. Each of them upholds Genesis 3:15 as a prescription of God's will for social arrangements today, even though they do not oppose labor-saving devices and do not insist on eating thorns and thistles, or at least a vegetarian diet, as consistency would require of them (Gen. 3:17–19). But if they were making rules for a future society in which they themselves might be born as women, we can be sure that it wouldn't take them very long to see things differently.

Nobody with any credibility would attempt today to uphold Deuteronomy 23:1 as a way of blocking people with handicaps from entering churches or synagogues or even from holding leadership roles. Yet a similar attitude does persist in the widespread fear and social avoidance of people who are physically or mentally handicapped. I remember at least one church debate concerning whether a candidate who limped might be accepted for ordination; but at least nobody attempted to *use the Bible* to argue against his candidacy. Fearing that we might not be born physically and mentally perfect, as futuristic planners we naturally would prefer the pluralistic-sounding assessment of Jesus to our own possible exclusion on the basis of Deuteronomy.

The Bible is very much a factor in current debates over the ordination of openly lesbian or gay candidates, and in debates concerning whether or not a church or synagogue should provide rituals for celebrating same-sex covenantal unions. (A bishop of the Episcopal Church recently said that since the church blesses fox hounds before hunts, it ought to be able to bless homosexual relationships — but his insight is not sitting well with a good many Episcopalians, despite the fact that this denomination, to which I belong, prides itself on being a place where a person does not have to check her mind at the door.) 1 Corinthians 6:9 is one of several passages now being utilized to block access to equal religious status for those lesbian women or gay men who are open and honest about their orientation.

For instance, a March 1990 letter from Habitat for Humanity explained that any unmarried person hired by Habitat must sign a pledge of celibacy. But Habitat officials deny that this requirement discriminates against homosexuals, because heterosexual single people must also sign the pledge. What the officials choose to ignore, of course, is the fact that marriage is always an option for heterosexuals but is unavailable to homosexuals, at least in any form that an organization like Habitat would recognize. Habitat officials claim that their celibacy policy was formulated to uphold Christian understandings of the Bible. And they are not alone. Many Protestant denominational policies, as well as the official policy of the Roman Catholic Church and several branches of Judaism, join Habitat for Humanity in an interpretation of Scripture that blocks openly les-bi-gay people from first-class citizenship.

The final passage in the left-hand column of our list, Mark 7:27, would hardly be cited today as justification for viciously nationalistic policies; yet the policies themselves persist. One of the worst aspects of war is the crude us-versus-them attitude it fosters. As I write, people are sporting lapel ribbons urging me to "pray for our troops," as if Iraqi troops were not just as much the offspring of God Herself as the troops of America's coalition. The old us-versus-them standoff between communism and capitalism has been defused by *perestroika,* but it remains to be seen whether the newly democratized nations of Europe will respect tolerance and each other, or whether they will allow old nationalistic and religious loyalties to split them into mutually antagonistic tribes (Michnik, 44). In the United States recently, racism and anti-Semitism have repeatedly demonstrated that they are far from dead; and the outpouring of violence against women and children is horrifying. In Christianity, perhaps the chief holdover of the us-versus-them attitude expressed in Mark 7:27 is the assumption that nobody can hope to get to heaven except those who have converted to Christianity; and that attitude is still very widespread indeed. The great English poet Alfred, Lord Tennyson was not at the top of his form when he wrote "Better fifty years of Europe than a cycle [a thousand years] of Cathay [China]," but plenty of United States citizens are no less chauvinistic than Tennyson was. Nevertheless, if there were a chance that we ourselves might eventually be born in an underdeveloped nation, as futuristic planners we would quickly enough move away from the judgment of Mark 7:27 to align ourselves with the universalism of Acts 17.

The passages in the left-hand column of our imaginative exercise illustrate the emphases of people we might call traditionalists, since their goal is to perpetuate the traditional hierarchies of heteropatriarchy. Their interpretations might justly be called repressive, since they block the access of some people to the power, respect, and privilege enjoyed by other people.

Because I am still evangelical in many ways and because I am a professor of literature with great respect for the written word, I must observe that every passage in the left-hand column looks quite different when it is placed within its historical and literary context. Then it is either open to a more liberating interpretation or else forms a historical record of earlier understandings of God's dealings with humankind. By contrast, every passage in the right-hand column retains its liberating, nonoppressive, universally positive face value when it is placed into its historical and literary context. These facts are worth pondering carefully when people are deciding whether to choose the traditionalist or the liberationist hermeneutics as their normative, basic, habitual method of interpreting the Bible, and other literary works as well.

Future society or no future society, the passages in the right-hand column would still be preferred by people who consider themselves liberationist, wholistic, feminist, New Age, pluralistic, sensuously spiritual, or humanistic. Although secular humanism has been the subject of vituperative attack from the Religious Right, it is important to remember that there are also Christian humanists, Jewish humanists, and humanists from other religious traditions. For instance, church Reformers like Luther, Melanchthon, and Calvin were Christian humanists. The term simply means that emphasis is placed on human experience, values, and dignity rather than on ecclesiastical theorizing. Many *secular* humanists, who deny supernaturalism, would probably not read a book like this because they have a severe allergy to the word *spirituality*. If by some means they got into reading this book, they still might skip this chapter because they would consider the Bible irrelevant to the structures of society. On the other hand, some secular humanists might indeed be wise enough to read this chapter, because many people are influenced by what they are told is biblical, whether it is or not, and whether or not they have ever read the Bible for themselves. Too often society hears about "what the Bible says" only from the traditionalists. It is time for some strong prophetic words from the pluralistic and humanist perspective.

Biblical Themes That Promote Pluralism

There are at least ten biblical themes that apparently provide support for those who want to honor and affirm human diversity: (1) One God as the source and sustainer of all the variety in the universe; (2) the movement of creation away from a single androgyne into a human race of similarity but not sameness, male and female; (3) the movement at the Tower of Babel from one language and culture to many languages and cultures; (4) the trinitarian nature of God, relational and egalitarian; (5) Jesus' injunctions to love friends and enemies alike, in imitation of God's indiscriminate grace; (6) the normative Hebrew and Christian love ethic, by which we are to love our neighbor as we love ourselves; (7) the image of the Body of Christ or the New Humanity, with many members and differing gifts but one divine Source (Head); (8) God's jealousy concerning idolatry — that is, worshipping anything smaller than the One-Who-Encompasses-All-Diversities; (9) God's omnipresence, within creation as well as surrounding it — "above all, through all, and in all"; (10) God's relinquishment of control over humankind. None of these are highly controversial themes. Although a traditionalist might *word* some of them differently, in all honesty traditionalists as well as liberationists would have to admit that these themes are either explicit or else strongly implied in Scripture. So let us think about them together. Themes not explicitly discussed in this chapter are examined elsewhere in this book.

Monotheism and Pluralism

The traditionalist interpreter assumes that because there is only one God, there is only one right way of doing things and only one right answer to every question. And of course what is right is determined by the group in power, which in the United States is a white, male, heterosexual, affluent group. (The group includes a minority of gay men, but they are deeply closeted.) By contrast, the wholistic, liberationist, or sensuously spiritual interpreter assumes that because there is only one God and yet so much variety in the universe created by that one God, God must be in favor of variety and pluralism.

The apostle Paul certainly implied as much in his words to the Greek philosophers on Mars Hill, as recorded in Acts 17. If some of these words seem familiar, that's because they are included as one of the right-column choices in our imaginative exercise:

> From one ancestor [God] made all nations to inhabit the whole earth, and [God] allotted the times of their existence and the boundaries of the places where they would live, so that they would search for [God] and perhaps grope for [God] and find [God] — though indeed [God] is not far from each one of us. For "In [God] we live and move and have our being"; as even some of your own poets have said, "For we too are [God's] offspring." Since we are God's offspring, we ought not to think that the deity is like gold, or silver, or stone, an image formed by the art and imagination of mortals. (Acts 17:26–29, NRSV; inclusive God-language mine)

Throughout history, monotheism has been used to legitimate countless wars and millions of deaths. As I write, Saddam Hussein assures his people that Allah fights on their side and that death in battle means instant heaven, while George Bush assures Americans that God is on our side. So much for the notion that the human race has come of age, taking full responsibility for its own choices! It would be easy enough to blame all this aggression on the biblical concept of "One God only," and many scholars (feminists included) have placed the blame right there. Indeed traditionalists do seem to assume that monotheism is the enemy of pluralism. For instance, although American traditionalists are forced by the Constitution into at least a grudging acceptance of social pluralism, throughout the 1970s and 1980s we have witnessed some astonishing attempts to create a civil religion. One method was the publication of "biblical scorecards" that rated politicians on whether or not they measured up to traditionalist interpretations of the Bible. Other methods include court cases to censor textbooks, the sometimes violent "pro-life" movement to deny reproductive choice to women, and organized opposition to civil rights protection for gay women and men. It is ironic that religious groups, themselves protected by our democratic pluralistic polity, should be so eager to deny similar protection to other groups of people!

As I understand it, the essence of a pluralistic society is that no one particular political, ideological, cultural, or ethnic group is automatically and permanently dominant. Democratic pluralism logically implies, and I assume, that the only way to honor human diversity is to work toward a society in which everybody has equal access to those things we ourselves would not want to do without. To borrow Jesse Jackson's image, the goal of democratic pluralism is a level playing field. Nobody should be forced to compete uphill!

There is nothing about monotheism that necessarily opposes democratic pluralism, and a great deal that supports it. Where problems arise, they stem not from monotheism itself, but from the arrogant notion that any one person or religious or political group knows all there is to know about what is correct and therefore can dictate the rules to everyone else. *Heteropatriarchal* monotheism has always assumed that its own version of a distant and controlling God-Father is the only admissible version, to be upheld by coercion, repression, and if necessary by physical violence.

But I would argue, and have already argued in my book *Godding,* that the concept of one Source affirms rather than denies pluralism. God's jealous refusal to give Her glory to another is not pridefulness, but an insistence that we give our attention to *all* that She is, to the entire human race and all the being and becoming of time and eternity, as opposed to our focussing on any one smaller segment or part of it. Ephesians 4:6 tells us that God is "above all and through all, and in us all." So when Shirley MacLaine teaches people to chant "I am God," she is correct — as long as she (and they) constantly remind themselves that everyone else and every other living thing, as well as much more we may not be aware of, is also God. (This is not pantheism, but panentheism, or radical omnipresence, meaning that everything exists in God and God in everything, but without limiting God only to the creation.)

A mark of genuine mysticism is the awareness that the Sacred One is not only within ourselves but also goes beyond anything we can find words for. Therefore to seek justice only for those who are like ourselves, or those whom we happen to like, is idolatry: it is giving the glory of the All-Encompassing One to something smaller than Her totality. According to the Bible, that makes Her *livid!*

Paul said on Mars Hill that *because we are all God's offspring,* we should not think that the deity is like any gold, silver, stone, or conceptual image formed by the imagination of human beings. Indeed, if we are the offspring of God, then any image of God more limited than every creature would be partial and idolatrous. As Paul implied, idols can be created in behaviors and in words as well as in artistic media. Chapter Six will be devoted to explaining how the Jewish and Christian traditions have developed and worshipped a controlling androcentric idol that has had disastrous results on human relationships. The assumptions that God is very old and very rich and of course white have also had disastrous consequences. In Christianity as in Greek philosophy the assumption that the deity is asexual, too self-contained and too "spiritual" to need any sensuous or sensual intimacy, has had disastrous results on human sexual attitudes, creating generations of body-haters and pleasure-haters who cannot care about justice for others because they are not fair even to themselves.

God Herself, who is above and through and in everyone and everything so that we live within a divine milieu, refuses to give Her glory to anything smaller than the whole. We had better learn to "bring *many* names" by which to address this God who is our strong Mother as well as our tender Father, a "young, growing God" as well as an "old, aching God," a "great, living God" who is "never fully known" even though She is "closer yet than breathing" (Wren, 137–38).

Relinquishment of Coercion

God's relinquishment of control over humankind is an important biblical theme in a culture where the religious and political Right seeks to legislate a single standard of morality — or failing that, to legislate punishment, such as forcing teen-age girls to bear unwanted babies as the penalty (for girls only) for premature sex. Despite such draconian measures, the Genesis creation accounts describe for us the self-limitation of God. Having created Adam and Eve in the divine image, God tells them to take charge of the world and all its creatures (Gen. 1:26–28). This was no small gesture. By placing humankind in charge of the world, God gave up the power to change society except through human agency. Another way of saying this is that having expressed Her infinite consciousness by the human male and female, God presented them with the whole divine milieu and gave them the freedom either to open themselves to the reality of God's presence everywhere, or else to deny God's presence and imagine themselves alone and self-sustained. The alternative to God's providing freedom to choose would have been a race of marionettes.

As we know from the story of the fall into delusion recorded in Genesis 3, humankind chose to trust the ego rather than the Self (chose to distrust our own deepest identity), and thus chose to imagine ourselves in alien bodies in an alien universe. We ate of the tree of the knowledge of good and evil, forfeiting our capacity to enjoy our birthright of knowing "Good by itself, and evil not at all" (Milton, *Paradise Lost* XI. 89). It was a major error, to be corrected only by learning once again to trust God's Presence in our Selves and in all Selves. This can be done only by turning away from the confused, partial, distorted perceptions of the ego and yielding ourselves to the fact that God is All in All. As T. S. Eliot put it, this is "a condition of complete simplicity/(Costing not less than everything)" ("Little Gidding," 256–57).

As infinite consciousness, God certainly knew that Adam and Eve would make the major error that each of us replicates until we awaken to our true identity. Nevertheless, God irrevocably gave us the right to choose, which means that we and God (inseparable as we are) are obliged to live with the consequences of our choices. It is therefore awesome arrogance for any segment of society to attempt to legislate away the moral agency or entitledness of another segment of society, unless that segment has identified itself as intent on undercutting the well-being of others. How dare anyone deny moral agency to pregnant women? (A complex issue, I know, which I will confront in Chapter Ten). How dare anyone deny civil and human rights to gay women and men (see Chapter Eleven)? How dare adults abuse the children or animals who are dependent upon them (see Chapter Nine)? How dare we "continue to tolerate economic priorities that value property more than people — that allow thirty children every minute to die of starvation and inadequate health care while the world spends one million, seven hundred thousand dollars in every one of those minutes, in preparation for war" (Lorde, "Survival," 12)? Clearly these injustices are all replications of that error recorded in Genesis 3: the error of thinking oneself separate from the All-Encompassing One and therefore of trying to get ahead through dominance over the "other" or simply unconcern for "the other."

It is not only in Genesis that the Bible speaks of God's relinquishing power and control over the human race. Throughout the Hebrew Scriptures, God is depicted as persistently yearning for a loving human response but without coercing that response. The Christian Scriptures depict God-in-Jesus as relinquishing the perquisites of divinity, taking on the limitations of humanity, calling his disciples friends, doing the job of a Jewish wife by washing his disciples' feet, and creating a discipleship of equals. As Brian Wren puts it,

> These moves toward a community based on mutual love . . . are anti-patriarchal, as is God's repeated option for the poor, downtrodden, excluded, and oppressed. This begins with the choice of a small, enslaved people in pharaoh's Egypt. It continues as the prophets assert the covenant rights of the poor against the oppression of kings, merchants, and corrupt judges. It is a central theme in the ministry of Jesus, as he welcomes and makes friends of people excluded or subordinated in his own society and issues God's open invitation to them. (132–33)

Learning to relinquish power over others and surrendering the ego's deceptive notion that we ourselves are somehow entitled to better living than others: these are basic to heart-felt pluralism. Our ego-natures inevitably perceive things relative to our own life experiences, including our families, socialization, education, religion, and temperament. For that reason we may always be in error about what is ultimately true, good, and beautiful ("God's will"). We must therefore avoid elevating our partial perceptions to the level of divine absolutes. By seeking power over other people, or

even by assuming we deserve better than they, we are placing ourselves as
superior to God.

From One, Many

Genesis 11 tells the story of those who planned to build a city and a tower
on a plain in Shinar. The tower was to reach to heaven in order to glorify
the single name of the group who built it ("let us make a name for ourselves," Gen. 11:4). The result of this attempt at ego-aggrandizement was
the furthering of pluralism — the confounding of the single language into
many languages and the scattering of the people across the face of the earth.
I understand this to mean that the fighting and divisiveness that occurred
during this project led to so much alienation that people formed their own
subcultures, developed their own languages, and went their own ways.

Just as God could have rested content with the single androgynous
earth-creature called Adam but instead divided that creature into the human
male and female, God could somehow have taught humility to the unified
group in Shinar, rather than permitting a multiplicity and confusion (Babel) of languages and nations. Myth, history, and science have reaffirmed
the Creator's pluralism in millions of instances ever since. Not one face is
the same as any other, not one thumbprint, not even one snowflake! Don't
these facts tell us something about the multiplicity of God's Self-expression?

From One, many. The direction is clear. For human governance, there
must be found a pluralistic protection of as many harmless ways of being
as God needs for Her manifold creativity. The fact that the many are also
ultimately one is not a matter for human legislation, although it brings
great peace of soul to those who know about it. We cannot force other
people to become healed or whole; we can only try to match our treatment
of one another to the fact that in our diversity we express a single Source.
Thus the prophet Malachi attempted to stop human beings from betraying
one another by crying out, "Have we not all one parent? Has not one God
created us? Why then are we faithless to one another . . . ?" (Mal. 2:10).

Trinitarian Relatedness and Coequality

Not only is God the Source or Parent of us all, but this One God is
depicted in the Bible as triune, radically one and yet "a co-equal unity-
in-relatedness" (Wren). Although they strongly emphasize monotheism,
the Hebrew Scriptures seem to imply the triune nature of the One in such
places as the triple benediction in Numbers 6:24–26, the seraphim's triple
cry of *holy* in Isaiah 6:3, the reference to a presence, a redeemer, and a holy
spirit in Isaiah 63:9–10, the plural form of *Elohim* (deity), and the spots

where the deity speaks with the deity. Similarly the Christian Scriptures also do not contain a formal statement concerning the triune nature of the One God. But both Jesus and the apostles attribute distinct personalities to a Father (Mother), a Son (Child, Offspring), and a Holy Spirit (Unger, 1307–8). Incidentally, the Great Mother has always been worshipped as Triune: Virgin, Mother, and Crone.

Centuries ago, the theologians of early Christianity concluded that the three "persons" of the godhead must be coequal as well as coeternal. But as long as Christians continue to worship a withdrawn, controlling, and dominating God-Father in Heaven, we will refuse to pay attention to the implications of our own Trinity — "the equality, mutuality, and dynamism of trinitarian relationships" (Wren, 130). Trinitarian doctrine is therefore one of the strongest undergirdings for pluralism on the part of Christian believers. If the Council of Nicea (325 C.E.) could see the danger of Arius's hierarchical Trinity and came down on the side of a consubstantial Three-in-One, why cannot modern Christians see the error of social hierarchies, which elevate some children of God and oppress others?

Loving Our Enemies

Then there is the remarkable teaching of Jesus in Matthew 5:43–45, and 48, which I quote from the New Revised Standard Version:

> You have heard that it was said, "You shall love your neighbor and hate your enemy." But I say to you, Love your enemies and pray for those who persecute you, *so that you may be children of your Father [Mother] in heaven;* for [God] makes [God's] sun rise on the evil and on the good, and sends rain on the righteous and on the unrighteous.... Be perfect, therefore, as your heavenly Father [Mother] is perfect. (emphasis and inclusive God-language mine)

Because God provides sunshine and rain without discriminating between just and unjust people, those who wish to be known as Her children are instructed to love and pray for their acquaintances without discriminating between their friends and enemies. Now that's pluralism!

Jesus even implies that it is precisely *through* loving our enemies that we *become* God's children — which would make sense, since through the eyes of eternity we are all one family and there *are* no enemies. ("Enemy" is the projection of a frightened ego.) Jesus seems to imply that failure to share life's necessities with "the other" endangers our recognition of our own at-oneness with God. This interpretation is supported by Jesus' further urging that we "be perfect [complete, all-embracing] as your heavenly Father [Mother] is perfect [complete, all-embracing]" (Young, 745; Douglas-Klotz, ix). The passage does not mean that we must somehow like people we don't like or allow people to walk on us, but it does mean that a creative response to those who are unjust to us would be one that helps to bring them toward harmony with us and therefore with the universe, rather than driving them deeper into alienation (Douglas-Klotz, 85).

This would be a good time to look back at the quotation from Mark 7:27 in the left-hand column of our imaginative exercise. When we look at the context of that passage, we can discover where Jesus learned the pluralistic nature of God's love. (Either that, or we glimpse a rare moment when Jesus forgot to implement something he already knew, and then was reminded of it by the Greek woman.) Mark 7 gives us the only recorded instance in which a human being confronted Jesus and caused him to change his mind. At first he refused to heal the daughter of the Greek woman because he was thinking his mission was confined exclusively to Israel. (We all know what it is to be forced to set priorities.) But because the woman was desperate for her daughter's healing, she became assertive and creative, and her assertiveness caused Jesus to change his mind and extend his healing ministry across nationalistic and religious borders. Hence, although out of context Mark 7:27 seems to justify nationalistic and religious exclusiveness, when the passage is interpreted in context, it has the opposite effect.

One Body, Many Interpretive Communities

The New Testament image of the One Body of the Christ is another powerfully pluralistic image. This Body (which in interreligious language could be called the New Humanity) is made up of many members with varying gifts, but all the diverse gifts come from the one Holy Spirit (1 Cor. 12:4–13). The image is more that of a rich and complex orchestra than that of a regimented unison. Galatians 3:28 indicates that in this Body there are no classist barriers, no racist barriers, and no sexist barriers. Extrapolating from the pluralism already present in Galatians 3:28, we could extend it to say that the Body of the Christ is *She* as well as *He,* poor as well as affluent, handicapped as well as fully abled, lesgay and bisexual as well as heterosexual, of many colors, many nations, many religions, and many interpretive communities.

In Chapter Twelve of this book I will go into further detail about interpretive communities and the contrast between a liberating, sensuously spiritual method of reading the Bible and the more traditional interpretative method. Here I want only to explain why I myself switched from the traditional hermeneutics I believed for the first thirty-five years of my life to the pluralistic hermeneutics I have outlined here. In the first place, as a woman (and a *lesbian* woman at that) I was desperate. Like the Greek woman who became creative and assertive because she was desperate for the healing of her daughter, I was desperate for authenticity, for the healing of my self-esteem, and for the use of my gifts. If you watched your own mental process as you filled out your imaginative exercise, you will remember that the vulnerability of not knowing what your individual status would be in the future society you were planning taught you to respect everyone else's status in that society. Regardless of how bigoted we might be, we wouldn't want to chance oppressive rules against people of color, people with handicaps, women, or les-bi-gay people, when we ourselves might turn out in the future to be one of them! Wise parents often tell contentious children that whereas one of them may cut the cake into slices, the one who does the cutting will get the last choice of a serving. The result is that the child who cuts the cake suddenly develops a very keen eye for what equal pieces look like.

From first to last the Bible tells us we are to love our neighbor as we love ourselves, a pluralistic statement if ever there was one. Moses said it in Deuteronomy 5:10, Jesus said it in Matthew 5:43, Paul said it in Romans 13:9, James said it in James 2:8, and it was repeated word for word in four other Bible passages. Anything stated unequivocally eight times in the Bible, implied in countless other passages, and even expanded by Jesus into loving our enemies, seems to me an adequate norm against which all other writings and all other suggestions for behavior may be measured. And since what I wish for myself is life, liberty, and the pursuit of happiness (a pursuit that involves respect for my civil and human rights) I must seek to extend the same to all my neighbors everywhere. "As one unites the 'dwellers' within [one's own unconscious being], one also becomes more responsible about and for those who dwell around one on the outside. Put another way, there is no proof of the inner spiritual work without corresponding action in community" (Douglas-Klotz, 82).

So that's the second reason why I switched, however gradually, from a traditionalist to a more inclusive hermeneutic: not only because I was desperate for my own healing, but in response to the normative love ethic that you shall love your neighbor as yourself. Third and finally, I chose the pluralistic hermeneutic because I discovered that it is more honest, contextual, and scholarly than the traditionalist method. The meaning of that statement will be clarified in Chapter Twelve, as I discuss the existence of different interpretive communities and the almost insuperable difficulties of communication between them. It is inevitable and perhaps even in a sense positive that there should be schools of differing interpretation for a text as complex as the Bible. The great eighteenth-century thinker Samuel Johnson explained it this way:

As a question becomes more complicated and involved, and extends to a greater number of relations, disagreement of opinion will always be multiplied, not because we are irrational, but because we are finite beings, furnished with different kinds of knowledge, exerting different degrees of attention, one discovering consequences which escape another, none taking in the whole concatenation of causes and effects, the most comprehending but a very small part; each comparing what [she] observes with a different criterion, and each referring it to a different purpose.

Where, then, is the wonder, that they, who see only a small part, should judge erroneously of the whole? or that they, who see different and dissimilar parts, should judge differently from each other? (quoted in Booth, ii)

All the more reason why we must nurture one another's ability to differ and *be* different!

Biblical Narratives and the Pluralistic Perspective

At any rate, I have suggested here ten different overarching themes and image-clusters by which the Bible lends support to pluralism and the honoring of human diversity. Cynthia Ozick, writing about the biblical book of Ruth, reminds me of how many of the Bible's *narrative* details might be enlisted in the same cause. Ozick points out that three millennia before the concept of a democratic pluralist polity, Naomi was a kind of pluralist. For although Naomi was a Hebrew and a monotheist, she urged her widowed daughters-in-law to return to their own people *and their own gods*. Like Mother Teresa in our own day, a Catholic nun who will read from the Koran to a dying Muslim, Naomi "does not require that Orpah accept what is not natural for her, in the light of how she was reared, to accept" (Ozick, 374). Naomi does not require it of Ruth, either; but Ruth follows Naomi back to Israel and takes Naomi's God as her own, not only out of loyalty and love for her mother-in-law but out of her own ontological understanding: "She knows, she knows directly, prophetically — that the Creator of the Universe is One" (Ozick, 379). In this way a Moabite woman becomes part of the royal bloodline of King David.

Cynthia Ozick points out that the Moabites were "an enemy people, callous, pitiless, a people who deal in lethal curses" (365). According to rules set forth in Deuteronomy 23, the children of the wild hunter Esau (the Edomites) and also the children of the enslaving Egyptians could in the third generation finally be admitted into Israel's congregation. But *not the Moabites* — not even in the *tenth* generation — "because they did not meet you with food and water on your journey after you left Egypt, and because they hired Balaam . . . to curse you" (Deut. 23:4–5). Yet out of this totally despised and repudiated country comes Ruth; and because of her love and loyalty to Naomi and her recognition of the One Universal God, she becomes the great-grandmother of the greatest king Israel ever knew.

Not only that, but she becomes part of the "genealogy of Jesus the Messiah, the son of David, the son of Abraham," according to the first chapter of Matthew's Gospel; and she is one of only five women whose names are specified in that illustrious bloodline.

What if Naomi had refused to permit Ruth to return to Israel with her? What if Israel had refused to accept Ruth because of her birth in despicable Moab? Like many other biblical themes and details, the story of Ruth indicates that we reject, marginalize, or oppress other people at our own expense.

Chapter Five

FEMININITY, MASCULINITY, AND HUMAN FULFILLMENT

———— ≈ ————

My major goal in life could be called a Christian humanist concern (*Christian* only because that is my faith-tradition, not as a way of excluding people from other traditions or none at all). My Christian humanist goal is to make it possible for everybody to feel fully alive. I assume from my own experience and observation that feeling fully alive involves at least the following factors: access to basic human necessities; some sense of control in our work and our lives; the ability to relate authentically with one another and our environment; and a sense of spiritual connectedness with God, humankind, and the natural creation. According to the second-century bishop of Lyons, Irenaeus, "the glory of God is human beings fully alive," and I am convinced that his statement is true. By that standard, anyone who wants to "do all to the glory of God" (1 Cor. 10:31) would need to work toward sharing basic human necessities with everyone in the world and creating structures that would make authenticity and connectedness possible. Human spirituality is rich to the degree that we feel fully alive — which is to say, to the degree that we are able openly to honor what the Universal Consciousness is expressing through each of our particular lives.

In order for twentieth- and twenty-first century people to *remain* alive, let alone *fully* alive, surely we must transform our social structures from the dominator model of relating (currently in place) to a genuine partnership model of mutual egalitarian give-and-take. As Riane Eisler comments in her important book *The Chalice and the Blade,* "the way our society structures the most fundamental of human relations [between males and females]...has a profound effect on every one of our institutions, on ourselves, and...on the direction of our cultural evolution, particularly whether it will be peaceful or warlike" (xix). Dominator societies like our own assume that the two halves of humanity must relate according to a one-up, one-down ranking, which could also be called an "imperial power motive" (Eisler, 145). But there is another organizational principle that was lived in several prehistoric societies and later was taught and also modelled by Jesus and the discipleship of equals who traveled with him — the linking of the two halves of humanity in mutual supportiveness and concern, what Eisler calls a "partnership motive" or an "affiliation motive" (145).

In order to facilitate and expedite the urgently needed shift from a dominator to a partnership society, it is vital for us to understand the ways in which distorted concepts of human sexuality, gender distortions, and misconstructions of our God-language have blocked human freedom and healthy relationships and therefore have stunted any possibility of feeling fully alive. Only after accurate diagnosis of what is ailing us can we hope for an adequate cure.

Sex, Sexuality, and Gender

Our heteropatriarchal assumptions have fostered severe confusion concerning sex, sexuality, and gender. The term *sex,* properly understood, refers to a person's biological identity as male or female. By contrast, the term *sexuality* goes beyond biology to include the totality of a person's sexual orientation, including feelings and fantasies as well as behaviors. The term *gender,* properly understood, refers to a socially constructed set of categories called *masculine* and *feminine.* These categories are not created by biological necessity, but rather are created from a complex interwoven dynamic of emotional, cognitive, and social forces. Heteropatriarchy assumes that sex, sexuality, and gender automatically flow into one another so that for all practical purposes they are the same. But if we want to enhance human peace and freedom and the ability to relate and feel fully alive, we must distinguish carefully among these three terms.

Let me illustrate. Heteropatriarchal socialization teaches that a biological male "naturally" acquires the behavioral norms of his society (that is, he "naturally" behaves in ways considered appropriate to the masculine gender). It also teaches that a male's sexuality "naturally" evolves from his hormones. Any deviation from this norm is by definition *ab-*normal and *un-*natural. The same concept would apply to biological females and femininity. But I'm going to stick to male illustrations for the moment because so much of our trouble stems from the masculine gender constructs.

For several reasons, I cannot give credence to heteropatriarchy's conflation of sex, sexuality, and gender. First of all, concepts of masculinity and femininity vary a great deal from culture to culture and from one historical period to another, and therefore have no necessary biological connection. Second, sexuality is an extremely complex phenomenon, as far as we now know shaped both by social and personal experiences and by both nature and nurture. Except for a few women who refer to themselves as "political lesbians," I know of no one of any sexual orientation who can remember choosing their sexuality. Our sexuality is something we discover, an unchosen condition within which we must learn to live responsibly.

One person whose sex is male may prefer to become a nurse, defying heteropatriarchy's current gender expectations that call nursing a feminine occupation; but the same man's sexuality may be heterosexual. Another person of the male sex may become a professional football player, fulfilling our society's gender expectations, but may manifest a bisexual or perhaps gay sexuality. Yet another person may be anatomically male, yet may feel himself to be internally female. He may even be willing to undergo an expensive operation in order to become the sex that feels appropriate to his inner being. These three hypothetical men illustrate the following facts: that bodies are not always reliable signifiers; that gender roles may not match biology; and that rigid gender designations may be causing millions of people to lead lives of quiet desperation.

If a few brave souls are willing to undergo transsexual operations to make their anatomy match their inner experience of sex, sexuality, and gender, to what lesser but significant degree are the rest of us suffering constriction in the areas of gender and sexuality? Jan Morris, the journalist who successfully changed from James to Jan, has expressed doubt that she would have submitted to the sex-change operation "if society had allowed me to live in the gender I preferred" (Showalter, 2).

To live in the gender I preferred: this striking phrase causes me to think about the native American shamans who were permitted to live and dress like the other sex without stigma and with a great deal of respect for their spiritual power. Jan Morris's terminology gives the lie to the heteropatriarchal notion that our biological sex causes us to gravitate toward whatever happens to be considered gender-appropriate behavior. I know a man who to this day remains fully convinced that all women love to wash clothes and dishes and clean houses simply because they are women, despite many indications to the contrary from the women in his life. Such a belief happens to be very convenient politically, relieving him of any guilt about leaving such repetitive and boring tasks to women. And his case provides a good illustration of how gender constructs serve political purposes. When self-interest masquerades as truth, it must of necessity exclude the self-interest of the other person or group, insisting that there *is* no alternative view (Belsey, 84).

Gender Constructs as Mythologies

In her book *Reflections on Gender and Science,* Evelyn Fox Keller describes

> the deeply rooted popular mythology that casts objectivity, reason, and mind as male, and subjectivity, feeling, and nature as female. In this division of emotional and intellectual labor, women have been the guarantors and protectors of the personal, the emotional, the body, the particular, whereas science — the province par excellence of the impersonal, the rational, the mind, and the general — has been the preserve of men. (7)

Although Keller does not say so, the gender designations she refers to go all the way back to Plato. They became part of Christian assumptions chiefly through the Alexandrian Jew Philo, who flourished about the time of Christ. But even before Philo, manuals on how to translate biblical language into the language of Greek philosophy equated Adam with Natural Reason and Eve with the Senses (Bruno, 638).

In short, men have defined culture and spirit as masculine, and nature and body as feminine. This basic dualism has fostered other gender dualisms in turn: the "masculine" is public, abstract, spiritual, and impersonal, while the "feminine" is private, sensual, instinctual, and personal. The political results of this human splitting have been catastrophic for intimacy and even for public relationships. Having dumped their own most dreaded characteristics onto the "other" (the subordinated sex), men felt it very important that the public and impersonal sex must always control and govern the private, sensual, and therefore dangerous sex. But of course these traits are not actually allocated according to sex at all: they are gender constructs, just as the idea that science is neutral and value-free is a construct.

Anyone doubting that heteropatriarchal gender distortions have done violence to both women and men would need only to ponder the insults hurled at male recruits during hazing in military academies. They are routinely called names like "vagina-face," "douche bag," "used Kotex," "abortions," "little fat vaginas," "afterbirths," and "scumbags" (Condren, 187). As on children's playgrounds, so in military academies: the most insulting association to apply to a male is anything female. In this way men are cut off from their own bodies, senses, and instincts, and tremendous blockages are placed across the road leading to tender intimacy with women.

Returning to the gender construct that science is neutral and objective (i.e., "masculine"): Einstein once referred to scientists as people who are "driven to escape from personal existence to the world of objective observing and understanding." And for that very reason, many scientists have actively preferred to picture reality as being "as impersonal and free of human values as the rules of arithmetic" (Keller, 10). But the habitual metaphors utilized by many scientists reveal that something very different is going on. In their language, Nature is almost always female, and she is to be mastered, controlled, and dominated by science. The objective sciences are referred to as "hard" in an implicitly sexual metaphor, whereas the more subjective branches of knowledge are called "soft" ("feminine"). A woman thinking logically or scientifically is thinking "like a man," while a man pursuing nonrational subjective argument is acting "like a woman." Even computer language reflects gender dualism: when a computer is working, it is "up"; out of order, it is "down." The controlling and permanent equipment is "hardware," while the more changeable and transitory programs are "software."

Before I go any further, I'd like to make clear that my words about scientists refer to the central scientific establishment since the Renaissance. I am certainly *not* referring to the wonderful reforms pioneered by people like Werner Heisenberg, Geoffrey Chew, Fritjof Capra, and Paul Davies. Nor am I referring to the lesser known but effective people who are working to bring about a science that is "an interconnected network of mutually consistent models," each of them conscious of their own limitations (Capra, 69). I am thankful for these reformers. In a sense, it is because of their reforms that we can be clear about what has been going on for several centuries. But I think it is also important for us to become aware of the damage that has been done by established scientific attitudes.

Ernest Schachtel describes the aggression by which the traditional scientist "cuts off those aspects of the object which he cannot use for his purposes." The adversarial relationship to objects of study is reflected in scientific references to "attacking," "conquering," or "licking" various problems. Here is how one scientist described his favorite scientific reading: "I liked to follow the workings of another mind through these minute, teasing investigations to see a relentless observer get hold of Nature and squeeze her until the sweat broke out all over her and her sphincters loosened" (Keller, 123).

My main purpose here is not to indict science, about which I know very little. My interest is in confronting the destructive gender attitudes that have prevailed in the scientific establishment — one of the last places we would have expected to find such highly emotional imagery. Concerning the male scientist who relishes the thought of getting hold of Nature and squeezing her until she sweats and her sphincters loosen: it is hard to imagine him being able to come home to an egalitarian, mutually respectful relationship with an actual woman. For that matter, it is hard to imagine him coming home to a same-sex partner and engaging in sexual intimacy without despising the receptive, nurturant, "feminine" aspects of the relationship.

Even in such a stodgy classroom subject as how to analyze poetry in English, students are traditionally told that when single syllables rhyme together perfectly, that's "masculine, or strong, rhyme," whereas if two or three syllables rhyme with two or three other syllables, that's "feminine, or weak, rhyme." Thus, unconsciously, students receive the gender message that to be masculine, separate, and autonomous (psychically single) is to be strong, while to be feminine, connected, and in affiliation is to be weak. Gender messages are everywhere! I tell my students to drop the terms *masculine, feminine, strong,* and *weak*, and simply call the rhymes *single, double,* or *triple*. The result is simpler and more accurate and constitutes a refusal to go along with the dualisms that deform human relationships.

Brain Research and Gender Designations

Recently brain theorists have been discussing the biocultural roots of gender stereotypes that attribute to women passivity, intuition, nonrationality, and relationality and attribute to men a linear rationality and aggressive individualism. (As we have seen, these attributions are used politically to assign "real women" to the private, secondary, auxiliary sphere of activity.) Brain theory is helpful because it reminds us that both sexes have a whole brain, with the left lobe specializing in linear ways of knowing and the right lobe specializing in more wholistic ways. I can't help delighting in the fact that brain research has overturned traditional associations of the right side with everything masculine, linear, and good, and the left side with everything feminine, subjective, and evil.

Brain research has also revealed that females tend to develop an integration between right and left lobe brain processes, while males tend to bifurcate them because of their later development of language skills. Hence, in man, "non-dualistic, integrating modes of thought tend to be under-developed." And as we have seen, heteropatriarchal culture "reinforces and ratifies the male developmental tendencies" (Ruether, "Brain Theory," 263). In fact, heteropatriarchy tends to view wholistic perceptions as unreal and unrealistic.

But Rosemary Radford Ruether points out that brain theory has *not* established that these developmental tendencies are based in biological sex. Perhaps cross-cultural studies of male brain development in cultures that encourage visions and dreams will show us male brains that do develop the second stage of integrating left and right lobe functions. Right now, "we scarcely know what it means for men and women to be fully human, and cannot know as long as we [all] grow up in patriarchy" (Ruether, "Brain Theory," 264). So we can hope that the human race is not saddled forever with male inadequacy in wholistic thinking. Even if humankind should turn out to be limited in that way, however, we can stop reinforcing only the male developmental tendencies and can begin to honor wholistic perceptions in schools, boardrooms, and the halls of government. A movement toward greater respect for wholism is already underway, but much remains to be done.

R. W. Emerson's Gender Assumptions

David Leverenz has written an analysis of Ralph Waldo Emerson's thinking that reveals some of the dangers of heteropatriarchal gender dualisms. Emerson wrote in his journal in July 1834, "I wish to be a true and free man, and therefore would not be a woman, or a king, or a clergyman, each of which classes in the present order of things is a slave" (Leverenz, 138). Well, that's honest enough. But Leverenz's careful analysis of Emerson's public utterances and writings reveals an unconscious *compliance* with gender-based injustice that is disappointing in one of America's greatest prophetic voices. Not only that: Emerson's compliance with gender inequity undergirds his own self-destructive divorce of mind from feeling, and therefore his rejection of his bodyself.

To Emerson, feeling meant "pain, powerlessness, resentment, and the perils of the body," all of which he projected onto the laboring masses, including women. Leverenz points out that Emerson's "grand disdain for those whose sense of self comes from their daily tasks, needs, and relations reflects his discomfort with his own body and his fear of intimacy" (150). And of course Emerson is by no means alone in this alienation: among people who have believed the gender mythology of our culture (and especially among traditional men) discomfort with the body, fear of psychological intimacy, and alienation from feelings are commonplace.

At the beginning of his famous essay "Self-Reliance," Emerson writes of "the nonchalance of boys who are sure of a dinner" as being "the healthy attitude of human nature" (Leverenz, 136). That's a wonderfully powerful image. But Emerson does not seem to notice the irony that the boys' breezy freedom depends on being "sure of a dinner" rather than "sure of themselves." That is, in an essay called "*Self*-Reliance," Emerson's prime illustration of "*the* healthy attitude of human nature" reveals reliance upon invisible and unacknowledged female labor instead of *self*-reliance or even mutual *inter*-reliance! As for the females themselves, David Leverenz writes, "One can picture them in the kitchen [as] the angels of the house, getting more faceless and sexless by the minute while they put out the meals for their surefooted [husbands, sons, and] brothers. [In Emerson's unconscious meaning], to achieve a bold male self-reliance presumes a depersonalized female support system" (151).

Again, Emerson's attitudes are fairly typical of those who have bought into heteropatriarchal gender roles and attitudes. So are the internal results of these attitudes: according to his own essays and journals, Emerson thinks that experience teaches us that there is "a widening gulf between every me and thee" (Leverenz, 155). No wonder Emerson's wife Lidian endured thirty years of recurrent depressions! And many women have endured much more than depressions: "A cross-cultural study conducted by Shirley and John McConahay found a significant correlation between the rigid sexual stereotypes required to maintain male dominance and the incidence of not only warfare, but wife-beating, child-beating, and rape" (Eisler, 188).

Gender Constructs and Kenneth Rexroth

Lest anybody think matters have improved since Emerson's day, I will provide a contemporary illustration. One of my William Paterson College colleagues and friends, Linda Hamalian, has just completed the definitive biography of modern American poet Kenneth Rexroth. She was originally attracted to Rexroth's "unconventionally glamorous personality" and to his poetry, which often depicts beautiful loving relationships to women. But in the course of her research, Linda Hamalian was distressed to learn that Rexroth physically abused his female partners. She was further distressed to learn that various people are not particularly shocked to learn that Rexroth, after writing lovingly and respectfully of women, actually struck his wives, using force to win arguments he would otherwise have lost. (The gender construct that "real men" do whatever is necessary to control women will be discussed at length in the chapter to follow.) Rexroth's principal publisher remarked that he wasn't at all surprised to learn that Rexroth was violent, because "that kind of behavior was common."

Common to whom? One must conclude that Rexroth's publisher meant that control and dominance over women is so commonly achieved through the physical violence of men that it must be accepted with a complaisant shrug. It is the shrug of acceptance that is especially horrifying to me, and I would presume horrifying to anyone who is concerned about loving, peaceful, mutually supportive human partnerships and communities.

During the summer of 1989, Linda Hamalian reported at the National Women's Studies Association conference that the other Rexroth scholars, all of them men, were having a hard time coping with the fact that the first and definitive biography of Kenneth Rexroth was being written by a woman. They withheld information from her, they demanded that she turn over information to them, and they pestered her when she refused to share her original findings prior to publication. The point here is that men (socialized toward autonomy and separation) think it is all right for them to withhold information from the woman who is authorized to write the first Rexroth biography, where she would of course credit them for their contributions. But the same men are outraged when a woman "acts like a man" by withholding her findings until she can get them into print. (Many a woman's research has been published over a man's byline, so it is wise to be cautious!)

The Difficulties of Male-Female Partnership

In her recent book *Successful Women, Angry Men,* Bebe Moore Campbell has described the widespread phenomenon of husbands in dual-career marriages who at first appear to support and encourage their wives' professional development, only to turn upon them when the success of the wife's career seems to threaten the husband's happiness. Alvin Poussaint, associate professor of psychology at Harvard Medical School, comments that "disagreements about gender-role function become most acute after babies appear on the scene. Many men at this point revert to more traditional notions of a wife's role [than they had claimed previously], and many career women develop feelings of guilt and conflict over not being more available and attentive to their offspring" (Campbell, xvi). Thus both women and men are victimized by the socialization that raises radically different gender expectations for women and men, pinning childcare upon women, when in actuality everybody would profit from more balanced parenting. Pain, hurt, anger, and often divorce are the result of differing gender expectations in dual-career marriages; and the majority of marriages in the United States do have two working spouses.

Is there any real hope for better male-female relationships, for acting out of an affiliation instead of an imperial power motive, in a society so fraught with false definitions of masculinity and femininity, and with such skewed attitudes toward human sexuality and embodiment in general? My own heart tells me yes, there is always hope.

Part of the solution to male domination in our society is structural. The United States is the only modern industrialized country that has no federal policies concerning maternity, childcare, and daycare. Furthermore, American women still earn less than 64 cents for every dollar a man makes, whereas Swedish women earn 81 percent of male earnings, French women earn 78 percent, and Italian women earn 86 percent. Obviously, therefore, "corporate and governmental sexism is imperiling the survival of American families" (Campbell, 228–29). Such structural inequities can be addressed only through well-organized political effort.

But in addition to these structural changes, there are the attitudes toward gender and sexuality that are the focus of this chapter. Like Bebe Moore Campbell, I believe that the friendship men and women need in their partnerships can take place only between two equally powerful human beings. In *The Chalice and the Blade,* Riane Eisler has presented evidence that human equality brought peace to several prehistoric societies. She argues that what worked before can be achieved again by laying aside the blade of militarism and lifting up the chalice of mutual cooperation. It is ironic that opposition to feminist and partnership movements should so frequently come from Christian people, because the Christian Scriptures indicate that Christians are to submit themselves to one another out of reverence for the Christ (Eph. 5:20). According to this model, equality is achieved through respect for each other's subjectivity, for the Inner Spiritual Guide, the Holy Spirit, the Christ-nature, in each person; and in respect for the relationship as a whole. Certainly anyone who wakes up to the reality that all of us are manifestations or expressions of God's mind would understand the destructiveness of trying to dominate another person!

Gender and the Hatred of Lesgay People

Unfortunately, traditionalists in American churches, synagogues, and politics are putting up a tremendous resistance to any changes in the old gender constructs, and are doing so largely through attacks on homosexuality. Rosalind Pollack Petchesky explains the reasoning behind this intense resistance to change:

> Behind the New Right's antihomosexual campaign [lie the] political values that motivate the "profamily" movement, including the movement against abortion.... While it may be true that "prolifers" are hostile to sexuality as such, it is really the social aspects of traditional gender identities — and particularly the position of male paternal and heterosexual authority — that they are determined to protect.... Male homosexuality is even more dangerous than female... because it signals a breakdown of "masculinity" itself — or what one right-wing ideologue [Michael Novak] calls the "male spirit," or "the male principle." ...At stake in the New Right campaign against homosexuality is the very idea of what it means to be a "man" or a "woman," and the structure and meaning of the traditional family.... The meaning of "masculinity" (as of "femininity") — that is, of gender itself — has been defined historically through the structure of the family and the dominant position of the father within it. (quoted in Darling, 432)

Nothing less than the preservation of heteropatriarchy is at stake. If that means that the majority of the human race must live lives of subordinated desperation, the attitude seems to be that that is preferable to a breakdown of heteropatriarchal privileges for the white male heterosexual minority.

By definition, such an attitude is toxic to human equality and human fulfillment, and in turn it is based on gender-role definitions that are similarly toxic. As we confront those gender assumptions, we must constantly remind ourselves that "gender is... [only] a social construct, arbitrary, and varying from one society to another, related to sex but not identical with it; and [that] gender roles vary from one culture to another just as the words we use to signify our meaning vary from one language...to another" (Phyllis Rackin, in Showalter, 115–16).

The Joyous Struggle

What human society has created, human society can change. In the following chapter I will develop my contention that churchly language concerning God as King, Master, and Father has very much legitimated and encouraged the abuses of power in heteropatriarchy. But one sign of hope is that changes in God-imagery can also encourage greater health. A 1981 study reported by Len Sperry finds that men who have a womanly image of God "pray more often and intensely," "become more committed to social concerns," "have better relationships with women," have "more fulfilling sexual experiences in marriage," and in general are "more spiritually mature than men with exclusively masculine God-images" (Sperry, 5–8).

Because appropriate feelings are essential to clear thinking, radical divisions between our emotions and our intellectual labors are dangerous to human survival. For instance, greater emotional identification with the crew of the *Challenger* might have caused clear-headed decisions that would have saved some very precious human lives. And I was encouraged recently to see some newspaper articles saying that American servicepeople in Saudi Arabia were feeling empathy toward the Iraqi soldiers whom they perceived as being only human and afraid and homesick for peace just like themselves. If all political leaders felt similar empathy, negotiations would soon take the place of war. Well, then, the world must find a way to select or elect more empathetic officials.

Physicist Fritjof Capra wrote concerning his encounter with Germaine Greer's feminism, "Even as a man I was inspired by these exhortations, which made me realize that women's liberation was also men's liberation. I sensed the joy and excitement of a new expansion of consciousness....The struggle which is not joyous is the wrong struggle" (Capra, 222). If they became involved in the joyous struggle to create a partnership society, perhaps even the Lidian Emersons among us might be empowered to emerge from their depressions.

Chapter Six

GENDER CONSTRUCTS
AND THE HUMAN IMAGING OF GOD

———— ≈ ————

Montesquieu once quipped, "If the triangles made a god, they would give him three sides." I quote Montesquieu for several reasons: first, in the light of all we have seen concerning gender distortions of the meaning of masculinity and femininity, I hope readers will think about what happens when people with a distorted sense of masculinity are the ones who create God in the same distorted image. And second, I want to point out that even a brilliant philosopher like Montesquieu, who could imagine triangles creating a triangular god in their own image, could not bring himself to use the pronoun appropriate to his own metaphor: *it*. (The last time I looked, triangles were inanimate objects calling for the neuter pronoun.) So entrenched in the unconscious mind is the patriarchal belief-system that even a witty rationalist exalts the masculinity of God by his choice of pronoun!

Personally, I do not accept the reductionist notion that human beings created God in our own image. I believe that the Bible and other great religious texts are inspired in a very profound sense, and that the best of these texts (including the Bible) reveal to us a just and eternal One-Who-Is-All, One who lives beyond the human limitations of space, time, sex, race, and sexual orientation and who has expressed Herself by creating both women and men in Her Image. (That means, of course, that God is *beyond* human limitations in the sense of embodying Herself in *every* place, time, sex, race, species, body type, and sexual orientation.) But I also know that because of human alienation from the Ground of our own Being, we have developed gender definitions that are distorted. And then Christians — to narrow my focus to the religion I know best, the dominant religion in American society — have legitimated those gender distortions by settling exclusively into certain biblical metaphors for God until those metaphors have developed the force of an idol. We have spoken of God as our Father, our King, and our Master so exclusively that we have forgotten the many other biblical metaphors that depict God in ways that would undercut male primacy and female secondariness and teach us a partnership model of relating.

Documenting Androcentric Idolatry

For instance, British hymn writer and Reformed Church minister Brian Wren recently documented the Christian idolatry of the masculine that I've been referring to. He did so by analyzing the first 328 hymns in the 1983 *Hymns and Psalms: A Methodist and Ecumenical Hymnbook*. These 328 hymns were in a section devoted to the Nature of God, which was then followed by 104 hymns on God's World and 391 on God's People. In the 328 hymns on God's Nature, male or androcentric imagery was used 76.5 percent of the time, with some conceptual images (like Eternal) or nature images (like Sun) accounting for the other 23.5 percent. There were no female or gynocentric images of God whatsoever!

As for the pronouns, Brian Wren writes,

> If male and female humans were really believed to be created as an equal partnership in the divine image [as most Christian churches claim to believe], one would expect to find both feminine and masculine pronouns chosen for divine action. This is not so. In the 177 texts carrying pronouns, there are 1,423 pronouns for the divine. One is neuter, none are feminine, and 1,422 are masculine.... The fact that the genderless Trinity is prayed to and depicted in exclusively male images and pronouns must give humans a hooded one-eyed vision of God. (117–18)

Indeed. And it is in times of extreme crisis and transition that the political assumptions that undergird religious language are made explicit, whereas the rest of the time they tend to function on an unconscious level that is all the more powerful for being unconscious. For instance, in the seventeenth century, the theory that kings rule absolutely by divine right and therefore are vested with sacred authority was beginning to crumble. But it was at that very time, just as the theory of divine right was crumbling, that the theory also received its most strenuous and explicit articulations. King James I of England — the same James who authorized the King James Version of the Bible — argued that "Kings are justly called gods, for they exercise a manner or resemblance of divine power on earth" (Wren, 127).

According to King James, God has the power to create or destroy, to judge everyone and yet be judged by no one — and of course James assumed that as King of England he had the similar right of absolute control over his subjects. James's successor, Charles I, was defended by his Royalist followers as "the Lord's Anointed," as a modern King David against whom nobody should dare to lift a hand. Many of the Royalists also argued that a king is above the law (Hunter, 4:183–86, and 8:55–57). Like God Himself, the Royalists argued, a king *was* the law and could not be judged by it.

As for family relationships, John Hayward in 1603 was one among many who drew obvious parallels: as one God rules the world, and one head governs and controls the human body, and a state is governed by a single commander, in the same way one master governs each family unit (Wren, 127). The master, obviously, was the man of the house; and the ideal woman and wife was know by her "chastity, modesty, silence, and obedience" (Rose, xiv).

So powerful was the perceived correspondence between God-as-male, the human head, the mastery of the husband and father, and the head of the state, that the Renaissance Queen Elizabeth I was forced to define herself as both a man and a woman, both king and queen, both firstborn son and mother, in order to accommodate both her feminine body and her masculine regal position in the world. For instance, in her famous 1588 Armada speech she said to the English troops, "I have the body of a weak and feeble woman, but I have the heart and stomach of a king" (Marcus, 138). Thus she betrayed her bodyself and all other women in order to legitimate her authority.

Whenever Elizabeth I needed to enforce her will upon a group of recalcitrant men, she would appeal to her masculine authority as the embodiment of "sacred monarchy" (Marcus, 137–38). But obviously the average Renaissance wife could make no such appeal when her husband proved recalcitrant. He had on his side all the force of the parallels between God/king/the human head and the male control over wife and children. That is the very essence of the political system I am calling heteropatriarchy. This system requires heterosexual marriage in return for first-class citizenship and places the male at the top of the family hierarchy.

Through the centuries, heteropatriarchal God-language and its associated gender constructs have continued to support male supremacy. For instance, when Myra Bradwell was rejected by the State of Illinois for a license to practice law in 1873, Supreme Court Justice Joseph Bradley upheld her rejection with these words: "The paramount mission and destiny of women are to fulfill the noble and benign offices of wife and mother. This is the law of the Creator." In this way religion has acted to legitimate human social arrangements by projecting them into a sacred and cosmic frame of reference (Gray, 72–74).

Returning to our own century with these historical illustrations in mind, we are in a better position to appreciate the impact of Christianity's addiction to God-imagery that depicts the Holy One as King, Master, and Father, the controller of the universe and everyone in it. In his analysis of those 328 hymns about the nature of God, Brian Wren found that Jesus was called "king" 140 times and "Lord" 262 times, while "the First Person of the Trinity, and the whole godhead [was] seen as a male being who rules over [and controls] everything" (117 and 249).

Androcentric Idolatry and a Skewed Humanity

What is the effect of all this masculine-gender dominating and controlling God-language on human identities and relationships in our era? Scholars like Jean Baker Miller, Nancy Chodorow, Carol Gilligan, and Patrocino Schweikart have pointed out that whereas men tend to define themselves through individuation and separation from others, women tend to experience themselves in terms of their affiliations and relationships with others. Whereas traditional men tend to value autonomy more than interdependence, women tend to value interdependence and attachment more than separated autonomy. Whereas men tend to view personal interactions mainly as procedures for arbitrating conflicts between individual rights, women tend to be concerned in their dealings with others to negotiate between opposing needs so that relationship can be maintained (Perry, 297). Yet until very recently, the only acceptable interpretation of literary and religious texts has been the white middle-class male interpretation, so that our understanding has been skewed toward individualism and controlling one-upmanship.

Even to this day, the controversy about abortion continues to be stated chiefly in the masculine terminology of competing rights, as witness the widely used terms "abortion rights," "rights of the unborn," and "the right to choose." Yet women themselves, the central actors in human reproduction, do not tend to think in terms of competing rights. Rather, women think in terms of trying to negotiate solutions that will preserve the greatest possible number of relationships. For instance, a pregnant woman will try to balance the needs of the fetus with the needs of all the people she is already responsible for and accountable to. If she decides to terminate her relationship with the fetus, it is because she feels that by doing so she will better be able to meet her other responsibilities, including those to herself but by no means ending with herself.

At the time of this writing, the United States Supreme Court has taken several steps toward dismantling *Roe vs. Wade*. I believe that these triumphs for those who wish to limit the reproductive moral agency of women have come about partly because of society's adherence to the masculine mode of addressing the issue. If the issue is joined as woman's rights versus fetal rights, American law usually tends to give its protection to the apparently weaker or more helpless entity. But if the issue is joined in the more feminine-gender mode as the moral agency and responsibility of the woman in relationship to God and humankind, as opposed to the abstract power of the state, the outcome might be different.

Better yet would be for feminist thinkers to develop a completely nondualistic, care-based ethic as an alternative to heteropatriarchy's competition-based ethics. As Lauren Smedley points out,

> The terminology of "rights" and "interests" represents an ordering of the world that is inherently hierarchical, dualistic and competitive. . . . The notion of rights is dualistic, so that a right is a claim *to* something *against* someone. This notion implies a society of haves and have-nots. . . . Granting women, minorities or animals *rights* essentially makes them "honorary straight white men." (1 and 12, emphasis mine)

Smedley, an attorney, says she is all-too-familiar with "the phallic game-playing which results from legally battling 'right' against 'right'" (12). Everything in me responds positively to Smedley's observations. I think that works like Rosalind Pollack Petchesky's *Abortion and Woman's Choice* demonstrate the kind of moral field-thinking that is necessary for forming a consistent ethical system based on care rather than competition. For right now, however, we are stuck in heteropatriarchal systems and must try to inch closer to a care-based ethic by emphasizing relational responsibility rather than competing rights.

It is no accident that one of the strategies of the National Organization of Women has been to suggest that any state that denies a woman an abortion should be required to support the resulting child, so that those who make the decisions pay the tab. My slogan for this campaign would be, "Whoever decides, provides." I believe that any state agency or official that refuses to grant a moral agent the opportunity to govern her relationships according to the dictates of her own conscience should be required to support her throughout her pregnancy, to pay all the child's expenses until after college, and also to pay decent wages to the primary caretaker of the child. Whoever decides, provides.

I have said all this to illustrate female-gender thinking: the emphasis is on relationship and responsibility. If the state wishes to intervene between a moral agent and her God by forcing her to give birth to a baby she had decided she could not stay in relationship with (because of her other responsibilities), then the state must assume the responsibility of staying in relationship with the resulting human life. Relationship and responsibility are the keys to the way women (and feminist men) think about the world, *not* the competing rights by which women who need an abortion are labelled merely "selfish."

Can Gender Distortions Be Changed?

There are, then, some genuine gender distinctives or at least tendencies, whether they stem from biology or from the socialization process. My own assumption is that women have more flexible ego-boundaries and think primarily in terms of affiliation because we are living in a heteropatriarchal system that accords primacy to men and requires "real women" to marry men. Through the years, black people have been much more aware of white people than vice versa. Jews have been much more aware of Christians than the other way around. And for similar reasons of survival, women have had to pay attention to men in a way that men have simply not been compelled to pay attention to the secondary and subordinated sex.

So although there seem to be some genuine gender distinctives, I consider them to be mainly the result of socialization and therefore modifiable if and when human wholeness requires those modifications. I acknowledge that certain contemporary feminists would disagree. For instance, Barbara G. Walker argues that men by nature have such an inveterate drive to control women that equal partnership is impossible. According to Walker, the only hope for society is for women to seize control: "If the self-seeking powerlust of mature men were made subject to the 'intuitive' judgment of mature women, instead of the other way around, surely human life and society could be improved" (177). However, I believe that the human ego of either men or women becomes cruel when it imagines itself separate from its divine Source and therefore from all other people and creatures. And I believe that we human beings can more readily remember our holiness and interconnectedness when we are living in equal partnerships with one another. So I live in hope that by ridding ourselves of certain gender distortions, men and women can share the world together in a kinder and healthier way.

Perhaps the most serious gender distortion is the widespread belief that "real men" must control women and children even if it takes violence to do so. And it is my contention that that gender distortion is supported, aided, and abetted by Christian God-language. The results are disastrous: in one out of every four American homes, the woman is systematically battered by her husband. Rape occurs within 14 percent of marriages. Over 4 percent of American girls are sexually victimized by their own fathers, and an additional 12 percent are victimized by other male family members. By the time children reach the age of eighteen, one in three girls and one in seven boys has been sexually abused, with the perpetrators being male in the overwhelming majority of cases. Fully half of the abuse is incestuous (that is, occurring within the family).

In their 1984 study of incest, sociologists Linda Gordon and Paul O'Keefe commented, "The pattern we found consistently associated with incest was male domination of the family" (27–34). Exclusively masculine

God-language serves to legitimate such abuses, for as Mary Daly charged in *Beyond God the Father,* if God is perceived as fatherlike, fathers are perceived as Godlike: and absolute power corrupts absolutely.

The Role of Churchly God-Language

Instead of standing over against the heteropatriarchal system as a witness for justice and healthy human partnership, Christian churches, Jewish synagogues, and Islamic mosques have served as legitimators of the gender distortion that undergirds the abuses I've just been mentioning. I have been active in the religious inclusive language movement for many years, and I have sometimes been asked, most notably by Bill Gothard of the Youth Conflict Seminars, "If you teach that women need not obey their husbands, how will the human race know how to obey God?" To such questioners, the husband-controlling wife-submissive model is necessary in order to teach a proper human response to a controlling deity. So it becomes obvious that heteropatriarchal thinking has not changed in any significant way from King James I's concept that kings are gods who judge everyone and are judged by no one, or from John Heyward's contention that just as one God controls the world, the male controls his family and is beyond the law within the sphere of the family.

A newspaper columnist wrote recently that in domestic violence counselling centers, "The most striking thing counsellors notice is that abusers don't seem to understand that their behavior is wrong" (Campbell, "Violence"). They don't know their behavior is wrong because it coincides with society's gender distortion that a "real man" does whatever he must do in order to gain and keep control over a situation, and because religious language seems to imply that God, being male, controls humanity in the same way. For instance, certain people have blamed the AIDS epidemic on the anger of God at the behavior of gay men. And if that's what we think God is like, how can we expect angry men to behave any better? Make no mistake about it: those who are most insistent that God is a controlling, domineering Father are also those who support compulsory marriage and male supremacy and have no respect for gay men and lesbian women.

Please understand that I am not blaming masculine God-language for all domestic violence and sexual abuse. In fact, I think Michael Lerner is right that domestic violence is fuelled by dehumanized and frustrating conditions at the workplace. These are structural conditions that can be changed only by a revitalized and well organized, humanly concerned labor movement. What I *am* saying is that by clinging to the almost-exclusive use of masculine and controlling images of God as Lord, King, Father, and Master, Christian churches are exacerbating rather than helping to heal the gender distortions of society.

Resistance to Inclusive God-Language

Naively idealistic as I used to be, I thought that Christian people would only have to hear a thorough explanation of the human damage done by exclusively masculine God-language, after which the changes would be rapid and willing. But the National Council of Churches provided the first Inclusive Language Lectionary in 1983, with a crash course in inclusive language right between its covers; and resistance to its principles continues in 1991 to be quite phenomenal. It is instructive to trace the God-language debate as it has developed in just one church, the Presbyterian Church (U.S.A.). I cite this church not because it is the worst, but because it has done better than most.

Back in 1975, the Presbyterian General Assembly legislated that the language used concerning God's personhood must "affirm the personhood of all." Better yet, in 1980 the General Assembly stated that "our language about God should be as intentionally diverse and varied as is that of the Bible." But alas, the 1980 General Assembly backed away from its own liberating insight about diversity by stating that "although maternal qualities are ascribed to God in Scripture, the title 'Mother' is not applied to God in the Bible and its use is currently under debate." While this latter statement is technically accurate, it violates common sense concerning the historical conditions under which the Bible was written.

In a culture where people of power were almost exclusively male, authors would not think of addressing God as female or even of using female pronouns concerning Her. If their intention was to honor God, as clearly it was, then obviously they would do so by associating God with the people who were honored in their heteropatriarchal and monarchical society: kings, fathers, masters of the religious and intellectual realms, mighty soldiers, and so forth. The truly amazing factor is that Someone All-Encompassing was inspiring them to include very substantial amounts of female God-imagery: God as giving birth, as nursing mother, as midwife, as female pelican, as mother bear, as the Shekinah, as female homemaker, as female beloved, as the *Ezer* or helpmeet of humankind, as mother eagle, as mother hen, as bakerwoman, as Dame Wisdom, and so forth (Mollenkott, *Divine Feminine*).

Especially because the biblical authors feared and detested the Goddess-worship that surrounded ancient Israel and because of the power that heteropatriarchal socialization holds over the human mind, it is nearly miraculous for the Bible to include so much female God-imagery. Surely that inclusion should be our guide here at the turn of the century, not some literalistic shrinking from what is healthy for human beings because we can't point to a biblical proof text in which God is directly called *Mother*.

Similes vs. Metaphors

Getting back to the debate within the Presbyterian Church (U.S.A.), when it became apparent that those calling for inclusive God-language had some biblical precedent on their side and were serious about the issue, the champions of the status quo were not long in making their presence known. Roland Mushat Frye, emeritus professor of literature at the University of Pennsylvania, wrote a lengthy report in which he argued that when the Bible speaks of God as female, it uses *similes,* which are mere comparisons; whereas when the Bible speaks of God as male, it uses *metaphors,* which are superior to similes because they actually *name* in a normative, almost literal fashion. I quote Roland Frye: "whereas similes compare, metaphors predicate or name." Therefore, Frye argues that

> For the church to adopt inclusive feminist language for the deity would disrupt and destroy the careful, nuanced, and balanced formulations that for centuries have made it possible to proclaim the three persons, Father, Son, and Holy Spirit, whom Christians encounter as divine, within a single and undivided godhead. (45–57)

Clearly, for Professor Frye, keeping systematic theology carefully systematic takes precedence over the correction of social injustices and the healing of human pain. He is entitled to his opinion; but what he is *not* entitled to do is to falsify the definition of similes and metaphors in order to support the exclusively heteropatriarchal naming of God. I have been teaching English language and literature for thirty-nine years now, and it is simply not true that similes merely compare while metaphors name in what Frye implies is a literal and normative sense. Both similes and metaphors are figurative language; both of them compare, similes explicitly (with "like" or "as") and metaphors implicitly. If I use the metaphor "March is a lion," I have not "named" March any more than if I use the simile that "March comes in like a lion." Either way, any sane listener knows that I am comparing essentially unlike things for the purpose of clarity and imaginative power. (This particular comparison has gone flat — has lost its power — because of its familiarity, but I wanted to use something well known and easily remembered.)

It's true that metaphors are bolder and more striking than similes, and it is easy to understand why biblical authors socialized heteropatriarchally should usually use the more timid similes to describe God's female attributes. But in *God and the Rhetoric of Sexuality,* Phyllis Trible has shown that when the Hebrew Scriptures are analyzed with great care, they sometimes take us to the metaphorical level concerning God's "femaleness." So Frye's analysis is mistaken on two counts: because it is not true that similes and metaphors function as differently as he claims, and because the Bible uses both similes and metaphors to depict God's nature in female as well as male terms. As Janet Martin Soskice wrote in her scholarly study *Metaphor and Religious Language,* "metaphor and simile share the same function and differ primarily in their grammatical form" (59). When Jesus used a metaphor to say, "I am the bread of life," he certainly spoke more powerfully than if he had said, "I am like the bread of life"; but in neither case would a sensible reader expect to find literal loaves of "Jesus-bread" packaged for sale in the local supermarket.

As Sally McFague makes clear in *Metaphorical Theology,* metaphor always carries with it an "is not" as well as an "is"; otherwise it would be just a literal equivalent and would not stretch our minds. The point of all this is that according to the Bible, God is no more literally Father than Mother, no more literally male than female. One of our human limitations is that to be considered healthy and normal, we must be one sex or the other; but as Hilary of Poitiers said centuries ago, "we must not measure God's nature by our own."*

Pantheism vs. Panentheism

In addition to Roland Frye, the other major Presbyterian champion of the heteropatriarchal status quo has been Professor Elizabeth Achtemeier of Virginia Theological Seminary. She argues that to balance masculine and feminine God-language would lead the church into pantheism:

> As soon as God is called female, the images of birth, of suckling, of carrying in the womb, and, most importantly, the identification of the deity with the life in all things becomes inevitable, and the Bible's careful and consistent distinction between Creator and creation is blurred and lost. (108–9)

Apparently Professor Achtemeier has never heard of pan-en-theism, which defines God as being present within the creation without *limiting* God to the creation, as pantheism does. And apparently she has never noticed such passages as Ephesians 4:6, which tell us that God is *"above* all and *through* all and *in* you all." Or John 15:4–5, the words of Jesus: "Abide in me, and I in you . . . I am the vine, you are the branches." (I have listed many passages about God's presence in us and in the creation in my book *Godding: Human Responsibility and the Bible.*)

However, ignoring these many biblical indications that God is *with* us and *in* us and is glorified by the heavens and even the very stones of the earth, Achtemeier claims that "God is not bound up with or re-

---

* Brian Wren also discusses "How Metaphors Work" in his excellent book *What Language Shall I Borrow?,* 87–92.

vealed through the created world," is "not bound up with his creation in any way," and "stands over and above his world." Remembering our society's gender definitions that "real men" should stand separate from others in a controlling autonomy that precludes genuine interconnection and mutuality, we can see how Achtemeier's emphasis on God's separateness over and above his creation legitimizes such a gender construct. As Elizabeth Dodson Gray remarks, "In their philosophy and psychology [heteropatriarchal people] have created what have become cosmic theologies of separation, rather than of connection. And to live by cosmic theories of separation when you are actually within an interconnected reality-system is dangerous to the health and well-being of society" (120).

Concerning Elizabeth Achtemeier's claims about the Bible: I am not denying that the Bible sometimes depicts God as over and above the creation. But I am saying that the Bible also depicts God as very much within the creation, suffering with us and in need of our embodiment to do the divine work in the world. In her anxiety to support the status quo of masculine God-language, Achtemeier has ignored one pole of a biblical paradox, God's immanence, in order to pay total attention to the other pole, God's transcendence. The Bible is full of paradoxes, as life itself is; and it is important to keep both poles of any paradox in balance if we are truly interested in interpreting and applying the message correctly.

Although Elizabeth Achtemeier is certain that Judaism and Christianity are marked by "the absence of feminine symbolism" and that "the world is the object addressed by God the subject" (what a set-up for the objectification of women, bodies, and nature!), and although Achtemeier asserts that female God-language inevitably leads to pantheism, the Reverend Brian Wren is much closer to biblical usage in his assessment. He writes, "We *know* that God is both infinitely close to us and infinitely beyond the whole universe She has made. To speak of God as the Mother who carries the universe within Herself, or gives it birth into its own space and freedom, explicitly *denies* that God can be reduced to natural forces or nature itself" (163).

In other words, the biblical diversity of God-imagery, including God as Rock, Wind, and Water, teaches us not pantheism, but pan-en-theism. God Herself became incarnate in human flesh, enshrines Himself in the human heart, and manifests Itself in everything that lives. Perhaps if we remembered these biblical facts constantly, we would learn to love and appreciate our bodies more. Then we would be empowered to work for justice for every body, no matter how their bodies and behaviors might differ from our own. And we would learn to respect and love the earth and all the creatures in it.

The Feedback Loop:
Religious Language and Social Arrangements

The fewer communication skills and the less education people possess, the more vulnerable they may be to psychological and even physical victimization. Belenky, Clinchy, Goldberger, and Tarule, the authors of *Women's Ways of Knowing*, tell the story of Ann, who supported her family and raised the children without any help from her husband, who drank, battered, and stole the family's meager resources. Despite this reality, Ann was so brainwashed by heteropatriarchal gender constructs that she believed she would be lost without her husband. Having accepted that a woman is nothing without a man, for years she risked her own life and her children's lives in order to fit heteropatriarchy's internalized model (29). To the degree that women like Ann are religious, their oppression is intensified by God-language that renders them invisible and powerless.

Although I do not believe that human beings have simply created a nonexistent God in our own image, I *am* convinced that the way we image Her affects the way we behave toward one another. It's a "feedback loop. Changes in social patterns produce change in [the way we envision] the deity. Conversely, a change in the divine image can produce social change. . . . [Hence], religious images matter" (Walker, 173).

I have attempted to show the interaction between exclusively masculine and domineering God-language and the many abuses of power in our culture, especially the most basic gender distortions concerning masculinity and femininity. I am not encouraging exclusively *female* God-language, but rather a multiplicity of images with their appropriate pronouns, language that builds upon and carries forward the diversity of the Bible's God-imagery. My goal is an equal-partnership society in which all relationships are developed through mutual concern and supportiveness. I agree with the Filipina scholar Virginia Fabella: "If there are differences in the roles and functions [of women and men], they should be based on charisma and capability, not on gender" (88). Certainly the roles and functions of human beings should not be allocated according to distorted definitions of masculinity and femininity!

I am very grateful to pastor and hymn-writer Brian Wren for blowing the whistle concerning the unfair political advantages men have received from the language of Christian liturgy, hymnody, and theology. We women have been saying similar things for more than a decade; but this remains a heteropatriarchal culture, and Brian Wren has spoken in a heterosexual male voice some insights that heteropatriarchy will never hear in any other voice. So let us ponder together a very important passage from Brian Wren:

Linguistic images are more fleeting [than graven images] and leave room for the imagination. . . . No image [of God] is adequate. To select one image and bow down to it is idolatrous. If we draw on a variety of God-images, and let them balance, enrich, and clash with one another, we shall be following the instincts of biblical faith and the methods of many biblical voices. Allowing God-images to clash is important, because it reminds us that we are approaching that which is beyond all images. . . . [As we look at the biblical record], it is fair to speak of a direction of divine action, seeking to undermine and over-throw patriarchal structures. . . . The King abandons his throne, calls his disciples friends, and washes their feet. The Spirit creates a com-munity uniting gentiles and Jews, slaves and free citizens, in which there is a brief glimpse of women exercising leadership with men. (132)

It is this inclusive vision that provides the mandate for turn-of-the-century people. If we will seek to implement inclusiveness, abandoning hetero-patriarchal gender distortions in favor of allowing people simply to be themselves, we will enhance human fulfillment, health, and wholeness. What could be more important?

Chapter Seven

EROS IS A SPIRITUAL URGE

———— ≈ ————

I have argued in Chapters Five and Six that heteropatriarchal society has insisted on standards of masculinity and femininity that have severely limited and deformed human potential. If that is true, then it should come as no surprise that heteropatriarchal society, perhaps especially the religious segment of it, also tends toward body-hatred and pleasure-hatred, and hence erotophobia. The results have been painful for everybody concerned.

The philosopher Schopenhauer once remarked that "sexual passion is the kernel of the will to live." My own experience would indicate that that is true for many people, although I would prefer to say that sexual passion is one primary indicator of the will to live, at least on this planet we know as earth. From this perspective the attitudes of organized religion, and especially Christian attitudes toward sexual passion, have been too frequently devoted to death rather than life. For instance, in the *Canterbury Tales* Geoffrey Chaucer depicted a widespread medieval attitude toward sexual desire by having one of his characters refer to passion between a duly married husband and wife as "sin." If married lovers are sinful, what's left to call the rest of us? The Protestant Reformers restored sexual passion to respectability — but only within marriage. Many contemporary Christian churches, both Protestant and Catholic, uphold the Reformation attitude toward sexual passion: it is acceptable within the bonds of holy matrimony (especially in the service of procreation) but reprehensible otherwise.

If indeed sexual passion is one primary indicator of the will to live, most contemporary Christian churches and many synagogues have passed a death sentence upon the many single people who are not celibate. Their number includes heterosexuals who may remain unmarried for a variety of reasons, bisexuals, and the gay women and men for whom marriage is not possible. Of course the death sentence is not usually actualized: in reality, church officials pretend not to know how much extramarital passion is being enacted by their parishioners, and the only actual death is either teen-age suicide or the death of integrity. The integrity that dies is both the integrity of the churchly institutions themselves and the life integrity of those sexually active people who for one reason or another retain their place within religious systems by presenting either a celibate or a heterosexual pose, all the while engaging in secret and somewhat guilty passions.

No wonder many of our more candid contemporaries have felt constrained to sacrifice their spirituality upon the altar of their sexuality, walking out of churches, synagogues, or mosques, and into the bars and bedrooms of their choice. For instance, one mainline Protestant church has taken the official position that homosexuality is "incompatible" with Christian teachings. Now, if sexual passion is one primary indicator of the will to live, then such an official church position forces unmarried lovers to leave the church. Either that, or commit a form of psychological suicide by staying in the church. On the other hand, hundreds of thousands of lesbian or gay Christians have tried to sacrifice their sexuality to their spirituality, myself among them; but if we live long enough, the will to live more fully will assert itself, and sexual passion will triumph over abstract doctrines and promises. (Shakespeare put it this way: "The strongest oaths are straw/To the fire in the blood.")

By contrast to the religious moralists, sexual libertarians have promoted sex free of all responsibility, ethical values, and social consequences. But genuine freedom carries with it a set of responsibilities to the others with whom we live in community (*Reports*, 9). Because sex almost always involves at least a minimal level of human interaction, sexual libertarianism is unrealistic — and especially so in the age of AIDS.

Integration Rather Than Sacrifice

The major purpose of this chapter is to assert that there is an alternative to sacrificing sexuality to spirituality or spirituality to sexuality. That alternative is to build an integrated approach to sexuality and spirituality that enriches both by honoring both. The integration and honoring of both sexuality and spirituality can be achieved in several ways: a person can walk away from established institutions and develop a more independent form of spirituality, either through private meditation, study, and ritual, or through starting or joining an alternative spirituality group such as a witches' coven, a Course in Miracles study group, or a twelve-step group. Another method of honoring both sexuality and spirituality would be to attend services only in the context of established religious institutions that have positive attitudes toward all forms of sexual relating between consenting adults, such as the Universal Fellowship of Metropolitan Community Churches, the Unitarian Universalist Fellowship, or the lesbian, gay, and bisexual organizations within the various Jewish, Roman Catholic, and Protestant communities. A third method of honoring both sexuality and spirituality would be to continue to attend services within your own religious tradition, being completely candid there about your sexuality and thus challenging that institution either to change its stance by accepting you fully, or to implement its theories by forcing you out — or else to live with its own hypocrisy by accepting you on a personal level while rejecting you on a theoretical level. People who choose this third option are choosing to be catalysts for change, but they must be careful not to burn themselves out through constant contact with negative messages.

There is a fourth possibility. Sometimes local religious congregations take a stance that opposes the sexual negativism of the national organization they belong to. Among them would be the More Light Presbyterian churches, the Reconciling United Methodist churches, the les-bi-gay synagogues, and the occasional Catholic congregation that has a priest who is secretly supportive of human sexual diversity. Obviously it would be easier to honor our sexuality in such a spiritual context. But my major point is that whatever route we choose to take, including an eclectic route that uses several or all of the options I've outlined, it is vital that we never allow society's erotophobia to rob us of our sensuous spirituality.

Religion, Spirituality, Eros, Pornography

Although the dictionary tightly links spirituality with religion, it is important to distinguish organized religion from spirituality. I would define spirituality as the experience of the Sacred within ourselves, within our relationships, and within our entire environment. Spirituality refers to our ways of believing, belonging, and responding to the power and presence of Divinity, Holiness, the Higher Power, the All-Inclusive One who connects us spiritually to one another and the whole ecosystem. The experience of connectedness is too empowering and joyous to relinquish for any reason.

I have entitled this chapter "Eros Is a Spiritual Urge," and it is time to make good on the promise of that title. I am not using *eros* in the sense of a kind of love that must be differentiated from *sex, philia,* or *agape.* In the Western world, *sex* has been defined as lust or libido; *eros* as the drive of love to procreate or create; *philia* as friendship, or brotherly or sisterly love; and *agape* as charity, *caritas,* disinterested love devoted to the welfare of the other person, the kind of love God manifests toward humankind (May, 37). Everything in me resists this categorization, which separates passionate sexuality from the drive to love and create, from friendship, and from concern for the welfare of the other person. It is precisely that separation that has created the erotophobic culture we are living in today. Rather, I am using the word *eros* as a combination of all four traditional categories. I would argue that healthy and fulfilling erotic relationships include sexual passion, creative and caring love, friendship, and concern for the welfare of the partner. I would agree with Rollo May that "every human experience of authentic love is a blending, in various proportions, of these four [kinds of love]" (38). We do not feel or act upon sexual passion with all of our friends and family members, but wherever there is authentic love there is an erotic element: a mutual need to touch, a caring about the wholeness and welfare of the embodied person, and the desire to give and receive pleasure and mutual delight.

The black lesbian feminist poet Audre Lorde defines eros as "an assertion of the life-force . . . ; of that creative energy empowered, the knowledge and use of which we [women] are now reclaiming in our language, our history, our dancing, our loving, our work, our lives" ("Uses of the Erotic," 55). My hope is that men also will reclaim eros as a life-force of creative energy. Like Sigmund Freud in his later years, Audre Lorde identifies eros with "true life-instincts" (Heyward, *Touching*, 168, n. 19). She sees eros as the very opposite of pornography, which is often erroneously called erotic. I have never forgotten a porn show I once attended in London to educate myself on the subject. I expected loud stripper music, shouting, and excited appreciation of what was happening on stage. What I heard instead was a deadening and pathetic silence. I saw controlling men and puppet-like women simulating sexual intercourse in front of an audience totally lost in solitary apathy. There was no sense of wonder, no caring, no feeling, no aliveness. Needless to say, there was no sense of the sacred. It was humdrum. So my complaint about pornography is not only that it tends to be antispiritual, and not only that it tries to make male domination of women and children desirable, but that it also tends to be antierotic.

Recreational (Casual) Sex

I have no objection to the casual sharing of sexual pleasure and tenderness except to note that people who never get beyond recreational sex eventually report boredom with it. I have no objection to sensuality for its own sake, either, except to note that sensualists eventually become bored and somewhat jaded. John Keats captures the essence of jaded sensualism when he envies the figures of the lovers on the Grecian Urn. They are just about to kiss, but not yet quite touching. Keats's envy is based on the fact that the lovers are "Forever warm and still to be enjoyed / Forever panting, and forever young; / All breathing human passion far above / That leaves a heart high-sorrowful and cloyed, / A burning forehead, and a parching tongue."

Notwithstanding Keats's words, however, I believe that every honest attempt to relate to another human being is a good attempt, including recreational sex or sensuality for the sake of sensuality, if that is all a person can achieve. But relational modes that plumb spiritual depths and heights are more lastingly gratifying than exclusively recreational or casual sex. No use denying it: there really *is* a qualitative difference between the tinklings of a lovely music box and the full-throated sound of a symphony orchestra!

Audre Lorde clarifies the distinction between pornographic anti-eroticism and one-dimensional sex that is good for a while but not so satisfactory in the long run. She writes, "The erotic is not a question of what we do; it is a question of how acutely and fully we can feel in the do-ing" ("Uses of the Erotic," 54). Authentically felt eros empowers not only our sexual relationships, but all our relationships — not only to people, but to our work, to music and the other arts, to nature, to the universe we inhabit, to whatever Higher or Deeper Power we recognize. And in that wholistic sense, eros is distinctly a spiritual instinct, urging us toward rela-tionship on every level of our being, including the level of sexual passion but not focusing exclusively on that level.

Some of my readers may at this point be feeling that I am beg-ging the question, assuming that eros is an all-encompassing impulse toward the sharing of feeling, and therefore spiritual, without actually proving a necessary connection between eros and spirituality. I propose to prove that connection through five areas of evidence: classical mythology, the Bible, recent psychology, liberation theology, and the life experience of contemporary women and men. These sources are mainly European-or Western-world-centered, I acknowledge. I recognize that the Eastern world, Native Americans, and African cultures never fell into the same kinds of erotophobic dualisms as Western heteropatriarchy. Other cultures have different problems of their own, but they are not my focus here.

Eros in Classical Mythology

The classical myth of Cupid and Psyche reveals some powerful connections between eros and spirituality. Cupid, or Amor, is, of course, the Roman god of erotic love; his Greek name was Eros. Our modern depictions of the god of erotic love as a plump, roguish little boy with wings reflect later mythology; in earlier myth he is a beautiful young man who existed almost from the beginning of time and who was present at the birth of Venus rather than being her son, as later myth would have it. Far from being exclusively the property of heterosexuals, Eros was also worshipped as a god of love and loyalty between people of the same sex (Tripp, 232).

When Venus became jealous that people were worshipping Psyche in-stead of herself because of Psyche's beauty, she asked Eros to cause Psyche to fall in love with some unworthy man; but instead he spirited Psyche away to his own secret palace, where he would come to her only under a cover of darkness. As he explained to her, "If you saw me, perhaps you would fear me, perhaps adore me, but all I ask of you is to love me. I would rather you would love me as an equal than adore me as a god" (Bullfinch, 83). So immediately the myth expresses the importance of equality, of mutuality, of the reciprocal sharing of feelings, if passion is to flourish.

But Psyche is goaded by her jealous sisters to have a look at her lover. She brings a candle to bed in order to look at him while he sleeps, but when some hot wax falls on his shoulder, he awakens. Sorrowfully telling Psyche that "Love cannot dwell with suspicion," Eros flies away on his white wings. Not only does this incident show that trust is necessary if lovers are to stay together; it also shows that there is a certain mystery in erotic relationships that must not be violated. And, or course, it underscores the theme of equality. By inspecting Eros during his sleep, Psyche attempted to take power over him. Chaucer fully understood the significance of Psyche's act, remarking in the *Canterbury Tales,* "Love is a thing as any spirit free / When mastery cometh, the god of love anon / Beateth his wings, and farewell! he is gone." At this point the myth contains one of those reversals we so often find in heteropatriarchal literature: Psyche tries to take power over Cupid, whereas in the overwhelming majority of cases and in the basic structuring of heteropatriarchy, it is the male who assumes power over the female. But the point remains: *mastery destroys any possibility of love.*

After Psyche has been put through some impossible trials by the goddess Venus — trials Psyche survives only through the secret assistance of Eros and his emissaries — Venus is at long last placated. Psyche is permitted to drink ambrosia to become immortal and is reunited with Eros, who exultingly tells her that now their union has become eternal.

It is this eternal union between Eros and Psyche that establishes the mythological connection between sexuality and spirituality. Remember that Eros's Roman name is Cupid, from which is derived the English word *cupidity,* meaning intense desire or lustfulness. So lust or passionate sexuality is forever united with Psyche, whose name means both the human soul and a butterfly (Bullfinch, 89). In their transformation from worms to wings, butterflies are favorite symbols of spiritual maturation; so Psyche stands for the immortality of the human essence, the Self. From the union of Cupid and Psyche, sexuality and spirituality, a daughter is born. Her name is Pleasure. So the myth of Cupid and Psyche speaks to us across the centuries, implying that genuine pleasure results from a union of sexual passion with a strong awareness of the sacred soul in ourselves and our lovers. We are, of course, free to separate sex from spirituality, but classical myth indicates that in the long run the result will be loss of pleasure.

Time will allow me to cite only one other myth that makes a similar point. When the celebrated hunter Actaeon happened to see the Great Goddess Diana naked, washing herself in the woods, instead of falling down and worshipping her, he made a sexual overture toward her. She was so infuriated at his failure to recognize her divinity that she changed him into a stag, after which Actaeon's own hunting dogs tore him to shreds. The point of this version of the myth is, of course, that failure to recognize the sacred spirit in that which is sexually desirable will inevitably lead to fragmentation, a lack of central cohesiveness and meaningfulness in our human experience.

Eros in the Bible

Turning to the Bible, we find a much more sex-positive attitude than the behavior of contemporary religious institutions would lead us to expect. It is true that in the Bible, most of the passionate sexual experience takes place in a family context: but the forms of family are exceedingly varied, unlike the recent religious obsession with the nuclear family of "Daddy and me and baby makes three." I have listed forty different forms of the family that are mentioned or implied in the Hebrew and Christian Scriptures, not counting the nuclear family (see Appendix B). The Bible even records a same-sex family unit in the love relationship of Naomi and Ruth, a unit that later becomes an extended family in which Naomi is pronounced the mother of Ruth's son by Boaz. Furthermore, according to the Christian Scriptures, Jesus insisted upon defining family in terms of a common set of values, not in terms of biological connection. People who are barred by society from becoming legally recognized family units may take comfort from this fact: to Jesus, family meant a person's bonding with those who saw things in a similar fashion (those who heard the Word of God to them, and did it).

But our subject here is specifically eros, including sexual passion, and its intimate connectedness to the experience of the Sacred. How does the Bible touch upon this topic?

The most obvious biblical connection between sex and spirit occurs in the Song of Songs, often called the Song of Solomon, the most sensuous book not only in the Bible but in all the literature of antiquity. It consists of a series of love lyrics spoken by a highly charged duo, and I can find no sure indication that they are married to each other. In fact, since they are searching for one another during much of the book, it seems highly unlikely that they are married. Through the centuries, Christian exegetes have tried to find ways to allegorize the meaning of this gorgeous hymn to eros, because if the Song of Songs were taken at face value, then people would inevitably begin to question the traditional assumption about the spiritual superiority of a celibate priesthood. Even today, when the Song of Songs is taken more literally, most Christian and Jewish interpreters would still insist that the Song of Songs is about the holiness of *married* love.

I would agree with Rabbi Akiba (c. 100 C.E.) that the Song of Songs is the "holy of holies" of the sacred Scriptures (Phipps, 47). But at the same time I would insist that there is little or no evidence that the lovers are married. Even if they were, marriage at the time was a personal covenant between two people, not the state-mandate it is today.

In the Song of Songs, as in the creation stories in the book of Genesis, woman has an intrinsic value, and no mention is made of her ability to bear children. She is called not only spouse but also sister, indicating a psychophysical closeness, the recognition of a sacred equality between the lovers. As Lutheran pastor Dietrich Bonhoeffer wrote from a Nazi concentration camp, "Even the Bible could find room for the Song of Songs, and one could hardly have a more passionate and sensual love than is there portrayed. It is a good thing that that book is included in the Bible as a protest against those who believe that Christianity stands for the restraint of passion" (as quoted by Phipps, 66).

Because Christian interpreters have often differentiated sharply between *agape* and *eros,* disinterested godly love and mere human and sexual love, it is important to know that when the whole Bible was translated into Greek in the ancient version known as the Septuagint, the word *agape* is "used hundreds of times to express the whole spectrum of human relationships": for instance, the sexual yearning of Jacob for Rachel was translated *agape* (Gen. 23:20), and Amnon figured out a way to seduce Tamar because of *agape* (2 Sam. 13:1). The love David had with Jonathan was *agape* and wonderful, surpassing the *agape* of women (2 Sam. 1:26). God's love for humankind was also described as *agape* (Jer. 31:3). The point is that all love, whether human or divine, physical or spiritual, to the Septuagint translators could be expressed by the single Greek word *agape.* There was to their minds no great distinction between sexual desire and spiritual love. Furthermore, Professor William Phipps pointed out in his book *Recovering Biblical Sensuousness* that according to standard classical lexicons, in classical literature, "the word *eros* was also used to connote everything from what is now called erotic to a transcendent relationship with the divine" (105). Similarly, the ancient Jews did not separate the sacred from sexuality, the ultimate from the intimate. We moderns would be better off if we could reclaim for our contemporary world this more wholistic understanding of sexuality and spirituality. Instead we have allowed ourselves to follow Plato's differentiation between noble heavenly rational love and dishonorable bodily vulgar love (Plato's *Symposium*). We have read the Bible through Platonic lenses, and the results have been fragmenting and disastrous.

In 1970 the United Presbyterian General Assembly, responding to the biblical evidence that I've been talking about, declared that human sexuality "is truly a vehicle of the spirit and a means of communion" (*Minutes,* 897). A wonderful statement — but of course the General Assembly did not mean that love-making outside of marriage could be construed as "truly a vehicle

of the spirit and a means of communion." Like most other denominations, the United Presbyterian Church still officially denies the spirituality
of extramarital relationships, including lesbian or gay sexual passion — and
does so on the basis of the Bible. This is an injustice to all sexually active
single people, but especially to lesbian and gay people who are not *permitted* to marry. It also does not do justice to the Bible. The fact is that none of
the biblical authors knew about homosexuality as a lifelong unchosen and
unchanging orientation toward one's own sex. That orientation was first
discovered and named in the 1890s. So it is as anachronistic to turn to the
Bible for information about homosexuality as it would be to search for a
Bible passage concerning microcomputer chips (see Mollenkott, "Critical
Inquiry"). Same-sex behaviors are sometimes mentioned in the Bible, but
never in the context of an authentic sexual orientation. The overriding emphasis of the Bible is on loving our neighbor as we love ourselves — and
the word for love of neighbor is *agape,* the same word that the Septuagint
used for the love between David and Jonathan or Ruth and Naomi as well
as the love between women and men and the love between God and the
human race.

Eros in Contemporary Experience

So the Bible, like classical mythology, points toward the understanding that
human sexuality is most richly fulfilling when we recognize the sacredness
of our own bodyselves and that of our partners. Turning to modern psychology, I must because of space limit myself to one representative, and
I have chosen the book *Love and Will,* the best-selling masterpiece of humanistic psychologist Rollo May. He argues that at the moment of climax
in sexual intercourse, lovers are "carried beyond their personal isolation"
so that they "experience themselves as uniting with nature itself." He comments that in all but the most depersonalized sex, "There is an accelerating
experience of touch, contact, union to the point where, for a moment, the
awareness of separateness is lost, blotted out in a feeling of oneness with nature." He denies that this mystical transcendence is achieved only by ideal
lovers, maintaining that "it is an inseparable part of actual experience in
the love act" (316). The tremendous acclaim accorded to *Love and Will* by
leading physicians, psychologists, and theologians indicates how badly we
need this sort of reintegrated understanding of sexuality and spirituality.

To represent those feminist theologians who are calling for a sexual
theology that is affirming and healing, I have chosen the Episcopal lesbian
priest Carter Heyward. Even the subtitle of her 1989 book *Touching Our
Strength* makes the point that eros is a spiritual urge: *The Erotic as Power
and the Love of God.* Heyward outlines several sexual options open to all
of us: monogamy, celibacy, or "an openness to sexual relationships with

friends (which, for many in a sex-negative society, is considered promiscuous)" (*Touching*, 135). She admits that each of these sexual options has a history of alienation but argues that each also holds possibilities for transformation. And she comments, "Whatever ways we may choose to express ourselves sexually, we are obligated to approach each other's lives with a profound sense of tenderness, respect, and openness to learning with each other how we might become more faithful friends — in relation not only to each other but to the larger world as well, to helping make it a more just and peaceful resource of pleasure for all living creatures." Thus Heyward makes an important point about eros: sexualized spirituality is not a substitute for seeking a more just society; rather, eros empowers us to care about every *body*, and motivates our work on behalf of human justice.

Heyward uses the AIDS quilt to illustrate the fact that eros carries us even through and beyond death in passionate friendship that will never die (*Touching*, 138). My own favorite panel of the quilt contains a photograph of Billy Komasa inside a drawing of a burning heart, with a poem that beautifully illustrates that eros is a spiritual urge. The panel reads, "Radical doll, / You who thrilled so to light and the mysterious dark, / May you be dancing, dearest, somewhere / In a garden of secret, sweet delight."

The yearning tenderness of the AIDS quilt panels certainly provides evidence from contemporary experience of the interconnection between spirituality and sexuality, ultimacy and intimacy. Let me use one more illustration, this time from a brilliant lesbian novelist named Maureen Brady. Writing about her own early experience of female-perpetrated incest, Brady comments,

> For a child in [the situation of being sexually abused by an older member of the family] there is a contamination of both love and power. Trust is impossibly betrayed. And loyalty is demanded without being merited. While incest isn't about sex but about power, it's no accident that it moves in the realm of sexuality, because sexuality is closely akin to spirituality and instinctual expression. And it is this, the spirit, the true self of the child, which a perpetrator needs to overwhelm in order to experience possession, a taking of power against his or her own powerlessness. It sounds sinister and malicious. It is, regardless of whether the perpetrator had deliberate intent to injure or was unconsciously acting out of unowned wounds. (53)

Because of the largely unconscious damage caused by her experience of incest, for years Brady had to eke out her writing through what felt like a kink in the hose of her creativity. Eventually she realized that there was no kink in the hose she had been given; instead, there was someone stepping on the hose. And then she began the process of repossessing her own spirit, "creating autonomy where none [had been] respected." She does this partly through creating characters that become themselves, characters she as their author must release into their own existence. She comments, "Love does not possess but fosters a cycle of abundance instead" (53). Thus in both the damage done to her and her gradual control of that damage, the experience of Maureen Brady demonstrates that when someone is damaged in their sexuality, they are damaged also in their spirituality, their creativity, and their entire instinctual life. So the healing process must trace a similar trajectory: as we repossess our spirit and learn respect for our own boundaries and respect for the otherness of the other, and as we experience our personal power as manifestations of God Herself, we also become more open to sexual fulfillment.

Eros and Meditation

On the basis of what we have seen in classical mythology, the Bible, modern psychology and theology, and the life experience of our contemporaries, I think we can safely say that our sexual experience will become more pleasurable and satisfying as we develop our spiritual component in a sex-positive manner. Endocrinologist Deepak Chopra has written a powerful book exploring the frontiers of mind/body medicine. It's called *Quantum Healing*. He argues that through meditation, we enter a fourth and deeper state of consciousness than the ones we are used to, which are waking, sleeping, or dreaming. Chopra explains that when we go deep into the meditative trance, we automatically "contact the hidden blueprint of intelligence" and are able to change our previous negative patterns.

We have all heard of curing cancer and other diseases through visualization techniques, but most of us lack the strength of mind to be able to heal ourselves exclusively through positive visualization. Chopra argues that we can take the stress out of healing by "sinking vertically" into the center of our selves, into "pure, infinite consciousness," where we will learn to identify with the whole ocean instead of with only our one little wave on the surface of the sea. (This shift in identity is the awakening discussed in Chapter One.) And, says Chopra, "when the mind shifts, the body cannot help [following]" — a thesis that is perfectly logical if we really are spiritual beings who happen to be having human experiences at this time. I cannot take the space here to summarize the stunning evidence that Chopra offers for his thesis, but I recommend *Quantum Healing* to anyone interested in deepening her consciousness as a path to better health and more gratifying sexual intimacy.

With or without the theoretical grounding provided by *Quantum Healing*, I suggest that each day we spend some time paying attention to the universal process that is working itself out at the depths of our inner being. The Christian Scriptures say that God is "above all, through all, and in [us] all" (Eph. 4:6). Whether our term for the divine Presence is God, the Christ, the Goddess, the Higher Power, the Deeper Power, the All-Encompassing Larger Power, Energy, Love, or whatever, the important thing is to open ourselves to the experience of feeling that this power is in us and we are in this power, just as the ocean is in the wave and the wave is in the ocean. To put it another way, the important thing is to stop identifying with our ego personality that imagines itself separate from God and neighbor and to learn to identify with our Selves as partakers of the divine nature (2 Peter 1:4).

Although I am not greatly skilled at meditation, I do spend some time each day listening for whatever God may have to say to me. Discipline of the mind is not easy to learn, but it is necessary to discipline the mind in order to pay attention to God's Self. What happens is beautiful, but what happens to you probably won't be exactly the same as what happens to me. The best I can do is advise you to find out for yourself and be persistent. It is not enough to hear about and be theoretically aware of our divine connectedness; we must experience and feel that connectedness frequently if we are to be empowered in our spirits, in our sexuality, and in our attempts to bring about a more just society.

Learning to Be Erotically Honest

So, yes, eros is a spiritual urge. Unfortunately, however, not all spirits are positive and beneficent. I have a wonderfully honest friend, a Quaker, who currently is living in Belgium and trying to overcome her own addictive and co-dependent manner of relating. She writes,

> The erotic is my insurance policy. A deal. Once clinched, my survival is guaranteed. The clinch is the bedroom equivalent of the handshake, but it is more deadly than the handshake.... By way of the erotic, I get you to need me like oxygen, so I can continue to breathe. The erotic is a charm I work on you; it is an illusion with which I divert your attention while I empty your pockets. (White)

As my friend later indicates, it isn't easy to learn the honest use of sexuality after engaging in manipulative or addictive behaviors. It isn't easy to "retrain desire" into more spiritually positive channels. Yet for most of us that is the challenge that faces us in the realm of sexuality: how to be more honest with ourselves so that we can love and appreciate others. It is for this reason that we desperately need meditation or some other method of paying attention to our own inner process and feeling our connection to the sacred. It is only in relationships without abuse that healthy passion finds lasting fulfillment. As Psyche learned before her eternal union with Cupid, sexual experience that is gratifying in the long run demands that we approach our lovers as equals in mutual sharing and that we develop the spiritual qualities of trust and respect for each other's mystery. My Quaker friend puts it this way:

> I don't fool myself that this will be easy. The erotic will not suddenly trip fluently off the tongue. It's not possible to learn a language in a week. The mouth needs time to reform itself to the unaccustomed taste and shape of new words. It will be a long time before I am fearless with this language, before I am sure that I mean what I say with these lips.... I love the flesh and I intend to go on loving it, but I will not lie with it, however delicate and sweet the falsehood.

Perhaps we would all do well to join my friend in her resolve to learn to speak the language of the erotic without falsehood. As she recognizes, that's quite a challenge. But the reward is great. For we remember that when Eros finally achieved an authentic union with his Psyche and when Psyche achieved an authentic union with her Eros, the result was the birth of Pleasure.

Chapter Eight

THE SEX-LOVE-JUSTICE CONNECTION IN THE HEBREW AND CHRISTIAN SCRIPTURES

———— ≈ ————

TV talk show host Phil Donahue once quipped that many of our contemporaries have been taught the following sexual ethic: "Sex is dirty. So save it for the person you marry" (Scanzoni, 25). Although Donahue phrased that statement to reveal the absurdity of the teaching, church history indicates that our parents did not develop such sex-negative attitudes all by themselves. Take, for instance, the teachings of St. Augustine (354–430 C.E.). Augustine taught that any sexual activity always degraded the spiritual self, but could be forgiven if the couple were married and managed to despise their own pleasure and seek only to procreate. To this day, orthodox Roman Catholics reject contraceptive devices because to use them would turn even marital sex into grave sin, equivalent to fornication (Ruether, "Women, Sexuality," 4). Therefore, a fully Augustinian version of Donahue's remark would read, "Sex is dirty. So save it for making babies. And be careful not to enjoy it even then!"

However, such an attitude is far from biblical. The great English poet John Milton closely followed the emphasis of the Genesis creation accounts in *Paradise Lost*, where he depicts a conversation between Adam and the Archangel Raphael. Adam has been describing his passion for Eve, their perfect harmony and union of mind and body. Adam continues,

> "To love thou blam'st me not, for love thou say'st
> Leads up to heav'n, is both the way and guide;
> Bear with me then, if lawful what I ask:
> Love not the heav'nly Spirits, and how their love

109

> Express they, by looks only, or do they mix
> Irradiance, virtual or immediate touch?"
>   To whom the Angel, with a smile that glowed
> Celestial rosy red, love's proper hue,
> Answered: "Let it suffice thee that thou know'st
> Us happy, and without love no happiness.
> Whatever pure thou in the body enjoy'st
> (And pure thou wert created) we enjoy
> In eminence, and obstacle find none
> Of membrane, joint, or limb...."
>
> (*PL* VIII. 612–25; Bush 369)

Milton touches here upon many of the themes of Genesis 1 and 2: that it was impossible for the Earth Creature to be fully happy without a loving partner; that the body was created pure; that sexual intercourse is pure and undefiled as long as the living soul and body are in right relationship with their divine Source; that indeed, human sexual love reflects and derives from divine love. So convinced is Milton of all this that he assumes that even the angelic messengers of God make love in their astral bodies, unencumbered by the limitations of physical membranes, joints, and limbs.

Is Our Culture More Permissive Than Earlier Eras?

In his enthusiasm for the pleasures of sex, Milton was typical of the seventeenth-century Puritans. When some of them migrated to America in search of greater religious freedom, they brought with them their sex-positive attitudes. In fact, Andrew Greeley questions whether our society today is any more permissive than Puritan New England, "where the practice of 'bundling' was widespread and where serious Divines argued whether sleeping with one's betrothed was indeed sinful" (Taylor, 75). Those arguments about premarital sex were, we may be sure, carried on within a biblical framework, for the Puritans were very serious about the Scriptures. So it must give thoughtful people pause, here at the end of the twentieth century, that a society that is biblically illiterate has come to assume that Christianity teaches that sex is so dirty it should be saved for the person we marry!

Milton was particularly biblical in connecting sex with love. Although Milton's Adam asks about whether spiritual beings engage in sexual *intercourse,* the Archangel responds in terms of *love:* "Without love no happiness." Many in our society view the connecting of sex with love as a notion peculiar to women, but the Bible does not make any such gender-role distinction. I remember seeing a *Playboy* cartoon in which a man and woman were getting dressed, obviously after having sex. She looks at him hopefully, but he blusters, "Why speak of love at a time like this?" Sophisticates may consider that attitude acceptable in men today, especially in playboy-types and even in "liberated women"; but it is a far cry from the biblical understanding of sexual relations as creating one-fleshedness, which in turn implies justice achieved through equal partnership and mutuality. It was not the human female but the male who according to Genesis 2:23 said, "This at last is bone of my bones and flesh of my flesh." And the conclusion drawn from that recognition is whole-life commitment: "Therefore a man leaves his father and his mother and clings to his wife and they become one flesh" (Gen. 2:24).

Why Is a Predominantly Christian Society So Far from Biblical Attitudes?

Since the United States population is predominantly Christian, it seems fair to ask how our understanding of sex has strayed so far from the teachings of the book Christian churches claim as their norm, their standard-bearer, their moral and ethical guide. I have my own theory: I think "conservative" churches have been so busy upholding male supremacy and pointing out the evils of extra-marital sex, including homosexuality, that they have inadvertently polluted sexual pleasure even within marriage. Meanwhile "liberal" churches have been so embarrassed about misuses of the Bible (to justify slavery for instance) that they have tended to downplay the Scriptures altogether. Not only that, but acculturation to heterosexist and workaholic society has caused "liberal" people to back away from openly affirming physical pleasures. (It is one thing to enjoy sex in semiguilty secrecy but another thing to advocate such pleasure in public.) To heterosexists, one of the most hideous aspects of lesbian or gay sex is that it is engaged in purely for the pleasure and nurturance of the people involved, procreation being impossible. After all, capitalism urges productivity upon us as the be-all and end-all of living: if not making money, at least accomplishing some quantifiable task with a recognizable product. How can mere pleasure, mere tenderness, mere nurturing of a relationship be worth the investment of a good Christian's time?

The contemporary church has not entirely escaped the judgment of *Sex in History* that "the Christian *sense* of sin, which might have been a force for good, was diverted from areas where it could have been more usefully employed. By some mysterious alchemy, sexual purity came to neutralize other sins, so that even the moral oppression and physical barbarity that became characteristic of the Christian church in late medieval and Renaissance times scarcely appeared as sins at all in comparison with the sins of sex and heresy" (Tannahill, 161). In other words, the guilty fear of pleasure, bodies, and sexual passion served to deflect attention away from defining *sin* as *injustice, the unjust abuse of power*. Alas, in actual practice that has not changed very much.

All this has paid off in a sadly negative practical way. Family and sex therapists report that about 75 percent of their clients complain of a lack of interest in sex, and the American Psychiatric Association estimates that 20 percent of Americans are suffering from Inhibited Sexual Desire (Orr, 21). Both the pornography industries and the moralists thrive on the subordination of women. Unless we can eroticize equality, friendship, and justice-love, sexuality in America will continue to suffer malaise.

What Constitutes the Ethical Center in the Bible?

Despite contemporary misinterpretations, however, the Bible provides us with

> ...a steady insistence upon the personal qualities involved in all sexuality. There is no sexual act which does not have its source and its effect upon the center of selfhood. Or, to put it another way, there is no sexual act which is morally neutral, a merely instinctual contact. Every "contact" involves a relationship, and every relationship is characterized by certain qualities. These may be exploitative, protective, tender, casual, or commercial. Whatever they are, they affect both persons involved and their attitudes toward themselves and toward others.... Sex involves relationships, and the Bible is centered in relationships. (Cole 424–25)

So much does the Bible center in relationships that "the *only* pronouncement of 'not good' in the Genesis creation stories occurred when God evaluated human aloneness" (Scanzoni, 13). Heterosexual, homosexual, bisexual, even asexual: "It is not good that the [human creature] should be alone" (Gen. 2:18). We need companionship!

Christian churches could readily develop a consistent ethical system were they to define *sin* as the unjust abuse of power-in-relationship and *salvation* as right relationship, whether on the levels of human-divine relationship, interpersonal and family relationship, corporate relationship, or national and international relationship. Instead, many Christians have trivialized and fragmented ethical discussion by worrying about whether people have certificates before engaging in sex, whether people relate exclusively to the other sex, whether people utilize only certain approved positions, techniques, and body parts, and whether people obey traditional gender-role assignments. Such considerations conveniently deflect ethical discussion away from the focus of biblical concern: is this relationship just? honoring and nurturing to the Self of each participant? honoring and nurturing to God Herself?

That surely is the meaning of the apostle Paul's remarks in the first letter to the Corinthians: "Do you not know that your bodies are members of Christ? Should I therefore take the members of Christ and make them members of a prostitute? Never! Do you not know that whoever is united to a prostitute becomes one body with her? For it is said, 'The two shall be one flesh.' But anyone united to the [Sovereign] becomes one spirit with [God]. Shun fornication! . . . Or do you not know that your body is a temple of the Holy Spirit within you, which you have from God, and that you are not your own?" (6:15–17, 19, NRSV; inclusive language mine). This passage should not be read as an attack on prostitutes, for in its Genesis-based doctrine of one-fleshedness it elevates the status of the prostitute fully as high as the status of the customer. And we must remember that Jesus, who was mindful of the patriarchal inequities that undergird prostitution, always spoke kindly of prostitutes: like the publicans, they would enter God's kindom ahead of self-righteous people in respected professions.

The church has for centuries chosen to understand *fornication* to mean any sex outside of marriage. But from the standpoint of biblical ethics, such a position is too easy and too lax. It puts the emphasis on the letter of the law, which kills, rather than on the spirit of the law, which gives life. Rather, by *fornication* Christians should understand sex without a covenant of caring, sex without mutual respect and concern for the welfare of the partner, sex without justice and love in right relationship. Rape, with or without a marriage certificate, heterosexual or homosexual, would be one example of fornication. So would exploiting someone's vulnerability, even if she apparently consented under conditions where the social pressures of male primacy have rendered choice a mockery.

One-Fleshedness as Quality of Relationship

My point is that the Bible emphasizes the sexual joining of bodies as a one-fleshedness that is analogous to the way our spirits are one with God's Holy Spirit. This emphasis puts the focus on *quality of relationship* rather than on what positions or techniques we utilize. As William Graham Cole pointed out in his 1959 study, *Sex and Love in the Bible*, "there are no directions as to how or when a married couple should copulate. . . . Nor . . . are there prohibitions as to manner or posture of intercourse. The laws of many states rendering it a crime to engage in variations of position have no biblical warrant" (279). Cole goes on to point out the few exceptions to his statement, such as the Hebrew Scriptures' prohibition against sex during a woman's menstrual period; but his point is well taken.

Furthermore, although William Cole did not say so, the Bible's emphasis on one-fleshedness and therefore quality of relationship offers ethical guidance for sexual relationships outside of traditional marriage as well as within it. Since many Christian people are cohabiting outside of wedlock, this is a practical and important advantage. We must bear in mind that in the biblical culture, "neither priest nor state officer performed weddings" (Phipps, 91), for "there was no religious or civil ceremony of marriage in Israel.... Sex was itself the ceremony, as the law makes abundantly clear. "A man lying with an unbetrothed maiden made her his wife by that act" (Cole, 240). Furthermore, "betrothal [engagement; commitment; covenant] was tantamount to marriage, for the law was absolutely silent on sexual relations between a betrothed couple; no prohibitions were set up and no punishments provided" (Cole, 239).

For these reasons Bible professor William E. Phipps drove home the point I am making in his 1975 book, *Recovering Biblical Sensuousness:*

> A single person may manifest a more healthy and holy sexuality than one who is married. Moreover, a committed couple who "cleave together in one flesh" may be more "joined by God" than two who have obtained a clergyman's blessing and/or a state's license. If the latter are in a situation of permanent estrangement, it is they who are "living in sin." It is ironical that many in our culture who claim to receive their moral norms from the Bible have often regarded cohabitation to be wicked if it is not sanctioned by an official of the church or the state. Actually, neither priest nor state officer performed weddings in the biblical culture. (Phipps, 91)

What about Lesbian and Gay Relationships?

I am in a position to understand on my own pulse the truth of what Professor Phipps is saying. With the blessing of church and state, I lived in sin for years "in a situation of permanent estrangement" with my husband. Frightened and oppressed by fundamentalism's strictures, I dutifully committed fornication with him, denied my own nature, and debased the holy institution of marriage. Now, for the past eleven years, *without* the blessing of church, state, or society, I have lived in a healthy and holy covenant-relationship with a woman who encourages my spiritual quest and supports my ministry. My marriage was suicide by inches; my lesbian partnership is the peace, joy, and bliss of heaven-on-earth.

Unfortunately, like many other Christian thinkers, Professor Phipps concerned himself with the welfare of heterosexual Christians only. He acknowledged that Jesus was persecuted for saying that God loved all people equally (Luke 4:16–30; Phipps, 103). He even acknowledged that Jesus' story of the good Samaritan showed that a member of a scorned group could manifest neighbor love better than members of the more respected normative groups, and he quoted Edwin Markham's quatrain as illustration of the "Samaritan's viewpoint toward the Jew":

> [She] drew a circle that shut me out —
> Heretic, rebel, a thing to flout.
> But Love and I had the wit to win:
> We drew a circle that took [her] in!
> (Phipps, 103)

I could quote the same poem to a heterosexist church and society that denies me first-class citizenship because of my lesbianism. Although Phipps, Cole, and other Christian ethicists draw a circle that shuts out my people, and myself, we are drawing a sexual ethic in a circle that takes them in. It is the biblical ethic of sex in a context of caring and covenant, sexual union as one-fleshedness that parallels and illustrates the one-consciousness between ourselves and our Creator.

I am aware that my proposed inclusive sex ethic might seem blasphemous to those who assume that the Bible condemns all sexual activity except within marriage, which by definition means male-female intercourse. As we have already seen, marriage was not formalized by either church or state in the biblical culture; so the current Christian insistence on marriage is an unbiblical insistence. And the authentic homosexual orientation was unknown to the biblical authors, so it was impossible for them to condemn it. They knew only of certain same-sex *abuses,* which they condemned. It is not fair to take biblical condemnations of same-sex *abuses* and use them to condemn healthy, holy same-sex *love.* The Bible condemns heterosexual fornication and adultery, but nobody attempts to use those condemnations to attack loving heterosexual behavior or the entire heterosexual orientation!

As I write, an Episcopal Church commission has just recommended that bishops be allowed to ordain openly gay and lesbian noncelibate seminarians to the priesthood. Two days prior to the Episcopal recommendation, a special committee of the Presbyterian Church (U.S.A.) made a similar recommendation, coming to the same conclusions as a Presbyterian study group came to over thirteen years earlier. (The Blue Book recommendations of that previous group were defeated by the right wing's stacking the votes in the General Assembly, violating Presbyterian polity that delegates should be elected without prior commitment concerning the issues to be heard and voted upon in General Assembly. So much for doing everything "decently and in order"!) Both the Episcopal and the Presbyterian study groups listened to every available perspective before reaching their conclusions. I think it is remarkable that when people spend ample time studying the issues surrounding the homosexual orientation with open minds and include contextual biblical concerns in their study, they come to the conclusion that otherwise qualified lesbian women and gay men should be eligible for ordination, and that celibacy should not be a requirement.

As well they might. The apostle Paul said that *forcing celibacy onto other people is nothing less than heretical:*

> Now the spirit expressly says that in later times some will re-nounce the faith by paying attention to deceitful spirits and teachings of demons.... They forbid marriage and demand abstinence from foods, which God created to be received with thanksgiving.... For everything created by God is good, and nothing is to be rejected, provided it is received with thanksgiving. (1 Tim. 4:1–4, NRSV)

Unaware of the homosexual orientation or healthy lesbian and gay love, Paul specifies marriage as that which should not be denied to any Christian; nevertheless, his statement that "everything created by God is good" draws a circle that takes in les-bi-gay people. We did not choose our orientation; we discovered it. And we cannot change it, although we *can* force ourselves into inauthentic marriages or else attempt to live in a miserable and inauthentic celibacy. But according to a biblical sex ethic that emphasizes quality of relating, homosexuals would be included in Paul's interdiction against enforced celibacy.

Celibacy and Chastity

As Jesus implied in his word about eunuchs who have made themselves eunuchs for the sake of God's realm (Matt. 19:12), celibacy is an honorable state when it is freely chosen by those who possess a charismatic gift to remain celibate. By speaking well of celibates, Jesus in fact corrected the Hebraic view that celibacy is socially irresponsible (see Isa. 4:1 for a hint of the attitude that is conveyed mainly in extrabiblical Hebrew texts and traditions). In fact, celibacy was so highly honored in the early church that spiritual marriages were permitted through the end of the fourth century (Tannahill, 144). In those marriages, a man and woman could live together in every sense except for sexual intercourse. This practice of spiritual cohabitation is reflected in 1 Corinthians 7:36–37, which says that a man may marry "his virgin" rather than behaving improperly toward her; but if he is able to keep his desire under control, he does well to keep her permanently as "his virgin." (The New Revised Standard translators have put themselves into the position of supporting grave injustice by translating "his fiancée" instead of "his virgin." Trying to make sense of the text without reference to spiritual marriage, they now have Scripture advising life-long engagements with no wedding!)

All in all, however, Christianity made an honored place for celibacy and demoted marriage from the absolutely central position it had held in the ancient Hebrew culture; but *forcing* celibacy on anybody was taboo. Contemporary churches would be wise to retreat from their requirement that lesbian and gay people pledge celibacy in order to merit ordination.

Current church policies uphold an iniquitous double standard in which heterosexuals are automatically eligible for ordination and possessors of first-class citizenship, while homosexuals must purchase those privileges either by pretending to be heterosexual or by promising to live celibate. But accepting the biblical sex ethic of one-fleshedness and quality of relationship would do away with that unjust double standard. Not only that: it would introduce the more flexible yet more demanding biblical ethic of chastity. Back in 1935 a Scottish moral philosopher named John Macmurray explained that "what Jesus did was to substitute an inner and emotional basis of behavior for an external and intellectual one." The inner emotional basis, Macmurray explained, was chastity, defined as "sincerity in the expression of what we feel":

> Let me come straight away now to the one really positive thing I have to say about sex-morality. Its true basis is the virtue of chastity. And I want to explain what I think chastity really is.... In a word... chastity is emotional sincerity.... [Sexual intercourse] is a simple organic function to be used like all the others, for the expression of personality in the service of love.... If it is to be chaste, ... it must fall within a real unity of two persons — with essential friendship. And it must be a necessary part of that [emotional] unity." (as quoted in Macourt, 103 and 105)

Thus Macmurray upholds a standard of sexual intercourse or "one-fleshedness" as properly occurring only within the chastity of sincere friendship, which has often been defined as oneness of soul, or spiritual union. Macmurray's standard is a biblical one that is applicable both to heterosexual and homosexual relationships.

Monogamy and Relinquishing Judgment

Having established a single standard of morality, there can be little doubt that the biblical ideal for sexual experience is a monogamous lifetime or at least long-term relationship. Mark 10:2–9 records that Jesus upheld the Genesis ethic of "one-fleshedness" in the context of opposing the double standard that made divorce relatively easy for Jewish men but impossible for women. Romans 7:2–3 speaks of the laws of marriage as binding during the partners' lifetime; and 1 Corinthians 7 upholds lifetime relationships and assumes both monogamy and equal-partner mutuality.

But having acknowledged long-term monogamous relating as the biblical ideal, it is necessary to warn immediately against putting down various attempts to relate that fail to meet this ideal. Anglican priest and Cambridge professor Norman Pittenger says it well:

> Why do people frequent prostitutes, engage in "one-night stands," and the like? Not because they are wicked, but because they are lonely, in need of affection... wishing a release from sexual tension, and above all desiring a union of lives, however partial or imperfect. I dare not condemn those who engage in promiscuous or easy [casual] sexual encounters. But I would say to them that they are *really* wanting something else; they are really seeking for the sort of relationship which has about it the quality of true love... and... the joy which can be found in the widest and fullest sharing of life with another. (in Macourt, 89)

When I first began to speak at conferences involving large numbers of gay men, I asked my fellow-presenter John McNeill for advice concerning how to handle questions of sexual ethics. We had only a few brief seconds, but he gave me some marvelous advice: "Virginia, just be careful never to condemn anybody's attempt to relate." I have since read the statistics about the vast numbers of gay men who have been so stunned by society's disapproval and hatred that they have become totally asexual, living withdrawn, stressful lives of bitter loneliness. And I have thanked God and Her messenger John McNeill that I was never instrumental in adding to the sum of that human misery.

Christian Liberty

By contrast to moral judgmentalism the apostle Paul sets forth the principle of Christian liberty in passages like 1 Corinthians 6:12: "'All things are lawful for me,' but not all things are beneficial. 'All things are lawful for me,' but I will not be dominated by anything." Whereas the Hebrew Scriptures sought to delineate the areas of responsibility in their legal codes and the Catholic magisterium has made careful lists of what is permissible or prohibited and of mortal and venial sins, the apostle Paul and the Reformers "insisted on a highly dangerous commodity — what they call Christian liberty" (Cole, 426–27). Accepting all things as lawful but then discriminating between what is or is not beneficial, and being careful to avoid compulsiveness, is a highly demanding way of life. It inevitably requires individuals and their respective communities to discern what constitutes appropriate action in any given social context.

Roman Catholic ethicist Charles E. Curran writes about "the theology of compromise," which maintains that "because of the existence of sin in the world a person might be forced to accept some behavior that under ordinary circumstances [she] would not want to choose" (Taylor, 128–29). What Curran calls a theology of compromise, Joseph Fletcher has called situation ethics, Katie Cannon has called black womanist ethics, and I have called Christian humanist ethics.

By whatever name, Christian liberty demands that we assess situations carefully and ask our Inner Teacher, the Holy Spirit, what action or attitude is appropriate in each particular context:

> The gospel of Christian liberty offers escape from a rigid legalism which says implicitly, if not explicitly . . . that sex is shameful. Biblical faith proclaims the goodness of all the created world, including sexuality. It also declares, however, that [a human being] is . . . [her sister's] keeper, that [she] has a responsibility for [her] neighbor. . . . In every human encounter [she] meets God, who demands of [her] a response. Each encounter is absolutely unique, defying calculation or prescription by law. To walk through life according to the rules is to live by the letter which kills. One must walk in the spirit which gives life. One must trust in the Spirit and [Her] guidance, "proving all things" and doing all things to the glory of God. (Cole, 266–67)

The Immorality of Denying Pleasure to Others

Bernard Gert, who has proposed a rational foundation for morality in his book *The Moral Rules,* carries my argument forward in one of his observations. Concerning "nonmarital sex between mutually consenting adults," Gert comments,

> Unless it can be shown that nonmarital sexual relations between consenting adults cause harm to someone, public reason does not prohibit such activity. On the contrary, given that sex can provide some of life's most enjoyable moments, it would seem that the deprivation of this pleasure is itself immoral unless one can show that such deprivation is necessary for avoiding greater evil. . . . Certainly the burden of proof is on those who seek to deprive all unmarried people of the pleasures of sex. (113)

Since many churches today do seek to deprive all unmarried people of the pleasures of sex, a burden of proof as big as the national debt would seem to lie at the doors of the church. Should Christian leaders be held responsible for all the sex-related suicides of people driven to despair by their teachings? And all the lives of quiet desperation? Jesus warned against those who "tie up heavy burdens, hard to bear, and lay them on the shoulders of others; but they themselves are unwilling to lift a finger to move them" (Matt. 23:4).

Biblical Guidelines for Sexual Experience

Although the practice of Christian liberty requires us to use our minds and hearts to discern appropriate behavior in any given context, we are not without biblical guidelines. We have already seen that the sexual ideal of the Christian Scriptures, implied in several passages, is monogamous long-term relating. That ideal alone can serve as a guideline in many situations. Even more basic is the guidance provided in Mark 12:28–34, in which Jesus asserts that the greatest commandment is the apparently dual commandment to love God with all our hearts, souls, minds, and strength, and to love our neighbor as ourselves. (The duality is only *apparent* to those of us who believe that God is the only Person there is, the all-embracing consciousness of which each of us partakes, the Source from which every being derives. By this standard, loving God and loving self and loving neighbor are all the same act. No wonder Jesus said in Matthew 22:39 that the second commandment is "like" the first!)

As Giles Hibbert remarks, the commandments to love God and neighbor are "the absolute center of the New Testament." Therefore, "Any rules there may be about how loving should actually be done ... must be dependent upon [the commandment to love]; they cannot be conditions for its actuality. ... *How we love* depends upon *the reality of our loving,* and not the other way around" (Macourt, 96–97). When we have made an unrestrained commitment and have begun to practice the commandment to love, then and only then are we able to discover what laws should govern our actual loving. As always in discipleship, the commitment and beginning to practice come first; only after these acts of the will are we granted further knowledge: "Anyone who resolves to do the will of God will know whether the teaching is from God" (John 7:17).

The Christian Scriptures also provide us with a very clear picture of the purposes of sexual intimacy. Although Paul has suffered a very bad press in matters concerning sexuality, he is remarkably helpful in 1 Corinthians 7:2–5:

> Each man should have his own wife and each woman her own husband. The husband should give to his wife her conjugal rights, and likewise the wife to her husband. For the wife does not have authority over her own body, but the husband does; likewise the husband does not have authority over his own body, but the wife does. Do not deprive one another except by agreement for a set time, to devote yourselves to prayer, and then come together again, so that Satan may not tempt you because of your lack of self-control. (NRSV)

Not bad for a celibate bachelor!

First of all, this passage is notable for its even-handed treatment of male and female. As Evelyn and Frank Stagg have noticed, "Paul addresses the wife as directly as the husband, which is contrary to the usual pattern of addressing men and instructing women indirectly. Throughout this passage, duties between husband and wife are mutual and reciprocal; and there is no subordination of one to the other" (170).

Second, the passage says nothing whatsoever about procreation (St. Augustine, eat your heart out!). That sexual intimacy is intended to be pleasurable is implied by the phrase "conjugal *rights*" and by the warning "do not *deprive* one another." That sexual intimacy is intended to nourish and deepen the bonding is implied by the mutual authority the partners hold over one another's bodies. Here again we see the biblical concept of "one-fleshedness"; the body of each partner in sexual intimacy belongs to the other partner in the great mystery of divine/human oneness. The importance of sexual intimacy to the strength of the bonding is also implied in the warning about frequency: not even prayer should separate a couple for too long, because the relationship could be jeopardized by the celibacy forced upon the partner of the one who is devoted to prayer. Bachelor or no bachelor, Paul knew the facts of life: after a long, arid season of no sexual pleasuring, one person is liable to look outside the relationship for a more willing partner.

But What about Biblical Injustices?

All in all, the Bible is far more sex-positive than are the churches that claim to follow its teachings. I am not denying that in places the Bible reflects the hideous double standards of the society in which it was written. I will give just one example: comparison of Numbers 5:11–31 with Proverbs 6:27–35 reveals that for a woman, unfaithfulness to her husband brought severe physical punishment, and even his unfounded suspicion would subject her to a humiliating public trial; whereas for a man, unfaithfulness to his wife brought disapproval but no legal consequences. The inequity makes our blood boil, but nothing helpful for our own improvement can be gained by tracking down every instance of sexism, racism, classism, speciesism, ageism, and handicappism recorded in the Hebrew and Christian Scriptures. They trace, after all, a gradual evolution in human religious consciousness and moral conscience. Better that we focus on whatever is true, honorable, just, pure, pleasing, commendable, excellent, and praiseworthy (Phil. 4:8).

For our contemporaries, a very practical and painful biblical injustice has been the apparent demand that people stay within miserable marriages for the rest of their lives to fulfil the old adage, "You've made your bed — now lie in it." Although these days divorce is very widespread, even (or especially?) among Christians, it is often regarded as a somewhat guilty departure from biblical teaching that makes divorced Christians feel they are somehow in bad faith. Most Christians are not aware than in seventeenth-century England, the brilliant poet and theologian John Milton wrote four intricate, detailed defenses of divorce for incompatibility, all from a biblical standpoint. Nor do most Christians seem aware that many other highly respected thinkers approved of divorce on grounds other than adultery. Among them Milton lists Tertullian, Origen, Ambrose, Jerome, Augustine, Wycliff, Luther, Calvin, Erasmus, Melanchthon, Grotius, and Cranmer.

Milton's divorce tracts make heavy reading and his arguments are intricate; but they can be very liberating for people who respect the authority of Scripture and feel in need of a divorce. Rather than try to recount them all here, I will place my summary in an Appendix where it can be read by those in need of such detail. Here I will say only that Milton, who could read Hebrew, Greek, Aramaic, Syriac, Latin, and many modern languages, argues that in Matthew 9:3–9 Jesus was condemning only lustful and violent divorce (the kind Herod and Herodias had recently rushed through in order to marry each other). He was *not* speaking of divorce to relieve serious mental and spiritual incompatibility. As for Jesus' austere words recorded in Matthew 5, Mark 10, and Luke 16, Milton argues that *fornication* (KJV), *marital unfaithfulness* (NIV), or *unchastity* (NRSV) as the only ground for divorce is not limited to physical unfaithfulness but includes contemptuous behavior (psychological abusiveness) or natural and immutable dislike (profound incompatibility). In this way Milton insists on the biblical connection between sex, love, and justice and expresses disgust at those who would make the physical act of intercourse more important than a daily life of mutual loving-kindness.

Sex-Positive Elements in Scripture

Concerning the sex-love-justice connection, the Bible contains plenty that qualifies as true, honorable, just, pure, pleasing, commendable, excellent, and praiseworthy. For one thing, as even Augustine noted, the Bible assures us that "love is of God" (1 John 4:7) — that as much as love might seem to be coming from our own hearts, it actually stems from God Herself (Meeks, 230). Furthermore, as Augustine did *not* note, in the Greek New Testament, "the same verb is used of a husband who has carnally 'known' his wife as of Jesus being 'known' at Emmaus in the breaking of bread (Luke 24:35; Matthew 1:25). This suggests that both . . . coitus and the Eucharist afford participants a means for getting a deeper psychophysical revelation of one another" (Phipps, 88–89). In the Hebrew Scriptures, as we saw in the last chapter, the Song of Solomon enshrines passionate egalitarian sexual love in the holy Word. And when the Hebrew Scriptures were translated into Greek by the Septuagint translators, just as in the New Testament, the word *agape* was used to describe the sexual yearning of Jacob for Rachel, the desire of Amnon to seduce Tamar, the love of David and Jonathan, and the love of God for humankind. Although the Septuagint translators had a variety of Greek words that they could have used to describe various kinds of love — including *philia* and *eros* — they chose to delineate the whole spectrum of love and desire with the single Greek word most Christians currently reserve for disinterested God-like love: *agape*. Maybe they knew something we ought to learn!

Not only the Greek translators, but the Hebrew authors themselves utilized the same word, *'ahēḇ*, to denote God's love and human love. "The Old Testament knows of no bifurcation of affection into sacred and profane.... Hebrew life was throughout characterized by... 'holism,' the impetus to see life in terms of wholes rather than as parts, to unite rather than to divide. There was no separation of any aspect of existence into sacred and secular" — certainly not the love of God, love of neighbor, and sexual love (Cole, 53–54). For that very reason, the rabbis taught that Friday night, the beginning of the Sabbath, was "an ideal time" for a couple "to come together in the sexual embrace." In *The Jewish Way in Love and Marriage* Rabbi Maurice Lamm explains that "the joy of sex is not vulgar and merely tolerated. It is a joy appropriate to the holiest day of the week, a physical joy that is not merely the delight of the spirit" (Scanzoni, 47).

To Paul the apostle, as we have seen, sex was sacramental, to be engaged in with thanksgiving (1 Tim. 4:4 and 1 Thess. 5:18). Morton Kelsey likewise sees in deep and abiding relationships a harmony of closeness and distinction that expresses the mystical union of Christ and the church. And he comments,

> In the deep commitment and sharing of lives that we call love [married or not], another dimension of reality does open up. There are homosexuals, as well as heterosexuals, who have experienced this break-through and spoken of it in our own time. We may not like to face these facts, but in spite of the condemnation of the Christian church, they appear to be the religious facts. (in Taylor, 238)

From my personal experience and my knowledge of thousands of lesbian and gay Christians and cohabiting but unmarried heterosexual Christians, I can testify that those are indeed the religious facts.

In 1960 sociologist Ira Reiss published a book called *Premarital Sexual Standards in America*, in which he described the four sexual standards that coexist in the United States. The first is the formal standard: premarital sexual abstinence for both men and women. The second standard is the double standard, according to which men may do what women may not do. The third standard is permissiveness with affection; the fourth, permissiveness without affection (Scanzoni, 56–58). Of these four standards, only the first and the third show any respect for the biblical connection between sex, justice, and love. And only the third (permissiveness with affection) is inclusive enough to permit sexual pleasure to people who for some reason cannot marry. The standard of permissiveness with affection is already widely practiced among Christian people, and includes nonexploitation, being sure than both parties are operating under the same sexual understandings, and concern for contraception and avoidance of disease. I am suggesting that church leaders should recognize and honor this standard as biblically acceptable.

To put it another way: in response to the compassion of Jesus and the biblical emphasis on quality of relationship and Christian liberty, I am asking that church leaders cease and desist from tying up heavy burdens, hard to bear, and laying them on the shoulders of others. Today, no less than in the Garden of Eden, "it is not good that the [human creature] should be alone."

Chapter Nine

SOME BEATITUDES FOR TODAY'S CHURCH: TOWARD BECOMING MORE FUNCTIONAL CHURCH "FAMILIES"

———— ≈ ————

I am aware that for certain contemporary thinkers, the metaphor of the church as family is a dangerous one, too dangerous to be helpful. I can understand that reasoning. After centuries of patriarchy, the word *family* calls up a structure of inequity, with men dominating women and parents dominating children. Because of heteropatriarchal attitudes and the pressures of democratic capitalism gone awry, violence occurs in more than 28 percent of all marriages in the United States. One quarter of American adults approve of battles between husbands and wives — and the higher the educational level, the higher the level of approval (Engelsman and Pope-Lance, 7)! Emergency room nurses have been warned by their professional association that it is the nurses who must be alert to the signs of domestic violence — because half of the doctors are themselves involved in battering relationships (Thistlethwaite). Even without considering other forms of family dysfunctionality, we can see from these facts alone why certain thinkers get nervous about using family metaphors concerning the church.

But looked at from a different perspective, it is precisely *because* American families are in trouble that the metaphor of the church as a dysfunctional family working toward greater functionality might turn out to be very helpful indeed. For instance, Wallace Charles Smith makes extensive use of the family metaphor in his book on *The Church in the Life of the Black Family*. Explaining that "the black extended family is not just a gathering of nuclear families, but relationships linked either by blood or shared pain, history, and hope of liberation," Smith asserts that "the black church has always served as an extended family" (41). Although he is fully aware of the pressures upon black families and the problems within them, Smith utilizes biblical injunctions concerning equal partnership through mutuality to move both church and family toward fuller, richer functionality. My own goal for this chapter is similar: to look at the beatitudes as opened up for us by Neil Douglas-Klotz's translations from the Aramaic words of Jesus and to relate them to the problems of today's church "families," with an eye toward healing.

A Middle Eastern Mystic Speaks to Church "Families"

In the New Revised Standard Version, the first beatitude reads, "Blessed are the poor in spirit, for theirs is the kingdom of heaven" (Matt. 5:3). But Jesus, who was a Middle Eastern mystic, used Aramaic expressions that express "a fluid and wholistic view of the cosmos" and are difficult to capture in a brief English translation. Douglas-Klotz therefore provides five or six translations for each of the beatitudes in his book *Prayers of the Cosmos;* I will quote only two of each — enough to give the feel of the many levels of meaning in Aramaic but not enough to distract us from our goal of applying these to healing the dysfunctions of church "families."

The first beatitude can be translated this way: "Happy and aligned with the One are those who find their home in the breathing; to them belong the inner kingdom and queendom of heaven." The use of *kingdom and queendom* is apparently Douglas-Klotz's attempt to render the sexually inclusive connotations of Jesus' Aramaic words, and as a feminist of course I very much appreciate that attempt. But in order to get rid of the classist hierarchical connotations of royalty, I would prefer the common-gender term *kindom*. Simply by dropping the *g* in *kingdom,* we can achieve an image of an all-inclusive family, *God's kindom* (Gunther).

Another equally valid translation of the first beatitude would be "Healed are those who devote themselves to the link of spirit; the design of the universe is rendered through their form." Anyone who has read the work of physicists like Paul Davies, Gary Zukav, David Bohm, Werner Heisenberg, or Fritjof Capra will resonate to Jesus' words about the design of the universe as being a spiritual linkage. For instance, Paul Davies comments, "the world is not a collection of separate but coupled *things;* rather it is a network of *relations*" (112).

Well, then: do our contemporary churches qualify for the blessing of the first beatitude? As institutions, as structures, are they devoted to "the link of spirit"? Inasmuch as the members *are* the church, do we "find [our] home in the breathing" — in the one cosmic breath of life, the Holy Breath, the wind of the Spirit Jesus spoke about in the third chapter of John, that spiritual breath that is always so spontaneous, unpredictable, and yet appropriate?

Like Anne Wilson Schaef and Diane Fassel, I believe that "the mission of an organization should be supported by its own structure" (219). Church members (myself included) often quote Micah 6:8 as a description of the mission of churches and synagogues in the world: "[God] has told you, O mortal, what is good: / and what does the Lord require of you / but to do justice, and to love kindness / and to walk humbly with your God?" (NRSV). If then the mission of the church is to be supported by its structure, our churches must be restructured in such a way as to do justice to everyone, to love kindness toward everyone, and to walk humbly with our God within everyone. To the degree that our current church structures and policies exclude or marginalize any of our "family" members, our churches are dysfunctional "families," *not* at home in the breathing, *not* devoted to the universally connecting link of the Spirit.

Characteristics of Functional Families

John Bradshaw, the psychologist and theologian who has been giving healing presentations recently on public television, lists fourteen characteristics of functional families. If you are a member of a synagogue or church, as you read these you might want to ask yourself how many are characteristic of your home congregation and the national structure to which your congregation belongs. According to Bradshaw,

1. Problems in functional families are acknowledged and resolved [not just "studied" and "postponed" everlastingly].

2. All members [are free to] express their perceptions, feelings, thoughts, desires, and fantasies.

3. All relationships are dialogical and equal. Each person is of equal value as a person.

4. Communication is direct, congruent, concrete, specific, and behavioral.

5. All family members can get their needs met.

6. Family members [are allowed to] be different [and are accepted that way].

7. Parents [in our case, church leaders and officials] do what they say. They are self-disciplined disciplinarians.

8. Family roles are chosen [by the members themselves] and are flexible.

9. The atmosphere is fun and spontaneous.

10. The rules require accountability.

11. Violation of the values of other family members leads to [healthy] guilt [and correction].

12. Mistakes are forgiven and viewed as learning tools.

13. The family system exists for the individuals [not the individuals for the system].

14. The parents [or church leaders and officials] are in touch with their own [healthy] shame; [that is, they readily acknowledge their own limitations and correct their errors willingly]. (Bradshaw, 54–55)

Now I readily admit that national religious denominations are far more complex structures than individual family units. Nevertheless, if religious structures have grown so ponderous that it is no longer possible to attend to honest dialogue and feedback concerning what is proposed from the pulpit or from national headquarters, then perhaps they are just too unwieldy to carry out their mission. How well are our churches hearing everyone's concerns, valuing each person equally, affirming diversity, attempting to help *everyone* get their needs met (in other words, doing justice)? As the Mudflower Collective pointed out in *God's Fierce Whimsy*, "Pastors, teachers, scholars, parents [or administrators] who are indifferent to justice are not excellent pastors, teachers, scholars, parents, [or administrators]" (204–5). No matter whether the pastors and teachers can preach or teach like chained lightning. No matter how many respected books the scholars have written. No matter how many endowments the parents or administrators have laid by for the future. If there is indifference to justice, there is *no excellence*. None!

From the perspective of relating to the outside world, the essence of doing justice and loving kindness would be sharing the good basics of life with others, rather than hoarding institutional prestige or enormous endowments. As Sister Maria Jose Hobday has remarked, "Most Native American people feel that the most difficult thing American people have to work with is something in their blood that wants more than they need, whether other people have anything or not" (Hobday, 35). I for one must acknowledge the truth of that assessment. Are our religious institutions doing economic and social justice toward the outside world and thus devoting themselves to the connecting link of spirit in all people?

From the internal perspective of honoring each member, do our institutions utilize God-language that affirms girls and women as well as boys and men, encourages equal partnership, and assists members to recognize God's Spirit in one another and in the ecosystem we inhabit? Are we utilizing the Bible's many images of God as natural phenomenon, as child, as female? By the year 2000, it is probable that all Americans living below the poverty line will be women and the children they are trying to raise (Alperin,

170–76). Will our God-language be empowering to these women? If we use common-gender names for God, will we alternate between masculine and feminine pronouns? Or is the Creator, Redeemer, and Sustainer always *he,* so that half the human family members are linguistically invisible and disempowered? In the pictures on our walls, does God ever have breasts? red skin? black skin? yellow skin? In our structures, do clergy and laity co-create? Jesus said, "Healed are those who devote themselves to the link of spirit; the design of the universe is rendered through their form."

Emotional Turmoil within Church "Families"

The second beatitude reads, "Blessed are those who mourn, for they will be comforted" (NRSV). But Douglas-Klotz's translations from the Aramaic sound much more dynamic: "Blessed are those in emotional turmoil; they shall be united by love." Or, "Tuned to the Source are those feeling deeply confused by life; they shall be returned from their wandering." Apparently our turmoil and confusion are valuable because they cause us to turn toward our divine Source in order to ask for help so that eventually we see "the arrival of...what we long for" (Douglas-Klotz, 51).

The emotional turmoil and confusion felt in our churches often comes from being forced to listen to the demands of those whose voices have previously been ignored or silenced. This year, in many conventions and general assemblies, it will be the voice of gay and lesbian Christians asking yet once more for first-class citizenship and equal partnership in the church. For centuries in Christian churches, the heterosexual white male voice was the *only* voice, and that one particular perspective was elevated to the status of an absolute. For instance, when an Asian American Christian woman speaks, everybody instantly recognizes that she speaks from her particular perspective; but so does a heterosexual white male pastor of great prestige speak from *his* particular perspective. *Nobody* can claim to hold "the universally human" perspective (Welch, 62). Therefore churches and other organizations *need* the emotional turmoil of responding to minority voices.

I have been involved in the planning stages of a religious organization that I will not name but that I believe will eventually do a whole lot of good in the world. When I arrived at the first planning weekend, I was appalled to discover that everybody was white and the vast majority were men, and I said so. At the second organizational weekend, there still were no people of other colors and no additional women. I had to explain to everybody that this is *not* just a matter of political correctness; we are for sure going to overlook some vitally important aspects of organization if we do not immediately open up this board! Those we are excluding do not need us; *we* need *them!* And I promised myself and everybody else not to return for a third weekend unless greater diversity was achieved. (It was.) I tell that story because I think well-meaning church people sometimes get sick of the turmoil and confusion of listening to the formerly dispossessed and then trying to find ways to meet their needs without alienating too many others who really don't want to share their powers and privileges with yet another group. We need constantly to remind ourselves that Jesus said, "*Blessed* are those in emotional turmoil; they shall be united inside by love."

Other areas that often stimulate emotional turmoil are religious involvement in economics and politics. But perhaps corporate and financial institutions have become as corrupt as they have become because religious institutions have failed to raise moral issues as incessantly as they need to be raised. How many of our churches and synagogues have done battle with local banks concerning the policy of redlining, that is, the intentional and immoral denial of loans to persons living in certain areas? How many have confronted the stores and businesses that charge higher prices in poor communities? Or sought to outlaw the raising of prices in poor communities on the day the government checks are issued? If not, why not? After all, religious organizations are the only ones "whose vested interests lie in the area of corporate morality" (Smith, 92).

At Families 2000, an April 1991 conference sponsored by the National Council of Churches of Christ, I was asked, "Do we always have to be *against* something?" Clearly the asker was feeling some emotional turmoil over the thought of religious institutions entering the political and economic arenas as combatants for justice. And I had to reply that because systems are so rigged in favor of those who already *have* power and privilege, yes, it is necessary to take a stand. By apparently *not* taking a stand, we actually throw our weight on the side of the iniquitous status quo. For instance, to oppress their wives or sweethearts, men don't have to do anything at all; systemic sexism will do the oppressing. White people don't have to do anything at all to profit from the oppression of people of other colors; institutionalized racism will do the oppressing. People of the First World don't have to make an effort to profit from the oppression of people in the Two-Thirds World; economic policies already in place will do the job for us. So either we actively oppose injustice or we are profiting from injustice and therefore involved in it.

Gar Alperovitz, president of the National Center for Economic Alternatives, has pointed out that "the United States is so wealthy that if its gross production were divided equally among all its citizens today, each family of four would receive roughly $80,000.00" (20). But the fact is that the top one-fifth of American society receives about half of all the income, while the bottom one-fifth has to make do on less than 3.5 percent of the total income. And in 1988, a "mere one percent of American families at the very top had more income than the bottom 40 percent" all put together. If "democracy dies when inequality grows" (Alperovitz, 13), then American democracy is sick unto death. In the light of these facts, how can our religious institutions steer clear of economic and political involvement? Surely our churches must encourage small-scale co-ops, worker-owned firms, neighborhood corporations, and community institutions "in which consumer and worker cooperation overlaps, as it were, in one geographical area, so that the experience of community can be expanded in all aspects of life, steadily, over time" (Alperovitz, 15). And some congregations surely could align themselves with the concept of a state-guaranteed subsistence income, so that every citizen would have a basis for equal autonomy (Alperovitz, 17). If Alaska can acknowledge its community-wide interest in oil royalties by building up a permanent fund that currently yields a direct annual cash payment of almost $1,000 to each resident, couldn't church representatives help to devise ways that all major wealth would "regularly be returned to the community that ultimately made the creation of the wealth possible" (Alperovitz, 19)? I think about Isaiah's warning against heedless conglomerates of wealth: "Ah, you who join house to house / who add field to field, / until there is room for no one but you, / and you are left to live alone / in the midst of the land.... Surely many [such] houses shall be desolate" (5:8–9, NRSV). Cannot our congregations perform the prophetic function of issuing such warnings and seeking systemic correction of injustices?

Of course, these things make us feel uneasy, distressed, nervous. Who are we against so much corporate power? We are timid lest we make fools of ourselves. We are terrified of retaliation. But "Blessed are those in emotional turmoil; they shall be united inside by love."

Softening Our Rigid Attitudes

The third beatitude reads, "Blessed are the meek, for they will inherit the earth" (NRSV). In Douglas-Klotz's translations from the Aramaic: "Aligned with the One are the humble, those submitted to God's will; they shall be gifted with the productivity of the earth." Or, "Healthy are those who have softened what is rigid within; they shall receive physical vigor and strength from the universe."

It seems to me that rabbis, pastors, and denominational leaders could increase the spiritual health of their congregational "families" by specifically and repeatedly acknowledging the contributions of diverse "family" members: Native Americans, Asian Americans, African Americans, Latinos, Hispanics, people with physical or mental handicaps, lesbian women, gay men, and so forth. Perhaps people of good will think it is impolite to mention these distinctives, but the opposite is true. Of course, racial identities or physical handicaps can often be announced through a picture or the physical presence of the person or group involved. But where words are necessary, failure to pronounce them means that religious institutions are using peoples' good energy without publicly acknowledging the subgroup to which they belong. That kind of silence renders the subgroup as invisible or marginal as it has always been.

Whatever name people have chosen for themselves, let us empower them by naming the name publicly, with honor and respect. It does not matter whether we approve of the name or like the name, or even whether we consider the name an unwise choice: it is not anybody's province to tell other people what they ought to call themselves. To recognize and laud each other's contributions *by name* will force us to soften our inner rigidities and surrender our biases; but, says Jesus, "Healthy are those who have softened what is rigid within; they shall receive physical vigor and strength from the universe."

Another area in which religious thinking tends toward rigidity is the area of stereotypical attitudes toward family roles. Most churches beam their ministries chiefly toward nuclear family units, often assuming or acting as if the wife stays home to take care of children and domestic maintenance; but that is far from true. Homemakers currently represent less than one-seventh of all American women; and only about 2 percent of those who go out to work have fulfilling careers or work by choice. Most people (male or female) work because they need the money (Radl, 3). Yet, it is the working women who are accused of selfishness and at the same time expected to keep up with most of the childcare and domestic work.

One woman reported disturbance at the standard explanation for why so few men attend Parent-Teacher Association meetings. She was disturbed because men were excused on the basis of having to work; yet she and all the women she knew worked both outside and within the home and *still* were expected to attend P.T.A. and all other child-related events (Radl, 19). I remember my own disturbance when I was a young professional woman and was asked to bake cookies for a religious social occasion. I was the mother of a toddler, was taking several courses in graduate school, and was chairing a college English department. I hardly had time to catch my breath, let alone bake cookies for a church social! No one would ever have approached any of my male colleagues with such a request. Yet from what I hear, such stereotypical assumptions have not changed much in the three decades since the request was made of me.

Similar rigidity shows up concerning the form families take. Many preachers have bemoaned the demise of the family because of the diversity of family units in our society. But at Families 2000, the participants and I came up with forty different forms of the family that are mentioned or implied in the Hebrew and Christian Scriptures. Lists of these forms of family, including their location in the Bible, are provided in Appendix B. Here it is enough to mention that they include extended families; single mothers living with children; "trial marriages"; same-sex partnerships; related and unrelated single adults sharing a home; equal-partner, dual-career marriage; cross-cultural adoptive families; cohabitation without marriage; adults living with their parents; surrogate motherhood; blended families; "commuter marriages"; group-living of people with physical or mental disabilities; and several communes. Since all these forms of family existed in Bible times, at the very least we can conclude that there is no need to sing dirges about the destruction of the family. In the United States, as we have seen, unjust economic policies are putting desperate pressures on family units; but people will always bond together to help themselves get through life. And those with whom we bond are our family.

Although it may be difficult for some of us to realize that the nuclear family is a relatively recent development, and a Euro-American development at that, it will not hurt us to soften our rigid categories concerning what the family looks like. For as Jesus said, "Healthy are those who have softened what is rigid within; they shall receive physical vigor and strength from the universe."

Making Peace within Ourselves

The fourth beatitude reads, "Blessed are those who hunger and thirst for righteousness, for they will be filled" (NRSV). From the Aramaic, one translation goes this way: "Healthy are those who turn their mouths to receive a new birth of universal stability; they shall be encircled by the birth of a new society." Another reads, "Integrated, resisting delusion are those who long clearly for a foundation of peace between the warring parts of themselves; they shall find all around them the materials to build [that foundation of peace]."

One widespread delusion among contemporary church people is the idea that they can exclude one member or one marginalized or silenced constituency without damaging the majority. Rejection of others always leads to an inner dis-ease because we have simultaneously rejected the internal aspect of ourselves that corresponds to the externally rejected person or group. For instance, our entire culture is affected by erotophobia, as witness brutal and anti-erotic pornography on the one hand, and judgmental, hypocritical moralizing on the other. Church members are certainly not immune from erotophobia, body-hatred, and sexual dysfunctions. And their erotic dis-ease is exacerbated by religious failure to confront and deal openly with human sexuality.

A 1988 study run by eight evangelical denominations found that 43 percent of teenagers attending conservative churches have had intercourse by their eighteenth birthday (Orr, 201). So we may conclude that preaching about the sinfulness of sex outside marriage is not an adequate deterrent. The facts are that many teenagers and other unmarried heterosexuals *are* sexually active; lesbian women and gay men are not permitted to marry; many elderly people cannot afford to marry because of Social Security laws; people in government housing projects often cannot marry because if they do the government will increase their rent by reducing their subsidies (Smith, 94); and Christian theology has encouraged erotophobia. Because of all these carefully ignored facts, even married people are affected negatively: according to sex researchers Masters and Johnson, 68 percent of American marriages are sexually dysfunctional (Bradshaw, 152).

We cannot ignore or exclude concern for the well-being of others without blocking the flow of grace and wholeness to similar aspects within our own beings. But Jesus said, blessed, "integrated, resisting delusion are those who long clearly for a foundation of peace between the warring parts of themselves; they shall find all around them the materials to build [that foundation of peace]." Apparently, the more we extend ourselves to welcome other people into enjoyment of God's kindom, the more we welcome our own warring and repressed traits into an integrated wholeness at the center of ourselves.

Becoming Creatively Compassionate

In the New Revised Standard Version, the fifth beatitude is, "Blessed are the merciful, for they will receive mercy." From the Aramaic one translation is, "Tuned to the Source are those who shine from the deepest place in their bodies. Upon them shall be the rays of universal love." Or again, "Aligned with the One are the compassionate; upon them shall *be* compassion."

There are so many ways that congregational "families" could be more compassionate than we currently are! Do we show compassion for the struggles of those who have been so repelled by heteropatriarchal policies and language that they have been forced to organize their own Witches' Covens or other alternative spirituality groups? Or do we misrepresent them as pagans or devil worshippers? Do we supply hearing aids and/or translators for the hearing impaired? Ramps for those who cannot walk? When we ask congregations to stand, do we offer courtesy to those who cannot comfortably do so by saying, "Please rise *if you are able*?" Do we provide transportation for elderly people — not just to church, but to doctors' offices, shopping trips, and the like?

Do we provide community support for those who are undergoing separation or divorce? Do we assist in the adjustment that must be made when divorced people get together and bring into one home the children of their previous marriages? And for the sake of those previously mentioned people who either cannot or will not get legally married, couldn't our churches develop a ceremony that would provide community support for such relationships, leaving out the legal apparatus that excludes or else frightens off so many people? In fact, since most Americans believe in the separation of church and state, might we not be better off with purely religious ceremonies that leave the concerns of Caesar to state officials who are employed by Caesar?

I rejoice that many churches have been showing compassion to people who are homeless or hungry or who are immigrants without legal papers. My point is that we would be wise to seek out hundreds of other ways to show compassion; for as Jesus said, "Aligned with the One are the compassionate; upon them shall be compassion."

Supportiveness and Discernment in "Family Clusters"

In the NRSV the sixth beatitude is "Blessed are the pure in heart, for they will see God." From the Aramaic, Douglas-Klotz translates, "Aligned with the One are those whose lives radiate from a core of love; they shall be illuminated by a flash of lightning: the Source of the soul's movement in all creatures."

One of the ways our church "families" might become more fully functional — more sympathetic, friendly, and able to see God everywhere — might be to establish "family clusters." And not only "random" clusters, either, but seeing to it that each cluster contains several different forms of family: not only nuclear families, but singles with or without children, intergenerational families, multicultural adoptive families, gay or lesbian couples, and so forth. In that way, simply by learning to care for each other, cluster members would also be learning to honor diversity. And if adult cluster-members were also trained in the early warning signals of relationships turning sour, or signs of incest or physical or emotional abuse, timely intervention could be made in order to get professional help for everybody concerned.

Jesus told us not to judge one another, but he never told us not to be discerning. While it is important that we learn to see the holiness of one another, it is also a friendly office to assist one another in becoming all that we were meant to be. A good gardener is not blind to the weeds in her garden. It is precisely her loving respect for the health of her plants and flowers that causes her to get rid of the weeds. So "radiating from a core of love" does not mean mindless approval. It means willingness to be open to Love's guidance concerning the appropriate thing to do or say in order to support the well-being of ourselves and others. Diversified family clusters might be one way to get us sufficiently involved in one another's lives that such loving interaction would be possible. For as Jesus said, "Aligned with the One are those whose lives radiate from a core of love; they shall see God everywhere."

Peacemaking and Reproductive Responsibility

The seventh beatitude reads this way in the NRSV: "Blessed are the peace-makers, for they will be called children of God." Of five alternative translations from the Aramaic words of Jesus, here are two: "Healthy are those who strike the note that unites; they shall be remembered as rays of the One Unity." Or, "Healed are those who bear the fruit of sympathy and safety for all; they shall hasten the coming of God's new creation."

It may seem ludicrous to mention a divisive topic like reproductive freedom in the context of "striking the note that unites"; but I ask my readers to remember the imaginative exercise at the beginning of Chapter Four. If we ourselves did not know whether in some future society we might find ourselves pregnant against our will, we would be clear about the fact that the moral agency of pregnant women should be respected and supported, and that such support is an aspect of sympathy for, and the safety of, all members of the human family.

Although a fetus is potentially a human person, a woman is already fully a person. And whether we like it or not, responsible morality requires that we learn to think in terms of degrees and situations rather than remaining at the comfortable level of sweeping moral absolutes. (For further discussion of reproductive moral agency, see the following chapter.)

Women who are pregnant against their will have already been betrayed by sexist, racist, or economic pressures, or by poor information or contraceptive failure. They do not need to be betrayed again by religious institutions. So I pray that Christians and Jews will resist current pressures to withdraw their support for reproductive freedom as represented by the central issue of abortion rights.

Patricia A. Tyson might help us to understand why reproductive freedom represents "the fruit of sympathy and safety for all" of which Jesus spoke. Patricia Tyson is an African American and executive director of the Religious Coalition for Abortion Rights. She comments,

> Persons and institutions that oppose abortion have argued that the protection of the fetus is a civil rights issue. Their interpretation of civil rights is a contracted freedom where women, regardless of their health and/or economic condition, will be relegated to compulsory pregnancy. Their interpretation, contrary to what they state, will not extend equal rights to the fetus, but instead will extend superior status to the fetus. Anti-abortion persons who attempt to make abortion a civil rights issue do not understand the main tenet of civil rights — the belief that *all* groups and individuals are worthy and have a right to equality and self-determination. (Tyson, 2)

Thus, it is incumbent upon religious bodies to support reproductive freedom, which must include not only access to safe and legal abortion, but also access to good health care and pre- and post-natal care, thorough sex education (including AIDS prevention) and allied services. Jesus said, "Healed are those who bear the fruit of sympathy and safety for all; they shall hasten the coming of God's new creation."

Feeling Dislocated for God's Sake

Space requires me to give only one of the several Douglas-Klotz translations from the Aramaic for each of the beatitudes that remain. The eighth reads in the NRSV, "Blessed are those who are persecuted for righteousness' sake, for theirs is the kingdom of heaven." From Aramaic: "Tuned to the Source are those persecuted for trying to right society's balance; to them belongs the coming king- and-queendom." To them belongs the kindom of God. And the ninth beatitude is an extension or continuation of the same thought. "Blessed are you when people revile you and persecute you and utter all kinds of evil against you falsely on my account" (NRSV). From the Aramaic: "When you feel contaminated, dislocated, and feel an inner shame for no good reason, it is for my sake." Neil Douglas-Klotz explains that these two beatitudes refer to the fact that "society does not easily tolerate the prophetic spirit." In the face of social intolerance, Jesus tells us that if we are dislocated for justice-work, we can consider our new home to be the planet — or even the universe; and that we can "consider adversity as an incitement to take another step" (Douglas-Klotz, 69).

It seems to me that many contemporary religious institutions have acculturated themselves so thoroughly to the excesses of capitalism and heteropatriarchy that they stand little chance of being persecuted for the sake of justice and therefore of inheriting God's kindom. If we stood prophetically over against every single one of the economic and social injustices of our society, we would feel the kind of *passionate aliveness* with which Jesus closes the beatitudes: in the New Revised Standard Version, "Rejoice and be glad, for your reward is great in heaven, for in the same way they persecuted the prophets who were before you." In the Aramaic Jesus was saying something like this: "Then, feel at the peak of everything and be extremely moved; for your natural abundance, already in the cosmos, has multiplied around you (because of the blows on your heart)." Jesus is telling us that the blows on our hearts inflicted by injustice can be felt not only as personally painful, but as "an aid to opening a wider perspective of feeling and empathy with all [of] creation" (Douglas-Klotz, 73). In this way our personal pain is transformed into the joy of oneness with God Herself. By our stripes, we are *healed!*

It is my hope that our religious institutions and each of us individually will become willing to experience blows on our hearts for the sake of an expanded familial relationship with the universe and with the God who created us, one and all. Only in this way will God's kindom become a reality upon the earth.

Chapter Ten

PROCREATIVE SELF-DIRECTION
AND A MORE JUST SOCIETY

———— ≈ ————

For a sensuously spiritual woman who seeks her moral and ethical instructions from God at the center of her deepest Self, one of the least appealing aspects of modern American society is the movement to do away with legal and affordable abortion. It is not that she is irresponsible. It is quite the opposite: she does not want the state to interfere in the process by which she lives a life of responsible co-creatorship with God. Because a healthy young woman could possibly become pregnant more than thirty times, she must have control of her reproductive power in order to have control of her moral being. She cannot yield her whole self (body, soul, and spirit) to the will of God if the laws of the state deny her the opportunity to limit the scope of her relationships. Should responsible attempts at birth control fail, as they often do because of technological laxness or human error, the decision to abort is an admission that at this era in her life, another major commitment would be too much for her to take on. For a woman in such circumstances, abortion may be tragic, but it is a necessity.

Ethicist Beverly Wildung Harrison has written that the world of the 1990s is a world in which state-sponsored torture is the most visible means of social control, but in which less overt forms of social control are exceedingly widespread. Harrison writes,

> This whole pattern of bodily control and bodily violation calls out for a reconstruction of our moral traditions. We must insist that as never before the well-being of persons requires a new ethic of *touching,* an ethic for crossing the boundaries of human embodiment.... We must teach ourselves, our children, and all the people in this society that

139

there can be and will be no decent body politic, no common shared life, no community, unless we develop deep revulsion against bodily violations; and enforced pregnancy is such a violation. (20)

To my mind, Harrison's call for a new ethic of responsible touching (including self-disciplined restraint when appropriate) is important in many areas of modern concern — incest and child abuse, domestic violence, police and prison reform, clergy-congregant relationships, counselor-client relationships, and the like. But in no area is it more important than in the area of reproductive self-direction. An ethic of touching (of bodily integrity), by teaching respect for the boundaries of other people's bodies and our own bodies, would solidly support the right of reproductive choice without which pregnant women cannot exercise their moral agency. For instance, there seems to be a widespread assumption that it is a minor matter to force a woman pregnant against her will to carry a fetus for nine months in order to give it up for adoption. Such an assumption indicates that society has not yet developed a sufficient revulsion against the violation of peoples' bodily boundaries.

I am uncomfortable with the phrase "abortion rights" because in our society the rights of some are too often pitted against the rights of others in a way that reinforces us-versus-them dualisms. Because heteropatriarchy assumes that only one party to a conflict can possibly be correct, the pitting of fetal rights against women's rights is a particularly heteropatriarchal way of approaching the issue. But Harrison defines a "right" as "a basic moral condition of well-being that a community owes its members." By that definition, rights are not merely "liberties": rather, "they specify reciprocal relations between the community as a whole and its members" (18). And by this definition, to adopt a social policy of enforced child bearing would not only destroy the reproductive moral agency of women, but by doing so would make our whole society morally indefensible.

When "Choice" Is Constrained, Should We Call It Choice?

Even when women are accorded the "right to choose," however, the choice is often far from free because of the inequitable conditions under which women are forced to make their choices. For that reason I think that we who believe in procreative self-direction should not focus our energies exclusively on reproductive choice within these constrictive conditions. Instead we must simultaneously work to improve the conditions of society itself, so that reproductive choice might become more meaningful, more truly free.

No matter what their politics, ethicists have never questioned the fact that choice is essential to moral agency. For instance, an evangelical Christian dictionary of ethics points out that people "do have to make up their minds when moral principles conflict. There are times when the desirability of certain ends and the suitability of certain means have to be thoughtfully weighed. [People] who seek moral direction from Scripture are not relieved of the cognitive responsibility for discovering precisely what principles of moral action are taught there, for looking into their import in their original historical-cultural context, and then determining how the divine command relates to specific contemporary situations" (Paul, 168). So even conservative ethicists recognize the necessity of choice in moral dilemmas. But we need go no further than our desk dictionaries to discover that ethics centers in and necessitates choice. *Webster's New Collegiate Dictionary,* for instance, defines *ethics* as "the discipline dealing with what is good and bad and with moral duty and obligation." Good, bad, right, wrong, acceptable, unacceptable, appropriate, inappropriate: these choices lie at the very heart of ethics and morality.

To be sure, modern ethicists have debated about what degree of freedom is necessary before people can be held responsible for what they have apparently chosen to do. But the debate has usually taken place among well-to-do white European or American academic men, people who have never known what it feels like to be under severe constraints, forced to choose under agonizing conditions that one never would have chosen for oneself. Had these ethicists experienced what it is like to make "choices" as a slave, they would be very clear about the fact that a person should not be punished for decisions that were necessitated by factors wholly or largely beyond her control.

In fact, most ethicists *are* clear about the fact that for the most part a person's actions must be unforced by outside factors before she can be held morally responsible. Yet in spite of this ethical consensus and this clarity, a large percentage of evangelical and fundamentalist Christians, many Catholics, the far right in almost every major religious denomination, and the political rightists are all holding young women guilty for pregnancies that are often due to factors well beyond their control: lack of education, poverty, technological failure of poorly made birth control devices, and above all the socialization that stresses female submissiveness and urges males to show their strength by controlling women. Even in the most extreme cases of pregnancy due to factors beyond the woman's control many "pro-lifers" are willing to force the pregnant woman to carry the fetus and give it birth. This application of force to an individual conscience flies in the face of every ethical and moral comprehension of what is necessary before an individual can be held morally accountable and subject to punishment.

And, of course, it *is* a punishment to be forced to give birth to a fetus a woman never intended to conceive. Anybody who doubts that should try this experiment: tie a golf bag across your stomach for nine months, each month adding a new club until the bag is full. Wear the golf bag at all times, waking and sleeping. At the end of nine months, remove the golf bag, but undergo a major and life-threatening operation. And when all that is finished, have absolutely nothing to show for all your suffering.

If a judge handed down such a sentence to a robber or drug dealer or even a murderer, it would be labeled "cruel and unusual punishment" and, therefore, unconstitutional. But (apart from the tremendous emotional factors) that sentence is roughly equivalent to the punishment anti-abortionists wish to deal out to women who have had the misfortune of becoming pregnant against their will. As if it were a mere nothing, they are to be told to carry the fetus and give it birth and then hand it over for adoption. By contrast, Jesus said it was a mark of extreme and unusual love for anybody to give one's life, even for a friend (John 15:13). Yet betrayed young women are routinely asked to risk their lives by bringing to birth a fetus they did not choose to conceive and do not want to carry. Since giving birth is approximately seven times more likely to cause a woman's death than having an abortion, compulsory procreation is a very serious violation of a woman's bodily integrity as well as her moral agency.

Diversities within Catholicism

On the other hand, if it could be proved that the fetus is a human person from the very instant of conception, as American Catholic bishops and Protestant fundamentalists are currently maintaining, then elective abortion is indeed killing. Two factors would then have to be emphasized: first, that a fetus should not be accorded rights that surpass those of the woman involved. Nobody has an *absolute* right to life: if I were drowning and nobody would risk their life to save me, they could not be prosecuted for that refusal. Therefore a pregnant woman should not be forced to risk her own life in order to save the life of the fetus. Second, current law does permit killing as an act of self-defense. If a woman views giving birth as destructive of her physical or mental health, should she be denied an act of self-defense that would be permitted to any other person who is undergoing a life-threatening attack?

Many people have the impression that for two thousand years the Roman Catholic Church has steadfastly upheld the idea that all abortion is murder, but that is far from true. Only since the 1860s has the church gradually been developing the single inflexible position that is now being taught. And even today, "a strong minority of Catholic theologians believes that abortion is permissible in the early stages of pregnancy, and that the ban on abortion is based on faulty theology" (Hurst, 1).

As a Protestant, I do not feel comfortable about tackling Catholic teachings and practices, and I will spend most of this chapter dealing with general perspectives and with the biblical concerns that arise out of Protestantism's abortion debate. But I must confess to a certain relief in discovering that Catholic authorities like St. Jerome, St. Augustine, St. Thomas Aquinas, and the Council of Trent (among others) all believed that hominization (animation, ensoulment, the arrival of human-beingness) does *not* occur at conception. Furthermore,

> In modern practice, the [Catholic] church does not always hold to the doctrine of immediate hominization. It does not practice fetal baptism in all cases of miscarriage. It rarely performs baptism, extreme unction, or the funeral mass, even when a full-term baby is stillborn. It seems that the church makes a distinction, in every case except abortion, between the potential human being represented in the developing fetus and the actual human being which the fetus eventually becomes. (Hurst, 13)

It was precisely the distinction between the *potential* personhood of the fetus and the *actual* personhood of the woman that was the deciding factor concerning my pro-choice position, over which I agonized even though I was never pregnant against my will. On the score of potential versus actual life, I find myself in perfect agreement with Roman Catholic historian Rosemary Radford Ruether, who writes in *Conscience: A Newsjournal of Prochoice Catholic Opinion:*

> I believe that before viability one should regard the fetus as a potential human but not as having the same status as a person. This does not mean it is valueless or a "mere piece of tissue," as pro-choice extremists have put it. But its value cannot be put on the same level as a viable and birthed baby. (Ruether, "Women, Sexuality," 6)

As I explained in Chapter One, I have recently come to believe that God is far more radically omnipresent than I had ever been taught, so that God actually constitutes the essence of the human core, as the true light that enlightens every human being born into this world (John 1:9). From this perspective, even if hominization had taken place before an abortion, the soul that had begun to manifest God in that fetal embodiment would simply return to its Source. And from this perspective, to agonize about the abortion is to suffer unnecessarily. It would obviously be profoundly wrong to utilize this perspective in order to make light of killing anyone born or unborn. But when an abortion is necessary, looking at it from this angle can provide the peace of mind that is God's intended legacy to us all.

The Biblical Emphasis on Choice

In the Protestant Christian tradition in which I have spent my six decades, it is surely one of the great ironies that those who oppose abortion are frequently also those who claim that the Bible is their only rule of faith and practice. This irony occurs because no book on earth emphasizes the necessity of choice to the degree the Bible does. The necessity of choice is first introduced in the Book of Genesis, where Adam and Eve are placed in the Garden and put in charge of everything except for one tree, the fruit of which they are forbidden to eat. (The point I am making works equally well whether one takes the story literally or regards it as myth.) Surely a Creator who could create a universe and a world full of birds, animals, and fish and could make a human couple capable of reason — surely such a Creator could have made a Garden that contained no forbidden tree and, therefore, no temptation. Why was the possibility and the means of choosing to disobey the Creator provided for Adam and Eve from the very beginning? Because without an opportunity to say *no* to God, Adam and Eve could never have said a meaningful *yes* either. Moral agency requires choice — and requires it in the area of human reproduction, as in any other area. If God, foreknowing that Adam and Eve would yield to temptation, nevertheless gave them the opportunity to choose, how can modern religious people urge the state to do otherwise?

The fact that choosing to say *no* to God involved being cast out of the Garden symbolizes the fact that when we human beings choose to distrust our own center, the core of our own being (i.e., God's Self), we alienate and exile ourselves from a happy relationship with our environment. Precisely because God is the essence of our own being, genuine human freedom and happiness lie in aligning ourselves with the will of God. But the choice is ours: we can choose our own exile and ego-centered suffering if we are so inclined.

Joshua 24:15 is typical of the emphasis on choice, on decision making, which runs like a vein of iron throughout both the Hebrew and Christian Scriptures: "choose [you] this day whom you will serve." As Carol Gilligan demonstrated in her groundbreaking book *In a Different Voice,* when women are deciding whether or not to abort the fetus that is within their bodies against their will, they are not flippantly choosing between fetal liberty and women's liberty. They are, rather, making a complex ethical decision by weighing whether or not they can afford to stay in relationship with the fetus: whether their already existing relationships and responsibilities can, without sustaining too much damage, possibly be acclimated to a new relationship and responsibility. In other words, they are choosing whom they will serve. And it is quite possible that human life and, therefore, the Creator of life might be better served by an abortion than by a birth. Such a decision should be celebrated as an act of good faith, as a step in the service of God, not attacked and penalized as a selfish lack of caring.

From one perspective, it is true that no clear guidance concerning abortion can be found in the Bible. Any passage that has been utilized either by pro-choice or anti-abortion people has been rejected as evidence by the opposite camp. And that is perfectly understandable to anyone who grasps the principle of interpretive communities. I belong to the pro-choice interpretive community: that is, I share with that community certain assumptions that help to govern what I will admit as evidence and what I will reject. The same is true of the "pro-life" interpretive community, which cuts off ethical discussion by defining elective abortion as murder. So there is really nothing constructive to be gained by flinging Bible verses at one another.

But from another perspective, the Bible's overarching emphasis on choice should give honest Right-to-Lifers pause. In fact, it did give some of them pause when I presented a biblical case for choice at a meeting of the 1989 Evangelical Round Table, where Charles Colson and eight other speakers represented the anti-abortion position and I alone spoke in favor of choice. Some participants were surprised and a bit shaken because they could not deny that the Bible insists on human choice and commitment to God's will. What is a commitment to God's will, except a determination to take what seems to be the best course of action after carefully weighing the alternatives in a prayerful silence? And what else are many women doing when they agonize over whether or not to abort their fetus? Regardless of whether the women utilize religious terminology, they are human beings who are trying, within the limits of their own intellects and spirits, to decide what is the best course of action for everyone concerned, including but not stopping with themselves. And in that sense, they are trying to discern God's will for them. So in this larger sense, in the sense of an overarching biblical emphasis on the necessity of choosing, the Bible supports the work of the pro-choice movement.

Biblical Silences and a Differentiation

There is another sense in which the Bible supports the pro-choice movement, and that is in the sense that the biblical authors remained silent about abortion, contraception, and even infanticide. The killing of infants is repugnant to twentieth-century human sensibilities; yet, the practice becomes more frequent as soon as abortion becomes less available. Ever since the Hyde Amendment took away funding for poor women's abortions, the news media have been reporting more and more cases of abandonment, as well as the outright murdering of infants and youngsters by their parents. What that says to me is this: people who find infanticide repulsive should support birth control, choice, and the public funding of abortions for women who cannot afford them, so that infanticide does not become an appalling necessity in their lives.

During biblical times and at least until the beginning of the third century of the Common Era, it was customary to abandon younger siblings, female infants, and infants born out of wedlock, leaving them either in temples, latrine trenches, or the public refuse dump. While the New Testament was being written, infanticide was the birth control of the poor, while the more affluent had access to contraceptive potions and abortifacients (Waetjen, 62). Yet, knowing all that, the New Testament authors remained silent about all three: abortion, contraception, and infanticide. Could it be that an awareness of the pressures upon poor people and the extraordinary complexities of family planning in such societies led the biblical authors to maintain a discreet silence? Could they have known that oppressed people had to find some method or another of minimizing the pressures upon them? At any rate, it seems to me that because one of those early practices, infanticide, is abhorrent to our moral sensibilities, we had better not only permit but promote access to the less violent avenues of contraception and abortion.

The only other way in which the Bible legitimately may be used to cast light on the dilemma of a woman pregnant against her will would be by respecting the distinction made in Exodus 21:22–25. Here it is from the Revised Standard Version: "When men strive together, and hurt a woman with child, so that there is a miscarriage, and yet no harm follow, the one who hurt her shall be fined.... If any harm follows, then you shall give life for life, eye for eye, tooth for tooth, hand for hand, foot for foot, burn for burn, wound for wound, stripe for stripe." I am aware that evangelicals argue that what is at stake here is not a miscarriage, but only a premature birth. Yet, even the New International Version of the Bible, so beloved by evangelicals, gives "miscarriage" as a perfectly valid translation of this text; and the venerable King James translators knew exactly what the passage was about: "If men strive, and hurt a woman with child, so that her fruit depart from her, and yet no mischief follow, he shall surely be punished.... And if any mischief follow, then thou shalt give life for life." Clearly a distinction is made here between the value of potential life and value of actual life. Loss of the fetal life would result in a fine; loss of the woman's life would result in an execution. So, this passage, which values actual life over potential life, tends to support the values espoused by the pro-choice movement.

Although most twentieth-century human beings make our ethical decisions without hoping to find an explicit Bible prooftext to guide or support our actions, many Right-to-Life advocates do make exactly that kind of use of the Bible. So it is important for us to know that in three ways the Bible does lean toward the pro-choice position: in the distinction between the potential human life of the fetus and the actual human life of the woman in Exodus 21; in the New Testament's refusal to condemn abortion; and above all in the Bible's overarching emphasis on the necessity of growing up morally and taking responsibility as a moral agent in this world. If even God relinquished domination by placing the world and us creatures under human authority, as we are told in Genesis 1:28, then human beings would be well advised to relinquish domination over other people's moral and ethical decisions.

The Constraints on Women's Choices

But that brings me back to the context in which today's women must make their reproductive choices. As Rosalind Petchesky says in her outstanding book, *Abortion and Woman's Choice,*

> The critical issue for feminists is not so much the content of women's choices, or even the "right to choose," as it is the social and material conditions under which the choices are made. The "right to choose" means little when women are powerless.... [Like] the women employees at the American Cyanamid plant in West Virginia, they may "choose" sterilization as an alternative to losing their jobs. To paraphrase Marx, women make their own reproductive choices, but they do not make them just as they please; they do not make them under conditions they create but under conditions and constraints they, as mere individuals, are powerless to change. That these individuals do not determine the social framework in which they act does not nullify their choices nor their moral capacity to make them. It only suggests that we have to focus less on "choice" and more on how to transform the social conditions of choosing, working, and reproducing. (Petchesky, 11)

I have quoted Rosalind Petchesky at length because I think this point is powerfully important and absolutely necessary at this juncture in the history of reproductive choice and the anti-abortion movement. For here is some common ground that could be established between pro-choice advocates and those who sincerely believe that abortion is murder but who also sincerely care about the quality of life available to women and children in this society. Instead of caricaturing one another and vilifying one another, perhaps we could work together to "transform the social conditions of choosing, working, and reproducing."

One important task would be the vigorous promotion of sex education and contraception. Fran Avallone of the New Jersey Right to Choose wants public schools to discuss sexual practices sooner, and believes that contraception should be much more widely available, especially to teenagers. I agree, but would add that during classes in sex education and contraception, the danger of AIDS as well as pregnancy should be taught, so that students know not to resort to anal intercourse as a way of avoiding pregnancy, a practice that is widely used in the Hispanic and black communities. Unprotected oral sex is also a dangerous contraceptive ploy. I would also add that in addition to advising celibacy outside of marriage or serious commitment, the *reason* for all that should be taught — the joys of enhancing human dignity by taking each other seriously, and hence taking the pleasures of sex seriously. It seems to me that we would not be violating pluralism by teaching students that from a religious perspective, everybody is made in the image of the Sacred, as long as we did not insist on the exclusive naming of the Sacred as Jehovah, Christ, the Goddess, Allah, or even the human spirit; so that the right thing to do regarding sex would be to do what honors the Sacred in ourselves and each other. I do not think that would rule out mutual pleasuring in the right context; quite the opposite. Pleasuring may or may not entail sexual intercourse, but it would certainly entail responsibility and caring for the circumstances of the partner's life.

As a society, we must face the fact that some young people are going to have sexual relations no matter what we tell them; and for them, contraceptive knowledge and devices are essential. No matter how wrong we might consider teenage sex to be, surely most of us would not want to punish it with a death sentence! Yet through AIDS and the inevitable complications of teenagers giving birth, a death sentence is all too probable. From my years of experience in college teaching, I know that it is not usually the street-wise young woman who has sex without protection; it is the idealistic young woman who dreams of a little home with a husband and two kids and who considers herself much too pure ever to have intercourse outside of wedlock. When she is swept off her feet by either pressure from her male companion or passion for him, she is both ignorant and unprepared, and society has done her no favors.

Perhaps we could find common ground with some of the more humane people in the anti-abortion movement by uniting to pressure manufacturers to research and produce more affordable, more reliable means of contraception. I am particularly concerned about the 10 percent failure rate of the condom, not only because of the unwanted pregnancies that result but because of the possibility of transmitting AIDS. Surely a more reliable condom could be invented and manufactured! We who care for the quality of actual life need to work for the legal availability in the United States of the French pill, RU-486, and to oppose the Congressional move to prevent the Food and Drug Administration from approving the use of it. And we need to demand more publicity concerning how and where women can have access to Ovral, the morning-after pill that prevents pregnancy in the first seventy-two hours after intercourse. Although it is currently dispensed at rape crisis centers and by certain private physicians, it will do no good for desperate women unless they have heard of its existence and know where to get a prescription.

Lunatic Fringes vs. Humane Cooperation

It is my assumption that almost every social movement has its lunatic fringe but that there are usually many people involved who are sensible, sincere, and caring people. The pro-choice movement has its lunatic fringe: people who claim that a fetus is really nothing more than a part of a woman's body with which she is free to dispense, or people who shout insults at Right-to-Lifers and thus stir up tempers and possibly incite violence. I assume that the abortion clinic burnings and bombings are the work of the lunatic fringe of the Right-to-Life movement, and that there are many others in that movement who are pacifistic, kind, and humane people who really want to alleviate the sufferings of women but who cannot stomach abortion because they have been convinced that it is murder. Pro-choice moderates probably will never get anywhere with the lunatic fringe on either side, but it is quite possible that we could work together with the more humane Right-to-Lifers to achieve better sex education, better contraceptive devices, and social conditions that would make abortion less often necessary because life would be less desperate for women and children in the United States and around the world.

Among the improvements that are badly needed, and perhaps a common ground with our opponents, would be providing adequate family health services for the many people who cannot afford American health care; putting an end to compulsory or involuntary surgical sterilization of our sisters from the Third World; providing better funding for Third World family planning programs; facilitating the adoption of the more than 100,000 black, handicapped, or older American children who are waiting for homes; and providing adequate and affordable childcare centers for the ten million American children who currently need daycare. The United States is the only modern industrialized country in the world that has no federal policies concerning maternity, childcare, and daycare (Campbell, *Successful Women*, 227–29). That has to change. Furthermore, we might work together to provide shelters for battered or sexually abused women and children and counseling for both the abusers and the abused. Women of color tell us that their reproductive rights agenda includes access to adequate pre- and post-natal care and sterilization, AIDS prevention, and the pursuit of economic justice (Tyson, 1). Surely white people could work with them toward these laudable goals.

Making "Choice" More Meaningful

As for the larger picture, the social conditions that most need transformation if reproductive choosing is to become less constricted and constrained are conditions at the workplace and the male primacy that is still tolerated in American homes and still preached by the Religious Right. Part of male primacy involves a sexual double standard that causes at least a million teenage pregnancies annually in the United Stated alone. After failing in their many efforts to interest men over twenty-five in taking some responsibility for contraception, Planned Parenthood of Chicago discovered the reason for that failure by conducting a survey of over one thousand males between the ages of fifteen and nineteen. The survey revealed that 70 percent felt it was "okay to tell a girl you love her so that you can have sex with her"; 80 percent said a guy should *not* use birth control devices; yet 80 percent also said that if the girl got pregnant, she should not have an abortion, "because it's wrong" (Stoltenberg, 95). John Stoltenberg, co-founder of Men Against Pornography, draws some conclusions from such facts: "I believe that men as a class know that reproductive freedom for women is not in men's interest.... Men as a class know that if reproductive freedom for women ever became a reality, male supremacy could no longer exist.... Men as a class know that their social and cultural and economic advantage over and against women depends absolutely upon the continuance of involuntary pregnancy, involuntary gestation, involuntary parturition, and involuntary child rearing" (99–100).

Providing support for John Stoltenberg's assertions about men as a gender-class is the fact that male primacy is built into corporate life, where "the stereotype of the consummate corporate executive includes a wife who stays at home" (Campbell, *Successful Women*, 103). And facts from around the world also support Stoltenberg's thesis. Women form half of the human population, perform two-thirds of the work hours, earn one-tenth as much as men earn, and own only one one-hundredth of the property men own (Eisler, 157). Even in areas where women do 100 percent of the labor, they are permitted to eat only the male leftovers. Here in the United States, where sexism is more sophisticated and less flagrant, the pauperizing of women is getting more extreme every year. And among more affluent women, the choice for abortion still occurs primarily when they have no personal support system — especially no support from the man by whom they are pregnant (Lebacyz, 31). It is women's lack of resources, with the consequent inability to determine their own destiny, that is central to the decision to abort. Hence, to transform male primacy into human mutuality is to make abortion much less necessary than it currently is.

In my book *Women, Men, and the Bible*, I have shown that when interpreted contextually, the Bible supports human equal partnership rather than male dominance and female submission. It is overdue for churches, synagogues, schools, and mass media to make male-female mutuality and equal partnership into household words — and not only words, but reality.

As for the workplace, the United States needs a whole new labor movement that is truly concerned with creating a sense of solidarity, dignity, and pride among our workers. The American dream that anybody can get ahead if they try hard enough has locked too many of us into psychological isolation cells. We Americans may not be satisfied with the conditions of our lives and work, but we are afraid to tell each other about our lack of fulfillment because if the American dream is true, our unsatisfactory circumstances are our own fault. We blame ourselves for what is actually systemic, for conditions that can be changed only by organized and mass efforts. Whatever we can do to break down isolation, to get people talking openly with one another about their lives, and to create solidarity will help mobilize the energy that can transform the American workplace (Lerner, 87ff.). And whatever we do to humanize American working conditions will in turn make the reproductive choices of women more meaningful and more truly free.

To emphasize the oppression of women as I have been doing does not strip women of our moral agency. Of course women can say *no* to unprotected sex, provided they have the strength to resist their partner's importunities, which are in turn backed up by heteropatriarchal pressures toward female submission. It requires heroic strength to violate one's socialization, and not all have that kind of strength. Furthermore, women cannot control the carelessness of manufacturers of birth-control devices. And of course moral agents sometimes choose mistakenly or wrongly. The only way utterly to strip women of their moral agency is to pass coercive laws or to withhold from them the information necessary to an informed choice. Unfortunately, both of these assaults on the moral agency of American women seem all too imminent in the light of the Supreme Court's current political bent.

It is my conviction that people who believe in procreative self-direction must continue to defend reproductive choice against those who want to legislate it out of existence. But at the same time, we must work to change the conditions of society itself, the inequitable context in which women are currently forced to make their very limited choices. I am convinced that if enough of us have the will to make our society more just, more compassionate, and more mutually caring, we will also find the way.

Chapter Eleven

THE LESBIAN, BISEXUAL, AND GAY COMMUNITY AS SOCIAL TRANSFORMER

———— ≈ ————

A girl perhaps five years old sent the following letter to the Kids Section of *Woman Space,* a newsletter of the Women's Community in San Antonio, Texas:

> My name is Heime. I am this many. My mom is a lesbeing. I am a lesbeing too. It means we just like girls best. My mom is one single parent. It means she has only one child, me, and no woman. My mom asked me how I feel about if she gets a lover. I would rather get a grandmother or a dog. I would sit in the grandmother's lap, or ride the dog. My mom said those are nice ways to be close. She said I could find a way to be close to her lover, too. I hope she picks a grandmother who lets me ride her dog.
>
> We live in California for a little while. Lots of lesbeings here. Even boy ones named gays live here. I know because it is not a secret.
>
> We bought a lesbeing newspaper. My mom reads me the Kids Box. I can dial a story, take congo drum lessons, make a circus, or go to urban camp.
>
> I still like San Antonio best. I will always be a Texas lesbeing child. I will ask L.I.S.A. — maybe Texas lesbeing children can dial a story some day too.*

Heime's letter is full of the breezy naturalness of a child who has grown up in the midst of diversity and without sexual judgmentalism. Although

---

* My thanks to Suzanne Goodrich for sharing this gem.

she assumes that she will grow up to be lesbian like her mother, responsible research indicates that she probably will be heterosexual. After all, the vast majority of les-bi-gay people had apparently heterosexual parents; and Richard Green, who has conducted extensive studies of children being brought up by transsexuals and by lesbian couples, has concluded that "close proximity to adults of either homosexual or heterosexual persuasion does not in itself cause children to become either heterosexual or homosexual" (Scanzoni and Mollenkott, 99). So Heime's chances of discovering that she really is lesbian like her mother are probably no more than one in ten, like any other child's in the general population. But whatever she discovers about herself, she has no worries about being accepted and cherished just as she is. Heime is aware that lesgay people are often forced to closet their sexual identity, and she has noticed that things are different in her section of California, where even the "boy lesbeings" can be open about who they are. All of this is of interest to her as someone who likes to be "in the know." But her real enthusiasms are those of any other normal child: loving and being loved, playing with grandmothers and dogs, being consulted by her mother about their common future, dialing a story, taking congo drum lessons, making a circus, going to urban camp, and maintaining loyalty to the friends in her home town. Apart from her awareness of secrecy, Heime's breezy calmness about diversity reflects the way life could be for every child in a just society where heterosexuality was no longer compulsory.

Is Social Transformation Really Possible?

Will such a society ever be achieved? It would be achieved rapidly enough if we all woke up to the fact that what we do to other people, we are doing to ourselves. Jesus taught that what we give, we get (Matt. 7:1–2), and Paul taught that what we sow, we reap (Gal. 6:7). Even modern science supports these teachings: 98 percent of the atoms in our bodies change every year, moving into other bodies or back into the atmosphere. Our bodies constantly exchange water vapor with any other bodies within four feet of ourselves. So in a very physical sense we are all gay, we are all lesbian, we are all heterosexual, we are all bisexual — because we are all one. We could quite logically shift the wording of Jesus' commandment from "Thou shalt love thy neighbor as thyself" to "Thou shalt love thy neighbor, who *is* thyself."

Sooner or later, lesbian women, bisexual people, and gay men are going to be accepted as first-class citizens in the church and in society as a whole. If wolves and leopards will romp harmlessly with lambs in God's kindom (Isa. 12:6) then certainly heterosexuals could outgrow their fear of those whose orientation differs from their own. In such a world, bisexuals could work out for themselves an authentic and creative way of being in the world, and lesbian women and gay men could be themselves without fear of reprisal. So could everyone else who differs from societal "norms."

But how do we transform society into God's kindom starting from where it is at this very moment? Every chapter of this book represents some aspect of my answer to that question. In this chapter I will offer some of my observations concerning "bringing in the kindom" from the perspective of God's gay, bisexual, and lesbian Christian daughters and sons. To that end, I want to discuss three questions, speaking as a lesbian Christian chiefly to my les-bi-gay sisters and brothers, although anyone else is welcome to listen in:

1. Externally, what is blocking us from a central and comfortable position in human society?

2. In the Christian church, what is blocking us from first-class citizenship?

3. Internally, what is blocking us from feeling fully comfortable with other people?

The Glass Cage Called Heterosexism

Starting first with the external blockages, we discover the set of political assumptions (conscious or unconscious) known as *heterosexism*. These assumptions form a system of coercion that requires either heterosexuality or a pretence of it as the price of first-class citizenship in our families of birth, our churches, and society in general. The assumptions form an invisible but inflexible glass wall, and the walls are everywhere. When someone speaks as if everyone who dates is always dating a member of the other sex, that's heterosexism: it erases the presence of les-bi-gay people in the room, apparently assuming that because we're all decent here, there *aren't* any such people present.

If even les-bi-gay people are unaware of the constant heterosexist pressure they are under — and many of us *are* unaware of the extent of it — that's because the message is so pervasive as to become invisible except for those moments when we suddenly perceive it, and mutter "aha!" For instance, in a doctor's office I was idly leafing through *Sports Illustrated* when I came across a "cheesecake" photograph of tennis star Steffi Graf in spike heels and a very short, very revealing black dress. Steffi was bending forward so the viewer could get a good glimpse of her breasts. Here was the caption: "This Steffi Graf photo in April's *Vogue* turns more heads than a rally at Wimbledon. 'Even when I won the Grand Slam,' says Fraulein Hemline, 'I didn't get so many congratulations.'"

Now, we may well ask ourselves why a young woman would get more congratulations for one "cheesecake" photograph than for putting herself into all-time tennis history by winning the Grand Slam (the four most prestigious tournaments, all in one calendar year). The answer, of course, is heterosexism. "Cheesecake" photographs proclaim that the subject is available to the other sex, eager to please men, seeking her fulfillment from male approval and admiration. Whereas female tennis champions may be as ambitious as men, and may even love other women, by posing for this photograph Steffi Graf has proclaimed that she is heterosexual and available. And society has rewarded her with a great outpouring of relieved approval.

By contrast, tennis star Martina Navratilova has been called "a poor role model" in the mass media. Why? Because she is known to have romantic partnerships with women. Martina is generous on the court, kind and supportive to her opponents, and scrupulously honest about scoring — but still she is called a poor role model. And despite Martina's popularity on the women's tennis circuit, no other female tennis greats have had the courage to come to her defense, no doubt for fear of being labelled lesbian themselves.

The message that heterosexuality is compulsory is basic to maintaining the power men in general hold over women in general. Lorraine Hansberry was right on target when she remarked that we could not ever "begin to guess the numbers of women who are not prepared to risk a life alien to what they have been taught all their lives to believe was their 'natural' destiny — AND — their only expectation of ECONOMIC security" (as quoted in Rich, 19).

Traditional Christian churches are bastions of heterosexism and sexism. In her 1991 doctoral dissertation concerning conflict and change in the Episcopal Church, Pamela W. Darling explains why the issue of ordaining lesbian women and gay men is causing such consternation. At the same time she reveals some of the profound connections between sexism and heterosexism:

> Both the ordination of women and homosexuals fundamentally challenge the [hetero] patriarchal order of world and church, undermining male privilege by presenting alternatives to the traditional male/female dominance/submission model for all relationships, domestic and political. Ordaining women, gay men, and lesbians violates traditional images of the sacred, crossing the boundary fixed by defining heterosexual males as the norm for ordained ministry and hence the standard for all Christian living.... Women are linked with sexuality, which gay men and lesbians represent in its most uncontrolled form; [to the traditionalist], all [of them] must be excluded from the sacred precincts of the church. (Darling, 466)

Aided and abetted by religious sexism and heterosexism, the American economic system maintains a huge pool of cheap labor so that the money earned by their hard work can "trickle up" to the rich few. Wealthy people are able to capitalize on the vulnerability of those who cannot effectively demand decent pay because they are already victims of racism, sexism, ageism, handicappism, or heterosexism.

How Heterosexism Is Unique

But there is an important difference between heterosexism and the other -isms. If an employee can prove, for instance, that she has been victimized by her employer's racism or sexism, she has legal recourse. But if an employee is discriminated against because of suspicions that she is lesbian, in 98 percent of American society there is no law to which she can appeal. Furthermore, by seeking justice for herself the employee is courting the possibility that newspapers and other media will report on her case. Once her lesbianism is made public, she may well be subjected to ostracism, expulsion from school or housing or job, physical violence, or even murder.

A few years ago the National Gay Task Force surveyed 2,074 openly gay men and lesbian women in eight cities across the United States. Ninety percent of the men and 78 percent of the women had been verbally assaulted because of their orientation; 49 percent of the men and 34 percent of the women had been threatened with violence; and about 25 percent of both sexes had been physically assaulted because of their homosexuality (Cort and Carlevale, 13). While it might be possible to match those figures with those stemming from racial oppression, the big difference would occur *after* legal redress had been sought and publicity had been engendered. Whereas decent people everywhere would be outraged at verbal or physical violence inflicted because of the victim's race, many otherwise decent people would not be equally outraged at violence inflicted because of the victim's homosexuality — unless the victim turned out to be in fact heterosexual. The assumption goes this way: "Decent people are either heterosexual or willing to make a convincing pretense of heterosexuality. The victim must have been asking for trouble by flaunting her deviation from heterosexual appearances." As distinct from other minority statuses, there are in most areas no laws to protect this one endangered category of human beings.

The Source of Christian Heterosexism, and the Cure

In addition to the coercive system of heterosexism that operates throughout society, there are problems specific to Christianity that keep lesbian, gay, and bisexual people on the margins of the church. Some of these were mentioned in Chapter Nine, but this is the place to develop the ramifications for les-bi-gay people.

Of course there are the "clobber passages," the proof texts in the Bible that are often used out of context as evidence of the sinfulness of homosexual relationships. Letha Scanzoni and I have dealt with these in our book *Is the Homosexual My Neighbor?* and many other resources now exist for those who need to educate themselves about reading the Bible contextually. Here I want to look at the deeper theological issues that stimulate people to *misuse* the Bible as an instrument of judgment and rejection. Deepest of all, I believe, is an alienating understanding of sin and salvation.

Judging from the account in Genesis 3 of the fall of humankind, sin is the absence of trust in God, who is the ground or essence of our own being. The chief symptom of this absence of trust is *fear*. Adam and Eve became persuaded that they could not trust God to provide them with fulfillment if they obeyed Her by abstaining from the forbidden fruit. They thought they could do better for themselves by choosing on the basis of their ego-desires. And because they did not trust God at the depth of themselves, they lost trust in their own deepest being, in each other, and in their environment. Fear gripped their souls. The immediate result was hierarchy, with the male lording it over the female (Gen. 3:16). And all the other forms of human divisiveness had their inception in the same moment, in the fear that grows out of distrusting God's loving kindness toward humanity.

Church leaders seem often to act out of the belief that people must be shamed or frightened into seeking salvation. In particular, les-bi-gay people are told to repent of who we are in a message that can only drive us deeper into self-distrust and self-rejection. But it is crazy to assume that learning to distrust ourselves will teach us to trust the One who created us as we are, the One of whom we are the manifestations.

Pastor Robert Schuller got it right in his book *Self-Esteem*. He wrote,

I am humanly unable to correct my negative self-image until I encounter a life-changing experience with nonjudgmental love bestowed upon me by a Person whom I admire so much that to be unconditionally accepted [by that Person] is to be born again. (67)

In other words, if original sin is lack of trust in God's love at the depths of our own inner being, then *salvation* is being brought back into a trusting relationship by remembering Who We Are: God's children, never actually separated from God's love even though we had imagined we were. In the instant of remembering our true identity, we are *at-oned*, restored to a trusting relationship with God, with our Selves, with other people, and with the universe.

When Christian churches begin to teach such a reassuring concept of sin and salvation, there will be no further need for "clobber passages" by which to define other people as more sinful than ourselves. Judging boomerangs anyway. As Jesus implied, those who judge do so in order to project their guilt onto others (Matt. 7:4–5); and where there is no guilt, there will be no need for projection of guilt. What a relief!

Looked at from a slightly different angle, the church's negative message to les-bi-gay people overturns all traditional wisdom about the acceptance of God's will. Traditional wisdom is that "in acceptance lies peace." Peace for a person with a handicap lies in her accepting the limitation she cannot change, and dealing with it as creatively as possible. Similarly, males have been taught they should be grateful for their maleness, females for their femaleness, whites for their whiteness, blacks for their blackness. But les-bi-gay people are almost never encouraged to praise God for their lesbian, bisexual, or gay orientation. Instead, we are encouraged to rebel against God's will by repenting of being the people She created us to be!

In high school I was required to memorize parts of the Westminster Shorter Catechism. I memorized, believed, and still believe that the chief purpose of human life is "to glorify God and enjoy [Her] forever." Assuming that "forever" begins with here and now, how do I go about enjoying and glorifying God while I am a human being here on this planet? Surely I do *not* glorify and enjoy the Creator by rejecting and maligning what She has created. Rather, I glorify and enjoy God when I see Her in everyone and everything, and do my best to share my pleasure with all of God's embodied manifestations everywhere.

Poet Wendell Berry once commented, "You cannot devalue the body and value the soul — or anything else.... Contempt for the body is invariably manifested in contempt for *other* bodies — the bodies of slaves, laborers, women, animals, plants, the earth itself." And the great gay Christian poet W. H. Auden had his own way of saying something similar: "As a rule, it was the pleasure-haters who became unjust." I too have noticed that phenomenon during my six decades on this planet: those who hate bodily pleasure could not care less about justice for others because they are not doing justice even to their own bodies. Learning to love ourselves and others (including mutual pleasuring) is the greatest contribution we can make to the creation of a just society. And I am confident that the day will come when most Christian churches will teach a creation-positive method of glorifying God and enjoying Her forever. God's kindom *is* coming, on earth as it is in heaven!

In order to teach a loving, yielding trust in God's good intentions toward us all, Christian churches will have to develop a sexual ethic in which peoples' happiness *matters* (see Chapter Eight). The church cannot change the facts of God's creation, which include the fact that by about age four, 10 percent of males and females are oriented toward members of the same sex. The church could of course continue to *deny* the facts of God's creation by telling les-bi-gay Christians we do not exist because it is impossible (or incompatible) to be both les-bi-gay and Christian. But sooner or later sanity requires that we accept creation as it is and acclimate ourselves to reality.

If I so desire, I can defy gravity by flinging myself out a fourth-story window: but I will pay a steep price for that refusal to grasp and cooperate with the realities of God's creation. The price Christian churches have been paying involves a discouraging loss of grace, power, and integrity. Thoughtful Christians will not be willing to pay that price forever.

Internal Obstacles and Discomforts

But even if the church and the general society were to extend a warm and supportive welcome to all people who are lesbian, gay, or bisexual, we would not be able to enjoy that welcome unless we had first overcome the internal obstacles that keep us from feeling at home in God's universe. It is not that I am trying to minimize the external pressures placed upon us by society and the church. But I know that for gay, lesbian, and bisexual people, as for everyone else, the major enemy is the enemy within.

Everybody seems to suffer a certain amount of damage to their self-esteem while they are growing up — if not inflicted by parents, then by teachers or peers. Yet as les-bi-gay people, in addition to the usual self-esteem issues, we face the cruel exclusions of heterosexism that often force us into the closet. The dangers of being open about our orientation are real and life-threatening. Yet the closet is also a very dangerous place to be.

The Price of "Passing"

What it all comes down to is this: that les-bi-gay people are free to choose what form our victimization will take. Most Jews, blacks, Hispanics, Asians, or Native Americans cannot hide their identity, most women cannot hide their femaleness, most poor people cannot conceal their poverty, most children or older adults cannot conceal their age, and most people with handicaps cannot conceal their handicaps. But we *can* choose to hide our homosexuality, and bisexuals *can* choose to hide that aspect of their sexuality that is same-sex oriented. So "passing" is a greater temptation for us than it is for the targets of other societal oppressions.

Yet "passing" as heterosexual takes a terrific toll on our lives. As Audre Lorde has said, "passing" is "dishonesty by silence," and dishonesty erodes both our inner wholeness and our relationships to other people. I remember, for instance, years ago when I was living in a covenanted relationship with a grade-school teacher. Whenever we accidentally met someone from her school community, I was expected to fade into the woodwork, never to be introduced for fear our lesbianism might be suspected and her job security threatened. Each time she felt forced to deny me, our relationship turned just a bit colder and felt to ourselves just a little more disreputable.

For any reader who is heterosexually married or dating a person of the other sex, all that is necessary to catch the "feel" of the closeted experience is to spend a weekend carefully hiding the real nature of your relationship, never touching in public and pretending not to know each other if you should meet an acquaintance of one of you. Closets do nothing for self-esteem, either individually or as a couple.

Silence=Death

During the Third Reich, Hitler's troops rounded up anyone suspected of homosexuality and sent them to the concentration camps along with Jews, gypsies, and people with handicaps. There were very few voices raised in defense of any of the targeted groups, but least of all the homosexual people. Even in the camps, the pink inverted triangle placed on the gay men and the black inverted triangle placed on the lesbian women identified them as the bottom of the pecking order, the most despised among the despised. It is because the silence of society permitted the savagery of the Holocaust that contemporary les-bi-gay activists have taken as one of our mottos "Silence=death." It is intended to remind those of us who are still in the closet that failure to name ourselves and speak up for our rights could literally cause our deaths in some new purge. It is also intended to remind us that "dishonesty by silence" could cause death to our self-esteem and death to our relationships. And it is intended to challenge heterosexual people of good will to take an *explicit* stand in favor of the civil and human rights of les-bi-gay people — and all people.

In the nineteenth century, same-sex love was referred to as "the love that dares not speak its name." The "Silence=death" logo is intended to encourage us to dare to speak the name of our kind of love, and to challenge heterosexuals to speak its name with the respect due to every form of human bonding. Leonard Matlovich captured the irony of society's demeaning of gay love in what he ordered to be carved on his grave stone when he knew he was dying of AIDS. The stone contains two inverted pink triangles, the title "A Gay Vietnam Veteran," and the statement, "When I was in the military they gave me a medal for killing two men and a discharge for loving one." Although Matlovich is dead now, his stone continues to speak in the Congressional Cemetery, bearing witness to the craziness of a society that condones violence and condemns love.

I do not mean to imply that everyone should come storming out of the closet, as helpful as that would be in correcting our invisibility to society as a whole. I am well aware that integrity between our private and public selves is a luxury that is beyond the reach of many les-bi-gay people. For instance, since I have been "out," I have been approached secretly by a great number of lesbian or gay clergy in various mainline denominations.

For them, coming out would mean being dismissed from ministries they are called to and equipped to perform. After I had been publicly attacked by a Methodist bishop for identifying myself as lesbian, one of his own clergy whispered to me, "By your stripes we are healed." She was expressing what every courageous but closeted les-bi-gay person feels, what I used to feel, in relationship to those who are "out" and are taking the flak on behalf of the whole les-bi-gay community: profound appreciation, awe, perhaps even a little envy.

I understand that clergy in most denominations, many school-teachers at every level except for tenured professors in colleges and universities, and people engaged in many businesses are all forced by the heterosexist system to stay in their closets. But at the same time, I want closeted people to realize how much they are missing, and I want to urge them to come out just as soon as they are able — at retirement, perhaps, or even posthumously, but in any case just as soon as circumstances permit.

A Personal Coming-Out Story

Perhaps the history of my own coming out might be helpful. I grew up in a fundamentalist family, attended a fundamentalist high school and college, and believed the fundamentalist assessment of homosexuality as sin. Yet I knew I was attracted to girls long before I knew the name to call that attraction. And I experienced severe incongruity between the wonders of being in love and the terrors of what I thought was God's opinion of these feelings. How could the holiest, most transcendent sensations I had ever felt be *sinful*?

In high school I was told that my lesbianism was incurable (true) and that God had no use for people like me (false). I wept in the agony of rejection, and I tried to commit suicide, as so many lesbian or gay teenagers do. All through college I sublimated my sexuality in sports, studies, and many good works. Although I was always in love with somebody, I never went any farther than a few furtive kisses. At the urging of a Bob Jones University professor who assured me that I'd fall in love after I was married, at twenty-one, I married a fundamentalist man. Five years later, trying to shore up a marriage that was defunct from the start, I birthed a son. It was not until I was in my mid-thirties and became involved in women's liberation that I began to dig my way out of the heterosexist trap. (There is nothing wrong with heterosexuality if it is authentic to you; but there is something wrong with assuming superiority because of being heterosexual. By the same token, there's nothing wrong with belonging to a race — we all do — but there is plenty wrong with being *racist*.)

Because as a fundamentalist I prized the Bible so highly, my liberation had to begin with Bible study. For the first time, in my late thirties

I approached the Scriptures with the perspective that possibly — just possibly — the Bible did not condemn women to secondary status and homosexuals to hell, as fundamentalism teaches. The results of this study were twofold: first, a book called *Women, Men, and the Bible,* arguing for male-female equal partnership on the basis of the overarching themes of the Hebrew and Christian Scriptures. And second, a book co-authored with Letha Scanzoni, *Is the Homosexual My Neighbor? Another Christian View.* The latter dealt with the Bible as well as with medical, literary, historical, and social science research. It laid to rest my theoretical fears about my orientation.

But theory can do only so much, and a very important part of overcoming my heterosexist mind-set was meeting many other lesbian, bisexual, and gay Christians. In 1976 Kirkridge Retreat and Study Center (Bangor, Pennsylvania) began to offer a weekend event called Gay, Lesbian, and Christian. After several years of being too afraid to attend for fear of losing my lecture invitations, I finally signed up as a participant. When I saw a hundred other les-bi-gay people together on one plot of ground and felt the level of their Christian commitment, internal shifts began to happen. Gradually I began to name my lesbianism to important heterosexual people in my life. At first when I did that, I felt slightly soiled, as if I needed a good shower. Only later did I recognize that the soiled feeling was residual heterosexism. Finally I sensed (at the core of my being, where God Herself lives in us all) that I was ready to take a public stand with my own people, the les-bi-gay community. I have never regretted it.

Occasionally when I am making a public stand, I feel that old insecure soiled feeling come over me. But now that I recognize that it is only my ego, clamoring to be acceptable to everybody, I simply turn away from the sensation by reminding myself of my deepest identity as a daughter of God. From an eternal perspective, the sexual orientation of one brief lifetime seems rather unimportant, certainly nothing to get overly invested in one way or the other. My lesbianism does not make me any worse than anyone else, and neither does it make me better. It is simply a good gift, as all sexuality is a good gift. It is intended to be used responsibly, as one way of glorifying God and enjoying Her forever.

I wish that every les-bi-gay person could know for herself the kind of *empowerment* and *sense of community* that coming out has afforded to me. Even my reading of the Bible has been invigorated. For instance, I now identify with Queen Esther's daring to name her own Jewishness in order to save her people from destruction. I get a "shiver of solidarity" when I hear her promising to defend her community at the possible price of her own execution: she promised Mordecai's messengers, "I will go to the king, though it is against the law; and if I perish, I perish" (Esther 4:16). And I feel another "shiver of solidarity" when I hear her actually naming herself as a member of her community: "if it pleases the king, let my life be given me — that is my petition — and the lives of *my peo-ple* — that is my request. For we have been sold, *I and my people*, to be destroyed, to be killed, and to be annihilated" (Esther 7:3–4, emphasis mine). The solidarity that heterosexual people can take for granted can only be won by les-bi-gay people through a courageous *act* of solidarity. But it's worth the risk: "coming out" is also "coming home" to a solid sense of community.

Even those whose livelihood or calling prohibits them from being "out" can achieve partial solidarity with their people by becoming known as "justice freaks." If you object when racist, sexist, and classist jokes are told, nobody will think it strange when you also object to mockery aimed at les-bi-gay people. If you support and work to achieve fair treatment for everyone else, no one will question why you are also supporting and working to achieve fair treatment for lesbian women, bisexual people, and gay men. The healthiest "smoke screen" is an honest, across-the-boards, universal commitment to justice for everyone.

The Ethics of "Outing"

Unfortunately one result of society's hatred of les-bi-gay people is a dis-honest minority within the subculture. I refer to those people — almost always gay men — who with the help of the closet are able to become bish-ops of churches, chairmen of powerful boards, or influential politicians, and who maintain their closet by voting against policies that would benefit their les-bi-gay sisters or brothers.

Their unfortunate abuse of power has led to the development of a tech-nique known as "outing." Properly used, "outing" means publicizing the clandestine homosexual activities of the powerful and their injustice to their own people, unless they cease their opposition to les-bi-gay rights.

Obviously, the threat of "outing" is completely unscrupulous when it is used against relatively harmless and powerless people, or even against powerful people who never attempt to block les-bi-gay advances. Michelan-gelo Signorile recently "outed" a high Pentagon official in order to prove that rejecting lesbian and gay people from the military represents a double standard (Henry, 17). But unless that Pentagon official had been using his *personal* power to injure the les-bi-gay community, this "outing" seems to me to sacrifice an innocent person for the sake of a cause. Everybody is at different places on their coming out journey, and everybody (including Pentagon officials) should be allowed to respond to their Inner Guides in peace and safety. But when personal power is used unjustly, it is the role of the prophet to denounce that injustice, whatever form it may take, and to call for repentance. Closeted gay voting or lobbying against les-bi-gay rights is only one form of injustice, but like all other forms of injustice, it must be resisted — for the sake of the perpetrator as well as for the sake of the oppressed.

Since it is no small thing to violate the unwritten law that les-bi-gay people protect one another from public risk, I suggest the following process for "outing" when it seems absolutely necessary. First, a concerned openly lesbian, bisexual, or gay person should visit the powerful individual, warning him (or her) that unless they cease abusing their power by persecuting their own people, it will be necessary to describe their unjust behavior to the press. If that private visit does not suffice or if the individual refuses to meet, then a committee should make a visit to deliver the same warning. If admission is denied, a certified, return-receipt-requested letter should be sent. In both cases, the individual should be assured that if he (or she) were to "come out" voluntarily, they would be warmly welcomed into the community as valued members. But if they feel coming out to be impossible, all the community asks is that they stop opposing the community's civil and human rights, in which case the individual's privacy will be respected.

If the individual continues to abuse his (or her) power after the private and the committee visits (or letters), then the actual "outing" is the only hope of awakening the individual to justice toward both their own identity and that of the community. Ample evidence should be provided to the press of the individual's clandestine homosexual behavior and their public anti-homosexual stance. The emphasis should be on the abuse of power (the injustice), not on the individual's homosexuality, which we certainly do not regard as evil in and of itself, but only in any exploitative dimensions. And it should be emphasized that the individual will always be welcomed by the community when the exploitations and abuses cease.

Solidarity, Not Strife

In order to live together as a community, either within or outside our closets, it is necessary for all of us to learn to cherish and nourish ourselves and each other. Egotism, personality clashes, and power struggles between les-bi-gay organizations are counterproductive because they drain away energy that is needed for the struggle to achieve a just society. I for one am very grateful to les-bi-gay leaders for the creative and redemptive response they have made to the AIDS crisis, educating the community about safer sex and reaching out to help anybody who is stricken with the disease, regardless of their race, class, sex, or orientation. I am proud of the gay men who have turned away from the stressful life of sexual intimacy with a great many people and have explored the many other wonderful aspects of their bonding as men. (I was deeply moved when I heard a Chicago-based gay male chorus [the Windy City Slickers] singing a lesbian love song about cradling each other tenderly.) I am also proud of the many gay men and lesbian women who may have never experienced multiple sexual contacts but who opened their arms and hearts to those brothers who have been stricken with AIDS. The magnificent les-bi-gay response to the health crisis should become for us a paradigm of how community solidarity is achieved. As long as human beings are in need, cheap power struggles should be beneath us as we work for the common good of all.

Revving Up Our Social Transformers

If we take the time to heal our personal and communal self-esteem, we will be able to respond lovingly even to the very society that rejects us. We will not make doormats of ourselves, but we will struggle for justice with a "revolutionary patience" that will not take *no* for an answer but also will not fight hatred with hatred. Society needs us to help overcome its lopsided socialization, so we can develop more fully human people — wonderful "womanly men" like the liberated Albert, Harpo, and Jack in *The Color Purple,* and wonderful "manly women" like Sophia, Shug, and the liberated Celie in the same novel.

Psychologist Carl Jung once guessed that homosexuality might be related to "a distinct resistance to identifying with the role of a one-sided sexual being" such as the Total Woman or the supermacho male. He guessed that homosexuality "preserves an archetype of the androgynous original person," the Earth-Creature or Adam of Genesis 2. Whether or not Jung's educated guess is accurate, it is for certain that healthy les-bi-gay people have a lot to teach society about sex roles, equal partnership, and the achievement of inner wholeness in which our "masculine" and "feminine" components mutually support and empower each other. Which is, of course, one reason why we must be careful not to pit men against women within our common community. If we do that, we are turning against aspects of ourselves, our inner "contra-sexual" aspects, our "masculine" or "feminine" aspects. (I don't believe in eternally set gender characteristics, but during this transitional time such terms as "masculine" and "feminine" seem to be necessary.)

We cannot reject other human beings without feeling at some level that we are rejecting ourselves. For the same reason, I would like to see churches, synagogues, and mosques embrace their lesbian, gay, and bisexual members. Until that day, religious institutions cannot fully experience God's grace.

It is ultimately more important to love than to be loved, and we can offer our love to religious congregants and the larger society whether or not people are able to respond in kind. We can meet this challenge by taking time every day to nourish hope within ourselves. Hope is the great disturber of acquiescence and the great instigator of protest. Without hope we grow apathetic and despairing.

As we hear on airplanes, if we are traveling with someone who needs assistance and the oxygen masks drop, we must first put on our own mask before helping other persons with theirs. Why? So that we will have sufficient oxygen to assist them effectively. Hope is our oxygen mask. The reason so many activists burn out is that they are trying to help society put on its oxygen mask without first assuring their own steady supply of oxygen.

My own hope is constantly nourished by the promises of the Bible and the quiet knowledge that when I am centered, I am in tune with the universe, cooperating with the all-inclusive God who extended Herself to form the universe. I recommend that all les-bi-gay people take time every day for quiet prayer and contemplation, for knowing ourselves in the presence of God. Some of us had traumatic childhoods that weakened our spiritual immune systems so that we are highly vulnerable to attack from negative and unloving spiritual forces. For us, meditation on the fact of God-in-us is especially important.

Looked at from the horizontal standpoint of human relationships and structures, the tasks that challenge us as les-bi-gay people seem too enormous even to fathom. But looked at from the standpoint of the Eternal Now, from the standpoint of that loving spiritual energy that sustains us all, our task is already perfected, and ultimately defeat is impossible. We are in a divine comedy. We may be dead long before the end of the play, but it is coming eventually: a happy ending. There really *is* a new world coming. I know it because I do not believe that Jesus would have taught us to pray, "your will be done on earth as it is in heaven" if that were an impossibility. We need to go about our work in the world with a constant daily reminder of who we are: we are the dearly loved children of God who is our tender Father and our demanding Mother and then again our loving Friend, faithful Companion, and cosmic Lover. We are God's ambassadors in the world. We are co-creators with the One who restrained Her power over us in order to give us the opportunity to develop our creative strength in tandem with Hers. Although the challenges are tremendous, so are the spiritual resources. Let us cherish and nourish the seeds of the Spirit in ourselves and in each other and in the world we inhabit.

Chapter Twelve

BUILDING BRIDGES BETWEEN INTERPRETIVE COMMUNITIES

———— ≈ ————

Every human being belongs to an interpretive community. Inevitably, we must communicate from within specific situations. And to be in a specific situation is to be possessed by a "structure of assumptions, of practices understood to be relevant in relation to purposes and goals that are already in place." Any utterance is immediately heard "within the assumptions of these [confident and communal] purposes and goals" (Fish, 318; cf. 321). In his groundbreaking 1980 study called *Is There a Text in This Class? The Authority of Interpretive Communities,* Stanley Fish explains that "the self does not exist apart from the communal or conventional categories of thought that enable its operations (of thinking, seeing, reading)." Because *all* "conceptions that fill consciousness . . . are culturally derived," there is no such thing as a wholly free consciousness. Nobody's interpretive acts are exclusively her own; our interpretations fall to us by virtue of our position "in some socially organized environment" (Fish, 335).

Within the halls of contemporary literary criticism, there are many interpretive communities: among them, Freudian, Jungian, linguistic, deconstructionist, and feminist. Within biblical interpretation as in other literary interpretation, mimetic theorists tend to emphasize the world revealed in the literary work; autonomist theorists stress the text itself; expressive theorists stress the author's ways of inventing, imagining, and judging; and pragmatist theorists stress the experience of the reader (Johnston, 35). Because all of these critical strategies are subjective, they all have their weaknesses and are at least partially dependent on wider cultural forces (Johnston, 39). So the one really foolish assumption is that anyone could possibly arrive at a situationless, culture-free,

167

objective interpretation of any text, let alone a text as complex as the Bible.

An illustration is in order. Religiously speaking, I am a member of the "liberation theology" interpretive community, having been forced out of the fundamentalist community by the conditions of my life, especially my gender and my sexual orientation. Recently I was talking with someone who is still in the fundamentalist fold, a mimetic theorist who stresses the world that is uncovered by the text (that is, the "divine plan" or "God's timeless message" revealed in the Bible). He told me that he had never doubted the sincerity of my faith; his objection to me is simply that I am "not obedient in my discipleship." I did not respond at the time, but eventually I will continue that conversation by pointing out that from the perspective of *my* interpretive community, obedience to the will of God is absolutely central to my experience. I seek to hear and follow divine guidance in every circumstance of my life. The judgment that I am "not obedient" reveals the man's assumption that he knows God's will not only for himself but for everyone else. God's plan is revealed, he would say, in any literal and obvious face-value reading of the biblical text. As he sees it, I try to explain away the clear meaning of the text in order to justify my own "lifestyle" ("disobedience").

This judgment betrays a profound naiveté about the art of literary interpretation and the tremendous role of the interpretive communities to which we respectively belong. My critic anticipates no objection to his judgment because he assumes that his position is invulnerable to challenges, as indeed it *is* invulnerable within his own interpretive community. After all, within that community certain ideas of what is important, necessary, and desirable have been agreed to in advance, and he is safe unless he departs from "the party line."

How Interpretive Communities Screen Evidence

Gordon Fee and Douglas Stuart, both of whom teach Bible at evangelical Gordon-Conwell Theological Seminary, provide some excellent illustrations of the way interpretive communities work. (If a person never ventures outside her own interpretive community, she can become very smug, assuming that what she and her colleagues, friends, or co-religionists believe is the absolute truth and no doubt about it.) Fee and Stuart write,

... have you noticed how our prior theological commitments cause many of us to read that commitment into some texts while we read around others? It comes as a total surprise to some Christians when they find out that other Christians find support for infant baptism in such texts as 1 Corinthians 1:16, 7:14, or Colossians 2:11–12, or that others find evidence for a two-stage Second Coming [of Christ] in 2 Thessalonians 2:1, or that still others find evidence for sanctification as a second work of grace in Titus 3:5. For many in the Arminian tradition, who emphasize the believer's free will and responsibility, texts like Romans 8:30, 9:18–24, Galatians 1:15, and Ephesians 1:4–5 are something of an embarrassment. Likewise many Calvinists have their own ways of getting around 1 Corinthians 10:1–13, 2 Peter 2:20–22, and Hebrews 6:4–6. Indeed, our experience as teachers is that students from these traditions rarely ask what these texts mean: they want to know "how to answer" these texts! (Fee and Stuart, 59–60)

What Fee and Stuart refer to as "traditions," I am calling interpretive communities. In each community, there is an (often unwritten and unspoken) agreement about what constitutes evidence and what is irrelevant or beside the point. As Fee and Stuart's words illustrate, it is futile for us to fling accusations at each other about creating "a canon within the canon" (that is, emphasizing some Scriptures and jumping over others), because every interpretive community tends to do the same.

I liked a great deal about the Fee and Stuart book. But I couldn't help noticing how certain assumptions of *their* interpretive community caused them breezily to omit evidence for their statement that homosexuality is "*always* wrong" (66), that "the New Testament takes a singular position against it" (68), that "the whole Bible has a consistent witness against homosexual activity as being morally wrong" (69). By these statements, Fee and Stuart violate their own cardinal rule of interpretation: "*a text cannot mean what it never could have meant to its author or his* [sic] *readers*" (60). The biblical authors knew about certain same-sex *abuses*, but they did not have a clue about a life-long unchosen orientation toward one's own sex, within which the only authentic sexual responses would be same-sex responses. That orientation was not recognized and named until the 1890s. Hence the biblical authors never wrote about "homosexuality" at all — both the word and the concept were unknown. "Homosexuality" does not appear in any biblical text in any language; and modern translations that utilize the term are playing fast and loose with the text.

By their words about homosexuality, Fee and Stuart also violate their second basic rule for interpretation: "*Whenever we share comparable particulars (i.e., similar specific life situations) with the first-century setting, God's Word to us is the same as His* [sic] *Word to them*" (60). The prohibition against two men lying together in Leviticus stems partly from small and embattled Israel's need for population, whereas the world today certainly is not in need of population. So by Fee and Stuart's sensible rule, the Leviticus prohibition cannot apply. Paul's words in Romans 1 refer to the same-sex temple prostitution that he of course associated with idolatry; again, the specific life situation is drastically different. And despite the fact that Robin Scroggs has written a highly respected scholarly work (*The New Testament and Homosexuality*), which demonstrates that the only model of same-sex relating known to the authors of the Christian Scriptures was pederasty (man-boy love) with all its abusive possibilities, Fee and Stuart airily sweep aside Scroggs's evidence with the remark that "it simply has not been proved that the options for homosexuality differ today from those of the first-century" (70). Well, that's an example of how interpretive communities cause us simply *not to see* evidence that is very compelling to people in a different community.

Each community has its own "interpretive grid" that screens out evidence that might contradict its basic assumptions. Just as a horse wearing blinders cannot see the peripheral motions that might make it skittish, a person looking through her community's interpretive grid is protected from the evidence that might make her feel uneasy. I can illustrate from a story I often tell on myself. Although I had read Genesis dozens of times and held a Ph.D. in English literature, my fundamentalist belief in inerrancy had kept me from noticing the apparent contradictions between Genesis 1 and 2 until I was about thirty-five years old, when my armor was pierced by a feminist book. After that, I began to apply to the Bible the precise literary techniques I had learned during my doctoral studies (Mollenkott, "Exploring Fundamentalist Hermeneutics," 3). At first my realization that there were indeed two creation plots made me exceedingly upset; but perseverance yielded rich insight and rewards. So I am glad now that my protective grid was stripped away, although I certainly was *not* glad when my fundamentalist confidence first was shaken. (By "fundamentalist confidence," I refer to the "certainty" that there are no contradictions in the biblical text, that there is a chapter and verse for every problem, that God is clearly and *definitively* revealed in the Bible, and so forth.)

So what are we left with — myriads of interpretive communities forever, with each group confident of its own rightness and unwilling to credit the evidence offered by someone of a different persuasion? An unending Babel? A jockeying for political power in which communities align themselves on one side or the other of the Great Divide between "left" and "right," "liberal" and "conservative," "permissive" and "disciplined," or however else we decide to name the sides? Are we condemned forever to regard as enemies people from the interpretive communities on the other side of the Great Gulf? "We are they to them as they are them to us," as R. D. Laing said. Is communication across the gulf simply *hopeless*? Perhaps. But Jesus suggested a way out of the impasse.

Loving Our Enemies

Jesus insisted that it was no virtue to love those who love us — those of our own interpretive community — because anybody can do that much. Instead, Jesus said, we should pattern ourselves after the Most Holy One, who is "kind to the ungrateful and the wicked" (Luke 6:35) — which is how people from opposing interpretive communities can sometimes seem, especially when they trivialize or distort our position. According to Jesus, we are expected to be "merciful, just as our [Mother and] Father is merciful" (Luke 6:36). To anyone who has ever spoken to large groups of people of an opposing interpretive community, as I have, this can sound loony and even self-destructive, too idealistic to be of any earthly use. My phrase for speaking in "enemy territory" is "going into the lion's den." I don't do it very often, because at best it is an exhausting experience, at worst a battering one. Even a one-on-one conversation can sometimes be exhausting and battering! Yet I assume that Jesus was not only sane, but a wise and loving teacher who would not tell us to do what is impossible or harmful for us. So it is worthwhile to explore the meaning of this command.

Neil Douglas-Klotz, whose study of the Aramaic words of Jesus has been so helpful to me, gives us a translation of "Love your enemies" that tries to capture the many nuances of the Aramaic statement:

> From a hidden place,
> unite with your enemies from the inside
> fill the inner void that makes them swell outwardly and fall
> out of rhythm: instead of progressing, step by step,
> they stop and start harshly,
> out of time with you.
>
> Bring yourself back into rhythm within.
> Find the movement that mates with theirs —
> like two lovers creating life from dust.
> Do this work in secret, so they don't know.
> This kind of love creates, it doesn't emote.

> (Douglas-Klotz, 84)

Douglas-Klotz explains that the Aramaic for *enemy* conveys the image of being out of rhythm, moving with harsh movements that don't keep the beat, like a really clumsy dancer. What a great description of how people from opposing interpretive communities sometimes seem to us! And the Aramaic language depicts injustice with similar imagery — being out of tune, out of rhythm, and with an inner emptiness and vanity that causes the unjust person to seem to swell up like a boil (or maybe like a particularly gruesome zit!). Our personal "enemies" are all of these things *only in relationship to us:* "out of step, impeding, vacuous, and puffed up" (Douglas-Klotz, 85). The "enemies" of a whole interpretive community, or a nation, or the whole planet, are "out of step, impeding, vacuous, and puffed up" in relation to a much larger sphere. But *relationship* is always the key to understanding what "enemies" are. Because of the subjective evaluations involved in relationships, one person's enemy is another person's friend.

In the command to "Love your enemies," Jesus used an Aramaic word that suggests an impersonal force acting in secret to bring separate beings together to create new life. (The root of the word can refer to planting seed or to having sex.) But Jesus used a different word for love when he talked about loving our neighbor as ourselves: that word referred to having compassion and mercy on our neighbors.

In the context of interpretive communities, Jesus seems to be saying that to communicate across the gap between such communities, we must align ourselves with an impersonal and mysterious creative force that is beyond anything our "separated" egos can drum up. Therefore he is not telling us to placate our "enemies," to concede the whole store, or to let them walk all over us. Rather, he is talking about finding within ourselves and them a rhythm that can harmonize and thus perhaps move us toward greater harmony, as a very good dancer can help a clumsy partner to dance more smoothly. He is talking about searching within our common humanity to find something that would fill the inner emptiness of the "enemy" and then *addressing only that* within them.

Maria Arapakis tells a story that will illustrate what I understand Jesus to be saying. In the suffocating heat of July, a woman was trying to get into a crowded New York subway car. But the woman just inside wouldn't give an inch, apparently wanting to be able to lean against the door. She in fact became angry, telling the intruder to give her a break by staying outside. Instead of counterattacking, the commuter on the subway platform said, "I'm sorry, but I have to get home. I'd be more than happy to change places with you once I'm inside." And the woman did indeed move aside and allow the outsider to enter (Arapakis, 197).

What created this minor miracle? The woman on the subway platform found something to fill the inner emptiness of her "enemy": she spoke politely, apologizing for the disturbance, explaining her own need, and offering to allow the woman to lean on the door once she had made room for her. By finding a rhythm that harmonized with the other's, the commuter got her own needs met without assaulting the "enemy" who had stood in her way.

Jesus seems to me to be talking about making secret inner connections with our "enemies," connections that we probably will never reveal but that we utilize to bring the enemy closer to harmony with what is creative and positive in our universe. To illustrate how this may work among interpretive communities: when I speak on homosexuality in evangelical or fundamentalist contexts, I am sometimes accosted by Bible-thumping men who need to prove to me that self-affirming "unrepentant" gay people will go to hell. I do not say to these men, "you are afraid of your own sexuality and are trying to build fences to keep yourself from realizing what it is you fear you want." To say that would only terrify them, driving them deeper into their separation and judgmentalism. Instead, I continue to emphasize that gay women and men, like everyone else, are profoundly beloved manifestations of God's nature, and that nothing can separate *anybody* from the love of Christ (Rom. 8:35–39). Thus I am speaking to the man's Inner Reality (his Christ-nature) rather than to his frightened ego. He is giving me the opportunity to extend love (and thus receive love — not necessarily from him, but from God within myself). And I am giving his soul reassurance and the opportunity to choose authenticity, peace, and joy rather than terrified judgmentalism.

Finding the Innocence within Our Opponents

The Sufis (Islamic mystics) have a saying that "God is the receiver and giver of love, as well as the love itself" (Douglas-Klotz, 85). The word for *love* in that saying comes from the same Aramaic root used by Jesus in "Love your enemies." In other words, the impersonal force that acts in secret to create new life and harmony is nothing other than love, and "*God* is the receiver and giver of love, as well as the love itself." Since God is indeed everything that is loving, the command to "love our enemy" is a command to allow God to show us innocent Love even within our "enemy."

When we can see the innocent Sacred Presence even in the person we most despise, we are enabled to address that Presence within them. Rather than counter-attacking when we feel attacked, Jesus tells us to search within our common humanity for whatever motive might have caused the attack. We can unite with the attacker from the inside by assuming that from *their* perspective, their motives are no less human and understandable than our own motives seem to ourselves. Having recognized our common humanity and our common dependence on Sacred Energy, we are ready to find a movement that mates with theirs so as to do and/or say the appropriate thing and thus create peace.

I am certainly not saying that our "enemies" will all gladly change their ways and become our friends. Jesus himself was crucified, an outcome that hardly indicates that he turned all his enemies into friends and admirers. Nevertheless, on the cross Jesus loved his enemies by asking God to forgive them because "they do not know what they are doing." Jesus understood that cruelty stems from human ignorance and delusion about who we are, and that ignorance and delusion call for forgiveness and quiet correction rather than judgment and punishment.

So although loving our "enemies" in other interpretive communities may not cause them to agree with us, we will be giving *ourselves* peace and love, and we will be fostering our own joy and creativity, by making appropriate and connected responses to them. What they do with our responses is up to them, but *what we see in them determines our own happiness*. "Loving our enemies" is a gift we give to ourselves and to the universe. If we can discern the Divine Presence even in the most morally ugly person we can think of, then seeing the Divine Presence everywhere else will become easy indeed. We will find ourselves living in a divine milieu.

Harnessing for God the Energies of Love

The Divine Milieu was the title of a great book by the Catholic philosopher Pierre Teilhard de Chardin. Here is an arresting quotation from him: "The day will come when, after harnessing the winds, the tides, and gravitation, we shall harness for God the energies of love. And on that day, for the second time in the history of the world, [humankind] will have discovered fire." By telling us to love our enemies, Jesus was urging us to harness for God the energies of love, or rather to allow God as a force within us all to harness *us* in the energies of love, and thus to offer to our "enemies" the creative opportunity to come alive.

But whether or not our "enemies" choose life, *we* will be choosing life when we choose to unite with our "enemies" from the inside rather than to judge them and separate ourselves from them in order to justify vengeance against them. Only through such uniting can we overcome the dualism that causes us to feel cut off from God and neighbor, alone in a menacing universe.

Perhaps it would help us to remember how we feel when we are being lavishly entertained in someone else's home. Even if we disagree with them, we try to find a polite and gracious way to do so because we are dependent upon them as our hosts. Historian Lambros Kamperidis suggests that according to the Christian Scriptures, when we are called strangers and guests in this world, the meaning is that we are "to place ourselves in a state of dependence and to have a reverent attitude towards the world, as we do when we enjoy our host's entertainment" (Kamperidis, 8). Obviously, if we all behaved this way, our ecological, interpersonal, and intercommunity problems would be solved. Although communication would still be difficult across interpretive gaps, we would all treat our "enemies" as if they were our hosts and would treat the earth, air, and water the same way.

I want to reiterate that we are not asked to love the cruel behavior of our "enemies." We are *not* asked to pretend agreement with interpretations that we consider cruel, misguided, insupportable, or illogical. But we *are* asked (for our own benefit) to recognize and speak to the Divine Ground of our opponent's Being, a recognition that will make us happy because it is the same Divine Ground upon which we ourselves stand. And by speaking to the holiest and kindest, most decent aspect of our "enemies," we offer them an opportunity to implement that holiness, kindness, and self-respecting decency.

For instance, I have a delightful African American woman friend who used to run a maximum security prison. She gave orders that before any prison guard could take punitive action against a prisoner, she must be called to the scene to see what she could do. And this is the sort of thing she did: say, a prisoner was refusing to return to her cell. She was holding on to the bars from the outside, refusing to walk inside. My friend would be summoned by angry and impatient guards who felt they had more important things to do than to reason with an uncooperative prisoner. She would say to the prisoner, "Look, these guards are very eager to beat you up. After they bust your chops, they will throw you into your cell in a broken heap. Wouldn't you prefer to walk in there on your own two feet, with your head up?" And of course once she looked at it this way, the prisoner *did* prefer to enter under her own power. Thus my friend spoke to the human dignity of the prisoner and at the same time preserved the guards from unleashing their lower nature in violence. There were no riots during my friend's entire tenure as head of that prison.

For another example, I do not think Jesus would ask us to condone the behavior of the man Americans have recently "loved to hate," Saddam Hussein. He has slaughtered his own people by the thousands and has attacked the very ecosystem upon which his survival — and ours — depends. But I think Jesus *would* ask us to recognize in ourselves certain aspects of Saddam Hussein, such as our continued use of products that attack the ecosystem, or our ego's tortured desire to get even with those we feel have wronged us. And Jesus *would* ask us to recognize that as surely as Saddam Hussein is breathing, his being is sustained by the breath of God. Hussein's ego has denied his connection to the rest of creation, and in the resulting fear he has isolated himself to a terrible degree and has acted with great cruelty. But he is only an extreme example of what each of our egos is capable of doing if it can keep us convinced that we are separate from God, separate from other people, and separate from the ecosystem that supports our lives.

As an Episcopalian, I regret to admit that the president of the United States, also an Episcopalian, treated Saddam Hussein with a contempt that could only drive him farther into his delusion of separateness. In the United States, that turned out to be effective political strategy, but it was very poor Christianity. It was President Gorbachev who best illustrated Jesus' principle of uniting with the enemy from the inside and finding the movement that mates with theirs. Instead of taunting Hussein and thus driving him into greater cruelties, Gorbachev said to Hussein that he hoped he'd have the *courage* to pull out of Kuwait. Knowing that Hussein was exceedingly heteropatriarchal and macho, Gorbachev interpreted withdrawal as *courage,* making withdrawal something Hussein could have done without feeling he had lost status as a male warrior. It didn't work — but it stood a much better chance of working than Bush's macho and contemptuous challenges. And many thousands of lives would have been preserved if Gorbachev's appeal had worked.

Two Ways of Perceiving

When I am looking at others through the eyes of my ego (what St. Paul calls the "old nature") I am insecure, afraid, and consequently judgmental. I tend to be sure my ego knows what is right or wrong, good or bad, and I can't stand people who do things that are wrong. But when I turn away from my ego by asking the Holy Spirit to help me perceive correctly, everything shifts. I remember that in reality I am a spiritual being whom nothing can hurt, eternal and sinless and safe in God's love — in fact, an expression of God's love and therefore loveable — and that in reality other people are the same. If I deny the holiness of others, I lose sight of it in myself. It works the same way for everybody else as well. When they think they are only egos and bodies, on their own and vulnerable in a hostile universe, everyone gets as frightened and mean as I can be, and perhaps even more brutal than I. But none of that changes the essential holiness upon which their being is grounded.

Through the eyes of love I can still discern injustice or illogicality or inconsistencies of interpretation. Discernment is the human spirit's radar system; it is not the same thing as judging others to be worthless or essentially evil. Love does not require me to blind myself to my own inconsistency if I should claim that women must keep silent in church on the basis of 1 Corinthians 14:34–35 and yet simultaneously should oppose prophecy and speaking in tongues, practices that form the context for the "silence" passage (Fee and Stuart, 17). Love does not prohibit me from pointing out that it is wildly illogical and unjust to uphold prohibitions against homosexual acts on the basis of Leviticus 18:22 and 20:13 while sweeping aside prohibitions against marital intercourse during the woman's menses in the same two chapters (18:19 and 20:18). Or to argue that women should not wear slacks or shorts because they are "men's clothing" (Deut. 22:5) without also insisting that we must all build barrier walls around the roofs of our houses so no one will fall off (same chapter, verse 8) or desist from planting two kinds of seeds in one vineyard (verse 9; Fee and Stuart, 19). Love has to do with the tone I utilize in pointing out such discrepancies, and with the way I behave toward people as I try to teach them more adequate interpretive methods. And my tone and behavior depend on my being able to see God as the sustaining ground of my opponent's being. But love does *not* require me to send my mind into early retirement!

The Goal of Appropriateness

Loving our enemies (and friends too, for that matter) sometimes means confronting or correcting them. It means doing or saying what seems appropriate at the moment and in the situation. It certainly does not mean trying to be a people-pleaser, a moral chameleon. Sometimes Jesus loved his enemies by bawling them out in no uncertain terms, sometimes by letting them make their own mistakes, as when he let the rich young ruler return to his riches. Jesus loved that man, but he refused to threaten or coerce him into doing justice. Jesus just *let him go*. Sometimes Jesus loved his enemies by ducking out of their way in order to protect himself from their violence. Loving someone means doing what is appropriate to the situation and the individual.

I remember a moment when I was apparently "in the Spirit" and made a lightning-swift choice that surprised me but nevertheless seemed appropriate. I had been speaking in front of about eighty clergy, theological students, and faculty about a new sexual ethic and a whole society based on justice and equal partnership (see Chapter Eight). A young man said, "But I have a hard time believing that such a society is even possible." I shot back, "If you don't believe it's possible, then for you it is not possible. When you *believe* it you'll *see* it. You need *metanoia,* you need to be converted, you need to be transformed by the renewal of your mind!" When I got a moment to think about what I'd said, I was concerned that perhaps I had been too direct and harsh with the man. But hours later he was still present, still smiling, and still taking notes. Even if he hadn't stayed, however, I would have had to assume that those were the right words for him at that moment. It is not characteristic of me to speak quite that pointedly to an individual in front of a group, and as I said the words they did not feel entirely like my own words. But certainly they echoed my deepest convictions and were spoken out of loving concern for the young man's well-being — and the world's. Is this what it's like to be harnessed by God's love, somehow to find the movement that mates with the other's, and to create rather than to emote?

Some General Principles for Communicating across the Gap

I also remember a conference on the explosive issues surrounding human reproduction that brought together people from the "pro-life" and "pro-choice" movements. Facilitated by my friend Rose Mitchell and sponsored by the Synod of the Northeast of the Presbyterian Church (U.S.A.), the conference required all participants to promise in writing that they would give every speaker a respectful hearing. And almost everybody did as they had promised. While I do not know of anybody who changed interpretive communities as a result of the conference, I do believe that participants would henceforth be less likely to caricature each other as "heartless baby-killers" or "heartless woman-haters" after listening to each other's perspectives. At that conference we sought a common agenda, and certainly people found a small but significant core of objectives that they could work to achieve together. I believe that world peace would be furthered by our holding many more such conferences that bring together people from opposite interpretive communities.

To make such conferences successful, we would have to bear in mind certain principles. First, we would have to remember that *no* interpreter is objective (ourselves included), because *everyone* has cultural presuppositions. We are wise therefore to acknowledge our own presuppositions and to hold other people responsible for acknowledging theirs. Mendel Lieberman and Marion Hardie tell a good story about how this technique worked for one interreligious couple. The husband, Jewish, strongly opposed the introduction of a Christmas tree into the home. The wife, a Christian, placed both religious and sentimental value in having a Christmas tree for herself and the children. As this couple's consultants, Lieberman and Hardie offered no advice but simply role-played the conflict in front of the couple, mirroring the concerns of each partner and thus clarifying the convictions and intense feelings of each. No solutions were offered: just aesthetic distance that permitted clarity about preconceptions and concerns. But several days later the couple phoned to say that they had managed to work out a creative solution. They used twigs of holly and branches of evergreens to make a design on the wall, which they then decorated after the manner of Christmas trees. And everybody was happy (Lieberman and Hardie, 154).

A second principle to bear in mind is that it is not always necessary to change somebody's mind to get what you want. If we cannot get our "enemy" to switch interpretations, perhaps we can persuade them to change their behavior. Maria Arapakis tells of an affirmative-action program in one company that said to its male managers, "You don't have to change your opinions, you just have to change what you do." In other words, the company recognized that chauvinists are not going to change overnight, if at all; but it insisted that they cease *acting* unfairly and condescendingly toward women (Arapakis, 265). I think the les-bi-gay community is wise to take a similar stance toward society: if we are guaranteed the same civil and human rights as everyone else, we can live without needing everybody's approval. Even in the churches that claim that in Christ there is no "outsider," what we need is not theological approval as much as equal access to ordination, ritual, and so forth: in other words, our *religious* human rights. At Families 2000, an earnest African American man asked me to understand that although he did not consider himself homophobic, his interpretive community does regard my sexual orientation as sinful. I countered by asking him whether he would vote in favor of civil and human rights protection for les-bi-gay people and whether he would raise any objection if the government targeted us for destruction. When he answered yes to both questions, I agreed with him that he was not homophobic. We also agreed that we could regard ourselves as sister and brother despite our interpretive differences.

A third principle to remember is that we must give one another the benefit of the doubt because our assumptions tend to make things happen the way we expect them to happen (Arapakis, 167–68). Our beliefs tend to fulfil themselves. If we go to a party with a chip on our shoulders just daring everybody to show us a good time, chances are that we will be miserable. If we expect other drivers to be rude and inconsiderate, we will meet endless numbers of rude and inconsiderate drivers. If we assume that all students are cheats, many of our students will fulfil our expectations; but if we assume they want to do good work and provide support for them every step of the way, a remarkable number will come through with honest work. If we approach people from other interpretive communities with an aggressive, combative spirit, we will no doubt get even more aggressive combat than we had bargained for. But if we speak to the Christ in them with kindness and optimistic faith, we have a pretty good chance of being treated kindly in return. Trying to communicate will probably still be exhausting because of differing preconceptions, but the human connection can be richly rewarding.

I remember a time when I was chairing a meeting of Women of Faith, an interreligious dialogue group including women from the Protestant, Catholic, Muslim, and Jewish traditions. We were discussing the location of our next national conference, and some of us didn't want to use a certain center because the center had refused to host meetings of gay and lesbian people. A nun said, "We don't want to stick our necks out for people like *them,* do we?" I was stunned. A quick and angry answer flashed through my mind. But I gave her the benefit of the doubt, assuming that she spoke from ignorance both of my identity and of the existence of decent, religious les-bi-gay people. A few months later, at another meeting, I spoke to her privately, telling her who I am and how her remark had sounded to me. Now it was *her* turn to be stunned. She stammered about how highly she thought of me, and I asked her to revise her opinion of gay women and men of faith in the light of what she knew about my commitment to justice and peace. We shook hands on that — and I was grateful that I had given her the benefit of the doubt.

Trusting the Yearning for Wholeness

There are probably many other principles to remember when planning bridge-building conferences between interpretive communities, but I will mention only one more: that we should trust the fact that human beings "have within them a natural yearning and thrust toward health and wholeness" (Peck, 68). Although fear immobilizes that thrust and energy, when people feel themselves to be safe and unconditionally accepted, their defenses and resistances fall down, and their "thrust toward health" is free to pursue its path of self-improvement.

> Paradoxically, then, a group of humans becomes healing and converting only after its members have learned to stop trying to heal and convert. [Genuine] community is a safe place precisely because no one is attempting to heal or convert you, to fix you, to change you. Instead, the members accept you as you are. You are free to be you. And being so free, you are free to discard defenses, masks, disguises; free to seek your own psychological and spiritual health; free to become your whole and holy self. (Peck, 68)

When we can trust that even members of opposing interpretive communities harbor deep within themselves the same yearning and thrust toward health and wholeness that we have noticed in ourselves, we will be able to give them greater freedom to take off their disguises, masks, and defenses in our presence.

The concept of local church congregations is a wonderful one precisely because it offers us the opportunity of caring for each other on the long haul despite interpretive differences. I cannot speak for churches and synagogues of other eras, but I do know that in this era almost every congregation contains members who belong to differing interpretive communities, despite all that the pastor or pastors may do to try to achieve congregational consensus. Yet if people share a concern for each other's daily trials and triumphs — the birth defect of the Smiths' baby, the achievement of a doctorate by Ms. Jones, the car accident suffered by the Whites — there is something about the sharing of common humanity that can blunt the edge of differences of opinion and dogma. *If* we will allow that to happen!

Some Suggestions for Bridge-Building

I'd like to finish out this chapter, and this book, with a few other suggestions of ways to narrow the gaps between interpretive communities within and among religious denominations.

When a controversial issue such as sexual ethics or some specific church political involvement is up for discussion, I think it is wise to encourage the sharing of emotions *before* getting into the more abstract intellectual aspects of the issue. Participants in the discussion should be encouraged to describe their highest hope regarding the issue in question; then, their worst fear. In a nonjudgmental, uniformly supportive atmosphere, individuals should be encouraged to explore out loud *what it is* about the issue that stirs their joy, their fear, their pain, their anger. If these steps are taken in small groups, care should be taken that, if at all possible, each position regarding the issue is represented in each small group.

Next, there might be some discussion about the intensity of involvement of various participants. For instance, if a gay man or a lesbian woman feels called to the ministry and is in seminary, their involvement in the issue of ordaining self-affirming les-bi-gay people is going to feel like life-and-death to them. Should that enormous life involvement carry more weight than the desire of a traditionalist heterosexual thinker to keep her own moral categories clear-cut and simple? In a functional family, if one member's dignity or fulfillment is directly involved in a decision, whereas other family members are only indirectly involved, out of love the others will defer to the directly impacted member. Should it also work that way in the priorities of a functional congregation? When differences of interpretation threaten to split a local congregation, it seems to me that *community-building* (through listening to each other's hopes, fears, pain, joy, and anger), followed by a *discussion of priorities,* would be essential.

It might even be wise to set up a weekend workshop devoted to nothing other than community-building, bringing together some of the most articulate people from the various interpretive communities in a commitment to stick it out until genuine communication takes place across the gaps. Scott Peck describes the process of community-building in his book *The Different Drum: Community-Making and Peace.* It usually begins in pseudocommunity, a "boring mannerliness" in which everybody tries to fake acceptance of one another in order to avoid conflict (and nobody can beat Christians at *that* game!). Eventually, however, somebody expresses an honest reaction, and all hell breaks loose in a chaos of attempts to heal and convert each other. After a sufficient time spent in squabbling and perhaps even in mutual recrimination, the group must decide whether they want to organize a resolution (thus short-circuiting community) or whether they are willing to go through emptiness in order to achieve genuine community.

"Emptiness" means that participants must empty themselves of the "feelings, assumptions, ideas, and motives" that have been functioning within themselves as "barriers to communication." These could be stereotypes, theological or ideological rigidities, the need to control, or whatever else is getting in the way of genuine listening: "The transformation of a group from a collection of individuals into genuine community requires little deaths in many of these individuals" (Peck, 102). Could this be, for people of our time, one of the major meanings of taking up our cross and following Jesus?

Finally, as Scott Peck indicates, after the emptying comes community: each person speaking openly, vulnerably, truthfully, out of her or his own personal life situation. Peck comments, "When I am with a group of human beings committed to hanging in there through both the agony and the joy of community, I have a dim sense that I am participating in a phenomenon for which there is only one word. I almost hesitate to use it. The word is 'glory'" (Peck, 106).

I know the feeling. It is remarkable enough to build community among people who share similar preconceptions and interpretive attitudes, but there is something miraculous about achieving community with people who have come together wearing different interpretive grids. I agree with Peck that "community is the only catalyst that softens intransigence" (328), and that each of us should actively involve ourselves in building community. I also agree that the major guideline for community is inclusiveness. We need to seek out people who are different from ourselves because we need each other's gifts in order to be whole. White people need people who are black, brown, red, or yellow, and vice versa; Christians and Jews and Muslims need one another; rich and poor, Episcopalians and Baptists, Democrats and Republicans, hawks and doves, fully abled folks and people with handicaps, heterosexuals and homosexuals, "liberals" and "conservatives" *need* one another. If enough of us could learn to communicate across such gaps, lions would lie down with lambs in a creation born anew.

Using Books to Construct Community

Another method of bridging the communication gap is to begin with a specific promise of Scripture and then seek to work out the ramifications together. For instance, a single group containing people who differ drastically on certain issues might begin by claiming the promise of 2 Corinthians 5:19: "in Christ God was reconciling the world to [God's Self], not counting their trespasses against them, and entrusting the message of reconciliation to us" (NRSV, inclusive God-language mine). People might then enter into silence together, asking the Holy Spirit to teach them what steps they could take to become reconciled to the other people in the group, especially to those they differ with most concerning the currently divisive issue. After the silence, people could begin to talk about what they sensed about themselves during the silence, and how they honestly feel about what they think the Spirit is instructing them to do.

In 1982, psychotherapist Ralph Blair told a conference of Evangelicals Concerned that "Somehow, in Jesus Christ, God was reconciling that person next to you to [God's Self]. And somehow, in Jesus Christ, God was reconciling Jerry Falwell to [God's Self]. If we don't believe that, we cannot know that we ourselves have been reconciled" (Blair, 22). Jerry Falwell has used Christianity's fear and hatred of les-bi-gay people as one of his most lucrative fund-raising devices; so mentioning Falwell's reconciliation to God at a predominantly les-bi-gay conference was the equivalent of Jesus' praising the Good Samaritan in front of the Samaritan's archenemies. Blair was, I think, correct in his emphasis; unless the passage evokes in us a disturbing awareness of the places where we still hold resentment instead of reconciliation, it is not *gospel* to us. The purpose of the "silence-and-sharing" method I have outlined would be to elicit such insights from group members rather than to "lay them on" from an authority figure. People always remember best that which they work out on their own — or, more precisely, that which they are taught by God from the center of themselves.

Another useful strategy might be to contract with a group to meet once a month (even once a week) to discuss together a well-written conservative book on interpretation, such as the already-discussed *How to Read the Bible for All Its Worth: A Guide to Understanding the Bible.* Choosing a "conservative" book is important because people in the right-wing interpretive community tend to be more suspicious and fearful of differing views on how to read the Bible than people on the left. Study of such a book will reveal to everyone that Christians have a great deal of common ground on which to approach biblical interpretation, despite important differences. The fact that the chosen book is conservative would enable right-wingers to accept the facts that translations are interpretations, that different genres require different rules of interpretation, and that the Bible *does* need to be interpreted: "The antidote to *bad* interpretation is not *no* interpretation, but *good* interpretation" (Fee and Stuart, 18). The fact that Fee and Stuart obviously love Scripture and are up-front about interpretive squabbles *within* the "conservative" community would enable "liberals" to take their ideas seriously. Both sides could learn together some important principles of exegesis, hermeneutics, and the generic approach to literature. And both could then have a concrete foundation for discussing the inevitable differences concerning homosexuality, abortion, and perhaps other controversial matters.

Another book that is excellent for such discussion groups is Willard Swartley's *Slavery, Sabbath, War, and Woman: Case Studies in Biblical Interpretation.* Swartley's approach is to show how the Hebrew and Christian Scriptures have historically been interpreted to support slavery, worship on the seventh day of the week, war, and the subordination of women, and then to show how the opposite interpretive community interprets the Bible to oppose slavery, to affirm women's equal partnership, to support worship on the first day of the week, and to teach pacifism. Having studied Swartley's contrasts, the group could then split up to prepare a similar case study on homosexuality. Probably the most fruitful approach would be to have the left-wingers prepare the biblical case *against* lesbian or gay ordination and the ritualization of same-sex unions, while the right-wing prepares the biblical case *in favor* of them. In this way each side would have the opportunity of entering into the details of a position that is for-eign to them. After the cases were prepared, they could be presented to the whole group by a spokesperson from each side. The idea would be not to let the case rest until the right-wingers were satisfied that their view had been adequately represented by the left-wingers, and vice versa. This very process would be marvelous training in arguing fairly, and should have a good carry-over value into more intimate relationships. Even though con-sensus might never be reached, hearing each other out might lead to some marvelously creative solutions.

Learning Win-Win Conflict Resolution

A different approach to a controversial issue might be to spend some time applying to the situation at hand some of the suggestions of Lieberman and Hardie in their book *Resolving Family and Other Conflicts: Everybody Wins*. Especially important is for the group (inclusive of all positions, naturally) to decide together (1) who owns the problem, (2) what precisely is the problem, (3) whose behavior is the problem, (4) how important the issue is to each side, (5) how important the relationship between the sides is to each of them, and (6) whether everybody is committed to "fighting" fairly and effectively (Lieberman and Hardie, 96–104). On the issue of homosexuals in the Christian church, for instance, (1) les-bi-gay people own the problem because it is they who are being excluded from ordination and ritualized congregational support. Les-bi-gay people have owned this problem responsibly by asking year after year for church bodies to meet with them to find a resolution. (2) The precise nature of the problem is not a need for theological or personal approval, but a desire for full civil and human rights in the religious arena. (3) The behavior of the heterosexual majority is the problem, particularly their refusal to educate themselves concerning human sexual orientations. (4) The issue is very important to les-bi-gay Christians because, for many, their livelihood and fulfillment is at stake. It is important to their opponents because they feel themselves to be the defenders of biblical values. (5) The relationship of the les-bi-gay minority to the heterosexual majority *ought* to be important to both sides, and *would* be if everyone understood their essential oneness. As it stands, this is the point at which some gut-level confrontations need to take place. Do heterosexual Christians simply want les-bi-gay Christians to disappear, to ghettoize themselves, or are we to be valued and honored as members of the body of Christ Herself? (6) As for fighting fairly and effectively, that would involve taking responsibility for one's own feelings and for bringing matters to a clear resolution, being ready to make concessions if they are warranted, making equal space for the opposition, refusing to deny other people's reality, and so forth (Lieberman and Hardie, 106–9). None of that is easy to do, but it is vital to responsible adulthood as well as to reaching understanding across a gap between interpretive communities.

A less confrontational approach would be to conduct weekly Bible studies utilizing the methods set forth by Wayne Bradley Robinson in *The Transforming Power of the Bible*. Robinson suggests a group of from twelve to twenty people, and of course for our purposes it would need to include people from several interpretive communities. First of all the text (preferably a narrative) must be *actively* listened to, after which the group comes up with as many "hunches" as possible. ("Hunches" are intuitive, imaginative, creative responses to the text.) They will probably be released mainly by the facilitator's asking questions that emerge from the text and have been prepared in advance. After stimulating a large number of "hunches," the facilitator invites the group to do something that will help bridge the gap between the text and each individual: make a drawing or sculpture; write out a series of statements in which *each* participant compares herself to *each* character in the biblical story; or whatever may seem useful. Afterward, each participant shares verbally what she has learned about herself (but people are permitted to "pass" any time they feel they cannot talk about certain things). Step 3 is that each participant is invited to write down *what she has learned about or for herself* from steps 1 and 2 (but not what the text "means" in the abstract).

Step 4 involves challenging people to identify what they *want* to do about what they have learned about or for themselves (not what they "should" do, but *want* to do). Step 5 is to invite everyone to make short-term behavioral goals to achieve their wants. Step 6 involves covenanting with the group to carry out the goal and to let the others know how it went. Step 7 (taken at the beginning of the next group meeting) involves following through on Step 6 (Robinson, 8–10).

Studying the Bible together in this nonconfrontational method is premised upon the following assumptions: that people do have an inner directive toward wholeness; that they will be able to follow that directive in a safe, nonjudgmental environment; and that sharing growth experiences enhances understanding — even across the gaps between interpretive communities.

The Governing Assumptions of Sensuous Spirituality

Everything I have written in this book is based upon a set of supremely important assumptions about reality. On a personal level, people create social change primarily by *being* the social change they are looking for (Tuttle,

Conversations, May–June 1988, 5). Changes in social structures will inevitably follow when a sufficient number of people have realized their own inseparability from God and therefore from each other. But as anyone will realize who has read everything in this book, I do not believe this means that spiritual people should put forth no effort to change the unjust systems that deny to others the sensuous luxury of having enough time and health to be able to meditate, attend study groups, and enjoy heaven on earth. If activism is part of our nature and we feel a stimulus toward justice work when we are centered, then God wants to express Her loving justice through our activism.

But it is worse than futile to do anything that is incongruent with our own being and therefore with the movement of God's Being. Any action will be healing and appropriate if it arises out of congruence with our centered Self (that is, if we are "obeying God's will" or are "in the Spirit"). But if it arises out of a heady zealousness to cure somebody else or to save the world, our action may or may not be helpful — probably not, because our timing will usually be off. That is why we need to develop a constant openness to our Inner Guide, the Holy Spirit, who will tell us not only *what* to do or say, but *when.* And yes, that means we have to be paying attention to God's voice within our centered Selves all the time. Constantly. Without ceasing. *All the time.*

Christians try to take our behavioral model from Jesus as the ideal for humanity. But there's a problem with the "Jesus-standard": depending upon which interpretive community we belong to, we have hardened the fluid congruence of Jesus' behavior into several radically different sets of "rules." And no matter which set of unwritten "rules" becomes our guide, those "rules" distract us from constant dependence on the Holy Spirit within our centered Selves. Being "the Christ" does not mean performing any specific type of action, but rather it means being appropriate to this specific situation this moment — perhaps compassionate and supportive, perhaps as hard as tempered steel — whatever will provide clarity, sanity, transformation, and healing. Our proper question is not so much "what would Jesus do?" but "what am I to do?" If someone is trying to use or abuse me, I would only encourage their error if I were to cooperate. Although they might accuse me of lacking Christ-like compassion for their plight, it is in fact not helpful to cooperate with the ego's co-dependent games. Again, the only way for me to know what will encourage clarity and truth is to pay attention to God's still small Voice all the time. Without ceasing.

Perhaps that constant attention sounds like a major drag, too much work to allow for any fun. Perhaps it sounds more like morbidly serious spirituality than like joyously sensuous spirituality. If it sounds that way to us, we have a good indication that we have yet to know the feeling of consistently following the bliss of our eternal being, of experiencing complete integrity at every moment, of being in constant touch with God's Self deep within our centered Self. Yet this is the discipleship our Selfhood seeks, and this is the experience that fulfills the heights and depths of our humanity. This is heaven on earth. And perfect freedom.

Appendix A

MILTON'S USE OF THE BIBLE TO DEFEND
DIVORCE FOR INCOMPATIBILITY

–––––––– ≈ ––––––––

It seems to me important for contemporary Christians to be aware of the reasoning in the four tracts John Milton wrote concerning divorce: *The Doctrine and Discipline of Divorce, The Judgement of Martin Bucer Concerning Divorce, Tetrachordon,* and *Colasterion.* Many fundamentalist Christians believe that divorce (except for adultery) and remarriage (under any circumstances) are denied to them by Scripture. And many other Christians go along with society's acceptance of divorce but assume that they are forced to ignore scriptural prohibitions in order to care for human need. Partly because Milton's prose is heavy reading, his scriptural arguments in favor of divorce for incompatibility have been all but lost to the contemporary Christian community. So has Milton's awareness of the many great Christian thinkers who all understood the words of Jesus "to grant divorce for causes other than adultery," among them, Tertullian, Origen, Ambrose, Jerome, Augustine, Wycliff, Luther, Calvin, Erasmus, Melanchthon, Grotius, and Archbishop Cranmer (Patterson, 701–11). In short, many Christian people have either lived in lonely misery or suffered an uneasy conscience because of their ignorance of the history of Christian thought concerning marriage and its dissolution.

From the perspective of this book, Milton's views are important because not only did he invent the word *sensuous,* but he lived a life of sensuous spirituality. His divorce tracts are particularly important because they reveal the hermeneutics of a major learned poet and theologian who regarded the Bible as the ultimate external authority for humankind. Because he believed that "the Spirit of God" wrote the Bible, he also believed that any apparent discrepancies between Scriptures are reconcilable by those willing to

189

study carefully enough and that "it is a better work to reconcile the seeming diversities of scripture, than the real dissensions of nearest friends." It is out of this assumption of an overall coherence that Milton scorns narrow-minded "quotationists" — what we would call proof-texters — and the "letter-bound servility" of "precious literalism," calling instead for informed comparative study of the statutes of God.

For his supreme interpretive principle (the norm that governs all his other assumptions) Milton obeys the law of charity (love): "We cannot safely assent to any precept written in the Bible, but as charity recommends it to us." Citing Ephesians 4:14–15, Milton argues that "the way to get a sure undoubted knowledge of things, is to hold that for truth which accords most with charity." Again and again, Milton returns to this interpretive norm: "the Christian arbitrement of charity is the supreme decider of all controversy, and the supreme resolver of all scripture." Hence, he paraphrases what Paul said about circumcision: "marriage is nothing, and divorce is nothing, 'but faith which worketh by love.' " And he asks, "Who shall answer for the perishing of all those souls, perishing by stubborn expositions of particular and inferior precepts against the general and supreme rule of charity?" Who, indeed?

Because Jesus gave his word that the law would never be abrogated while the world stands (Luke 16:17), Milton honors the laws in the Hebrew Scriptures that either permit or command divorce: Deuteronomy 13:6–9, for instance, in which the rejection of the spouse is so total that it includes execution; or Deuteronomy 24:1, or Malachi 2:15–16 in "Calvin and the best translations," which read, "he who hates, let him divorce." Pointing out that Jesus called divorce a law in Mark 10:5, Milton argues at length that whatever was permitted by the holy laws of God cannot be sin.

Because he is aware that many Christians regard Hebrew divorce law as being transcended by Jesus' words in Matthew 19:3–9, Milton does phrase-by-phrase exegesis of these words, asserting that "the vehemence of this our Saviour's speech was chiefly darted against Herod and Herodias." Citing the story of Herod's divorce of his long-time wife in order to marry his niece Herodias (who was also married at the time), Milton contends that the Pharisees who questioned Jesus were hoping to get him to contradict Moses and condemn Herod's action so that Jesus might meet the same fate as John the Baptist. "No wonder then if the sentence of our Saviour sounded stricter than his custom was . . . what Christ intends to speak here of divorce, will be rather the forbidding of what we may not do herein passionately and abusively, as Herod and Herodias did, than the discussing of what herein we may do reasonably and necessarily." In other words, Milton sees Jesus as condemning all lustful, violent divorce, not divorce based on serious mental and spiritual incompatibilities that cause lifelong misery to one or both parties.

Milton argues that in the King James Version (the English version he usually preferred, although he also knew Hebrew, Greek, Aramaic, and many other languages), the Pharisees' question about "putting away" a wife sounds softer than it probably was. In the Septuagint's headnote for Psalm 34, the same Greek word rendered "to *put away* his wife" is used to describe Abimelech's *forcing* David out of his presence. So Milton agrees with Erasmus and Hilary that the Pharisees stated their question in terms of the man's rights alone, without the wife's consent. Jesus' response was therefore meant "not to condemn all divorce, but all injury and violence in divorce."

Milton also points out that the Pharisees asked about divorcing "for every cause." (The New International Version renders "for any and every reason," a translation that supports Milton's argument.) Thus, Jesus snapped back at the Pharisees a prohibition intended to forbid "divorce for casual and temporal causes... rashly, and on the sudden heat."

Jesus' reference to "the beginning," to "one flesh," Milton understands to be a reminder to the Pharisees of the real meaning of marriage. (Among all the poets who have written in English, no one celebrates specifically *married* love more gorgeously than John Milton.) And he asks his readers, concerning Matthew 19:6, to think about the meaning of the phrase "What therefore God has joined." Has God joined people who are living together in "unfitness, wrath, contention, perpetual loneliness, perpetual discord?" Or has human error joined them? Milton concludes, "if it be unlawful... to put asunder that which God hath joined, let [us] take heed it be not detestable to join that by compulsion which God hath put asunder."

Milton strenuously denies that Jesus' words in Matthew 19:8 are intended to sweep aside an inferior Mosaic law in favor of a higher, more stringent standard of morality. At no time was divorce permitted as a necessary evil, for God's holy law does not accommodate itself to human evil. Rather, Milton interprets "hardness of heart" to refer to humankind's original fall into sin and imperfection. Once that lapse had occurred, error in choosing life partners became possible, and thus divorce was a necessary and positive "remedy against intolerable wrong and servitude above the patience of [humankind] to bear." Furthermore, Milton recognizes that by permitting responsible people to correct an error through divorce, the law also "permitted by accident the evil of them who divorced against the law's intention" — that is, those who divorced without any real reason other than the lust or whim of the moment.

What, then, of Jesus' absolute and austere words in Matthew 5:31–32, Mark 10:10–11, and Luke 16:18? Milton argues that Jesus was offended by the Pharisees' reducing the Mosaic divorce law merely to the man's giving the woman a writ of divorce, as if that were *all* the duty the law required. On the contrary, Milton says, the law applied not to any "trivial, accidental" desire for divorce, but only to "the grave causes of natural and immutable dislike" (that is, deep-seated incompatibility).

Concerning the one cause of divorce Jesus accepts here, "fornication" (KJV) or adultery, Milton spends many pages showing that Jesus did not mean merely a physical act of copulation, which would give primacy to the body (the letter) rather than to the spirit, and thus would contradict the whole tenor of Christ's teachings. Fornication, Milton argues, refers not only to physical unfaithfulness but also to "such a continual head-strong behavior, as tends to plain contempt." He cites Judges 19:2, where the Levite's wife is said to have "played the whore against him," and yet Josephus, the Septuagint, and several rabbis interpret that whoring simply as "stubbornness and rebellion against her husband." Fornication is thus roughly equivalent to the "uncleanness" for which Moses permitted divorce.

Similarly, Milton emphasized the full significance of the words *wife* and *husband:* if a person has had a genuinely compatible partner and then divorces that partner and remarries, that would constitute adultery.

Milton raged at churches and courts that would permit annulments for frigidity or impotence, but not for spiritual incompatibility: "They may be pious Christians together, they may be loving and friendly, they may be helpful to each other in the family, but they cannot couple; that shall divorce them, though either party would not. They can neither serve God together, nor be at peace with the other, nor be good in the family, one to other; but live as they were dead, or live as they were deadly enemies in a cage together: it is all one, they can couple, they shall not divorce til death, no, though this sentence be their death. What is this besides tyranny, . . . to turn nature upside down, to make both religion and the mind of man wait upon the slavish errands of the body?"

That Genesis 1 and 2 show us the prelapsarian state of humanity and therefore the ideal marriage is part of Milton's overall insistence upon placing Scripture statements within their proper historical and social contexts: prelapsarian perfection must not be confused with postlapsarian attempts to approximate perfection. Therefore we are well advised "to follow rather what moral Sinai prescribes equal to our strength, [rather] than fondly to think within our strength all that lost Paradise relates." And, as we have seen earlier, answers given to hypocritical questioners must not be confused with straight answers given to sincere seekers after truth. The ultimate context for absolutely everything is, remember, the law of love.

Using Scripture as its own best commentary and expecting God's character and commands to emerge consistent, Milton insists that doubtful or singular passages must be interpreted in the light of clear ones; that it is illogical to assume that Law would be more graceful and caring about marital misery than gospel; and that Christians should not try to be more righteous than God by prohibiting what God permits. He attacks the selectivity that prohibits divorce yet permits usury (lending for interest), which Jesus forbade in Luke 6:35.

Milton also points out that in 1 Corinthians 7:15 Paul permits a deserted person to remarry, thus expanding the parameters of what Jesus meant by fornication. He recognizes that marriage is "not in the single power of any person"; hence, if there is no real mutuality, divorce is "loosening the outward and formal tie of that which is already inwardly and really broken, or else was really never joined." Since God "hates all feigning and formality" and expects us to live peacefully, divorce in such cases becomes actively positive. Finally, like the great poet and expositor he is, Milton pays attention to figures of speech, emphasizing the important role of hyperbole (overstatement) in the Gospels, where Christ often cures excess by utilizing a contrary excess.

Milton's detractors have charged that his divorce tracts were self-serving, since his first wife, Mary Powell, who was only seventeen when she married her thirty-three-year-old scholarly husband, went home to mother several months after the wedding. The divorce tracts were all published during that desertion, which lasted from July 1642 until the summer of 1645. Yet Milton did not seek divorce from Mary and accepted her back when she finally returned, living with her until her death in 1652, just after the birth of their third child. Surely Professor J. Max Patrick is correct to say that the divorce tracts are not merely self-justification, but form part of Milton's campaign for religious, domestic, and political freedom as "aspects of his effort to continue the Reformation" (Patrick, xvii).

Still, the very real suffering of that abandonment gives special poignancy to Milton's words and may have stung him into honoring human experience more than most seventeenth-century theologians tended to do. During those painful three years Milton learned all too thoroughly that even the wisest of people can make a mistake. His sympathetic imagination also taught him that "as no man apprehends what vice is so well as he who is truly virtuous, . . . so there is none that can estimate the evil and the affliction of a natural hatred [incompatibility] in matrimony, unless he have a soul gentle enough and spacious enough to contemplate what is true love." Out of personal suffering and strenuous study of Scripture, Milton created his argument that when error or disaster have joined people together, it is charitable, wise, *and biblical* to permit them to disjoin.

DIVERSE FORMS OF FAMILY MENTIONED OR IMPLIED IN THE HEBREW AND CHRISTIAN SCRIPTURES

———— ≈ ————

1. *Patriarchal* (father-ruled) *extended families* including grandparents, servants, etc.: Abraham's household numbered 318 men, not counting women and children — Gen. 14:14

2. *Polygamous marriage:* one man with several or many wives and/or concubines and their children — Deut. 21:15

3. *Monogamous husband and promiscuous wife:* Hosea and Gomer — Hosea 1–3

4. *Female-headed extended family:* Rahab and her household — Joshua 6:17,25

5. *Matrilocal families:* Jacob and Moses lived for long periods with the birth-families of their wives — Gen. 29–31 / Exod. 2:21–22

6. *Single parents* and their children:
   a widow and her two sons — 2 Kings 4:1–7
   a widow and her resurrected son — Luke 7:11–12

7. *Levirate marriages:* a brother marrying the widow of his deceased brother — Deut. 25:5–10 / Matt. 22:23–27

8. *Families in which the wife clearly held the prestige:*
   Lappidoth and Deborah, judge of Israel — Judges 4:4
   Nabal and Abigail, who saved the family by placating King David after Nabal's rudeness — 1 Sam. 25:2–35
   Shallum and Huldah, a prophet consulted by the King of Judah — 2 Kings 22:14ff.

9. *Monogamous marriage* and the ideal of "one-fleshedness" Gen. 2:24
   Matt. 19:5

10. *Same-sex partnerships:* (1) Naomi and Ruth, later Ruth 1:16–17
    modified to an extended family in which Naomi was
    declared the mother of Ruth's son
    (2) the two disciples on the road to Emmaus who Luke 24:29
    invited Jesus to "stay with us"

11. *"Trial marriages":* among the Hebrews, sex was not Exod. 21:8
    prohibited during the betrothal period, and even
    at weddings, the major ceremony was the sexual
    intimacy itself — cf. the Song of Solomon and the
    "premarital sex" of Ruth and Boaz, Ruth 3:7

12. *Unrelated adults sharing a home:* the widows who Acts 9:36–39
    mourned Dorcas apparently lived in community

13. *Related single adults sharing a home:* Martha, Mary, and Luke 10:38–40
    Lazarus: Luke 10:38 indicates that Martha headed
    the household

14. *Celibate singles:* Jesus, John the Baptist, Paul (?)

15. *Spiritual marriages:* a Christian man and "his virgin" 1 Cor. 7:36–38
    cohabiting except for sexual intimacy — an approved
    practice until the end of the fourth century

16. *A "homeless household":* Jesus Matt. 8:20

17. *A Christian commune:* all property was held in common Acts 4:32

18. *An equal-partner, dual-career marriage:* Priscilla and Acts 18:2–3,18,
    Aquilla both traveled with Paul, team-taught the 26
    Bible, and were tentmakers by trade

**Additional Forms of Family Mentioned or Implied in the Hebrew and
Christian Scriptures Suggested by Participants at Families 2000,
A Conference Sponsored by the National Council of Churches
of Christ (Chicago, April 1991)**

19. *Immigrant families:*
    Joseph to Egypt; family followed. Gen. 42–46
    Elimelech, Naomi, and their sons to Moab Ruth 1:1–2

20. *Adoption within the extended family:* Hadassah (Esther) Esther 2:15,20
    was adopted by her cousin Mordecai
    Ephraim and Manasseh were adopted by their Gen. 48:6
    grandfather Jacob

21. *Cross-cultural adoptive family:*
    Moses was adopted by Pharaoh's daughter   Exod. 2:10
    Believers are adopted into God's family   Rom. 8:14

22. *Cross-class adoptive family:* Eliezer, a slave born in   Gen. 15:2–3
    Abraham's household, was adopted by Abraham

23. *Women living together in a harem* under the custody of   Esther 2:3
    a eunuch

24. *Cohabitation without marriage:* Samson and Delilah   Judges 16:4ff.

25. *Marriage in which sexual intimacy ceases* because of   2 Sam. 6:16–23
    alienation: King David and Michal

26. *Nomad families living in tents* in the desert:
    Jacob's family   Gen. 25:27 etc.
    Israel's forty years of wandering   Num. 14:33 etc.

27. *Widow living with her parents:* Orpah   Ruth 1:8,14–15

28. *Divorced man in second marriage:* King Ahasuerus and   Esther 2:17
    Queen Esther, after Vashti was rejected

29. *Women married by force:* the daughters of Shiloh   Judges 21
    abducted by the Benjamites; and women taken as the
    spoils of war

30. *Surrogate motherhood:*
    Hagar bore Ishmael for Abraham and Sarah   Gen. 16:1–15
    Bilhah bore Dan and Naphtali for Jacob and Rachel   Gen. 30:1–7
    Zilpah bore Gad and Asher for Jacob and Leah   Gen. 30:9–13

31. *Families established through incest:* Lot's children   Gen. 19:31–38
    conceived by his daughters

32. *Interracial/intercultural marriages:*
    Moses married Zipporah of Midian   Exod. 2:15–21
    Esau married two Canaanite wives   Gen. 27:46
    Ruth of Moab married Boaz of Israel   Ruth 4:9–10
    Ahasuerus, King of Medes and Persians, married   Esther 2:17
    Esther, a Jew
    Timothy had a Jewish mother and a Greek father   Acts 16:1–3

33. *Childless marriages:* Tamar's to Er and Onan   Gen. 38:6–10

34. *Blended families:* Jepthah was Gilead's son by a harlot;   Judges 11:1–3
    Gilead's sons by his wife rejected Jepthah.
    Herod Antipas and Herodias (with Salome, Herodias's   Luke 3:19
    daughter by her previous marriage)

35. *"Commuter marriages":* Peter, traveling with Jesus; his   Matt. 8:14
    wife and her mother living at home
    Joana, wife of Chuza (Herod's steward), traveling with   Luke 8:3
    Jesus

36. *Group living of people with physical or mental disabilities*   Luke 17:12

37. *Younger people caring for elderly people:*
    John and Mary, Jesus' mother   John 18:15–16
    Rufus and his mother   Rom. 16:13

38. *Religiously mixed marriages*   1 Cor. 7:12–16

39. *Unrelated people living in an ascetic religious community;*   Matt. 19:11–12
    adopting children to perpetuate community: the
    Essenes

40. *Unrelated people traveling with Jesus,* supported by   Luke 8:1–3
    several of the women

WORKS CITED

———— ≈ ————

Achtemeier, Elizabeth. "Female Language for God: Should the Church Adopt It?" *The Hermeneutical Quest*. Ed. Donald G. Miller. Allison Park, Pa.: Pickwick Publications, 1986.

Alperin, Mimi. "The Feminization of Poverty." *Women of Faith in Dialogue*. Ed. V. R. Mollenkott. New York: Crossroad, 1987.

Alperovitz, Gar. "Building a Living Democracy: A Whole New Way of Thinking about Politics and Economics." *Sojourners* (July 1990): 11–23.

Arapakis, Maria. *Soft Power! How to Speak Up, Set Limits, and Say No without Losing Your Lover, Your Job, or Your Friends*. New York: Warner Books, 1990.

Ardill, Susan, and Sue O'Sullivan. "Upsetting an Applecart: Difference, Desire, and Lesbian Sadomasochism." *Sexuality: A Reader*. Ed. Feminist Review. London: Virago Press, 1987.

Asiz, Sartaz. "Recollections of a Muslim Woman." *Woman of Power*. Issue Four.

Atwood, Margaret. *The Handmaid's Tale*. New York: Fawcett Crest, 1986.

Axelrod, Rise B., and Charles R. Cooper. *Reading Critically, Writing Well*. New York: St. Martin's Press, 1987.

Belenky, Mary Field, Blythe McVicker Clinchy, Nancy Rule Goldberger, and Jill Mattuck Tarule. *Women's Ways of Knowing: The Development of Self, Voice, and Mind*. New York: Basic Books, 1986.

Belsey, Catherine. *John Milton: Language, Gender, Power*. Oxford: Basil Blackwell, 1988.

Blair, Ralph. *Evangelicals (?!) Concerned*. 1982. Available from Evangelicals Concerned, Inc., 30 East 60th Street, New York, NY 10022.

Booth, Wayne C. *Critical Understanding: The Powers and Limits of Pluralism*. Chicago: University of Chicago Press, 1979.

Bradshaw, John. *Bradshaw On: The Family*. Deerfield Beach, Fla.: Health Communications, 1988.

Brady, Maureen. "Insider/Outsider Coming of Age." *Lesbian Texts and Contexts*. Ed. Karla Jay and Joanne Glasgow. New York: New York University Press, 1990.

Brown, Robert McAfee. "Protestants and the Marian Year." *Christian Century* (June 3–10, 1987): 520–21.

Broyles, William, Jr., "Why Men Love War." *Esquire* (November 1983).

Bruno, Gerald L. "Midrash and Allegory: The Beginnings of Scriptural Interpretation." *The Literary Guide to the Bible*. Cambridge, Mass.: Harvard University Press, 1987.

Bullfinch, Thomas. *Bullfinch's Mythology*. New York: Avanel Books, 1979.

Bush, Douglas, ed. *The Complete Poetical Works of John Milton*. Boston: Houghton Mifflin, 1965.

Cady, Susan, Marian Ronan, and Hal Taussig. *Wisdom's Feast: Sophia in Study and Celebration*, San Francisco: Harper & Row, 1989.

Campbell, Bebe Moore. *Successful Women, Angry Men*. New York: Random House, 1989.

Campbell, Carol Ann. "The Violence Lying Within." *The Record* (July 21, 1989), B-1.

Cannon, Katie G. *Black Womanist Ethics*. Atlanta: Scholars Press, 1988.

Capra, Fritjof. *Uncommon Wisdom*. New York: Bantam Books, 1988.

Chopra, Deepak. *Quantum Healing: Exploring the Frontiers of Mind/Body Medicine*. New York: Bantam Books, 1990.

Coats, Bill, and Catherine Randall Coats. "The Virgin Birth and Feminine History." *Plumbline* (May 1987).

Cole, William Graham. *Sex and Love in the Bible*. New York: Association Press, 1959.

Condren, Mary. *The Serpent and the Goddess*. San Francisco: Harper & Row, 1989.

Cort, J., and E. Carlevale. "Murder in Maine Renews Interest in Rights Bill." *The Advocate* (September 4, 1984).

A Course in Miracles. Farmingdale, N.Y.: Coleman Graphics, 1975.

Cowman, Mrs. Charles E. *Streams in the Desert*. Grand Rapids: Zondervan Publishing House, 1966.

Daly, Mary. *Pure Lust*. Boston: Beacon Press, 1984.

Darling, Pamela W. "'Tradition' vs. Women: Conflict and Change in the Episcopal Church, 1870–1990." Doctoral Dissertation, General Theological Seminary, New York, 1991.

Davies, Paul. *God and the New Physics*. New York: Simon & Schuster, 1984.

Douglas-Klotz, Neil. *Prayers of the Cosmos: Meditations on the Aramaic Words of Jesus*. New York: Harper & Row, 1990.

Eisler, Riane. *The Chalice and the Blade: Our History, Our Future*. San Francisco: Harper & Row, 1987.

Engelsman, Joan Chamberlain, and Deborah Pope-Lance. *Domestic Violence: A Guide for Clergy*. Trenton: New Jersey Department of Community Affairs, 1987.

Eschel, Shuli. *Women's Peace in the Middle East*. Videotape available for sale or rental from Shuli Eschel, 4831 Conrad Street, Apt. 2B, Skokie, IL 60077. Telephone (708) 679-6511.

Fabella, Virginia. "Mission of Women in the Church in Asia: Role and Position." *New Eyes for Reading: Biblical and Theological Reflections by Women in the Third World*. Oak Park, Ill.: Meyer-Stone, 1987.

Fee, Gordon D., and Douglas Stuart. *How to Read the Bible for All Its Worth*. Grand Rapids: Zondervan, 1982.

Fish, Stanley. *Is There a Text in This Class? The Authority of Interpretive Communities*. Cambridge, Mass.: Harvard University Press, 1980.

Frye, Roland Mushat. "Language for God and Feminist Language." *Interpretation: A Journal of Bible and Theology* 38 (1987): 45–57.

Gert, Bernard. *The Moral Rules: A New Rational Foundation for Morality*. New York: Harper & Row, 1973.

Gilligan, Carol. *In a Different Voice*. Cambridge, Mass.: Harvard University Press, 1982.

Gordon, Linda, and Paul O'Keefe. "Incest as a Form of Family Violence: Evidence from Historical Case Records." *Journal of Marriage and the Family* (February 1984): 27–34.

Gray, Elizabeth Dodson. *Patriarchy as a Conceptual Trap*. Wellesley, Mass.: Round-table Press, 1982.

Gunther, Sharon. Participant at Sisterly Conversations, Kirkridge, November 2-4, 1990.

Harrison, Beverly Wildung. "Situating the Dilemma of Abortion Historically." *Conscience: A Newsjournal of Prochoice Catholic Opinion* 11, no. 2 (March–April 1990): 15–20.

Henry, William A., III. "To 'Out' or Not to 'Out.'" *Time* (August 19, 1991): 17.

Heyward, Carter. *Speaking of Christ: A Lesbian Feminist Voice*. New York: Pilgrim Press, 1989.

————. *Touching Our Strength: The Erotic as Power and the Love of God*. San Francisco: Harper & Row, 1989.

Hobday, Sister Maria Jose. "Room for the Dance." *Parabola* 15, no. 4 (November 1990).

Hunt, Mary E. *Fierce Tenderness: A Feminist Theology of Friendship*. New York: Crossroad, 1991.

Hunter, William B., ed. *A Milton Encyclopedia*. 8 vols. Lewisburg, Pa.: Bucknell University Press, 1980.

Hurst, Jane. "History of Abortion in the Catholic Church." *Conscience: A Newsjournal of Prochoice Catholic Opinion* 12, no. 2 (March–April 1991): 1–17.

An Inclusive Language Lectionary: Readings for Year A, Revised Edition. New York: Pilgrim Press, 1986.

Interpreter's Dictionary of the Bible. Nashville: Abingdon Press, 1962.

Johnston, Robert K. "Interpreting Scripture: Literary Criticism and Evangelical Hermeneutics." *Christianity & Literature* 32 (Fall 1982): 33–47.

Kamperidis, Lambros. "Philoxenia and Hospitality." *Parabola* (Winter 1990): 5–13.

Keller, Evelyn Fox. *Reflections on Gender and Science*. New Haven: Yale University Press, 1985.

Knight, George, III. *The New Testament Teaching on the Role Relationship of Men and Women*. Grand Rapids: Baker, 1977.

Larson, Janet Karsten. "Margaret Atwood's Testaments: Resisting the Gilead Within." *Christian Century* (May 20–27, 1987): 496–98.

Lebacyz, Karen. "Abortion: Getting Our Ethics Straight." *Christian Reflections on the Issues of Abortion*. New York: Advisory Council of Church and Society, n.d.

Lerner, Michael. *Surplus Powerlessness: The Psychodynamics of Everyday Life . . . and the Psychology of Individual and Social Transformation*. Oakland, Calif.: Institute for Labor and Mental Health, 1986.

Leverenz, David. "Emerson's Man-Making Words." *Speaking of Gender*. Ed. Elaine Showalter. New York: Routledge, 1989.

Lieberman, Mendel, and Marion Hardie. *Resolving Family and Other Conflicts: Everybody Wins*. Santa Cruz, Calif.: Unity Press, 1981.

Lorde, Audre. "A Question of Survival." *Gay Community News* (August 13–19, 1989).

———. "Uses of the Erotic: The Erotic as Power." *Sister Outsider*. Trumansburg, N.Y.: Crossing Press, 1984.

Macourt, Malcolm, ed. *Towards a Theology of Gay Liberation*. London: SCM Press, 1977.

Marcus, Leah. "Shakespeare's Comic Heroines, Elizabeth I, and the Political Uses of Androgyny." *Women in the Middle Ages and the Renaissance*. Ed. Mary Beth Rose. Syracuse: Syracuse University Press, 1986.

May, Rollo. *Love and Will*. New York: W. W. Norton, 1969.

Meeks, Wayne A. *The Writings of St. Paul*. New York: W. W. Norton, 1972.

Michnik, Adam. "Notes on the Revolution." *New York Times Magazine* (March 11, 1990).

Miller, Casey, and Kate Swift. *Words & Women*. Garden City, N.Y.: Anchor/Doubleday, 1976.

Minutes of the General Assembly of the United Presbyterian Church in the USA, 1970, vol. 1.

Mollenkott, Virginia Ramey. "Exploring Fundamentalist Hermeneutics." Available from the Evangelical and Ecumenical Women's Caucus, Box 209, Hadley, NY 12835.

———. *Women, Men, and the Bible*. Nashville: Abingdon, 1977.

———. *The Divine Feminine: Biblical Imagery of God as Female*. New York: Crossroad, 1983.

———. "Critical Inquiry and Biblical Inerrancy." *Religion and Public Education* 17 (Winter 1990).

Mudflower Collective. *God's Fierce Whimsy*. New York: Pilgrim Press, 1985.

Orr, Lisa, ed. *Sexual Values: Opposing Viewpoints*. San Diego, Calif.: Greenhaven Press, 1989.

Ozick, Cynthia. "Ruth." *Congregation: Contemporary Writers Read the Jewish Bible*. Ed. David Rosenberg. New York: Harcourt Brace Jovanovich, 1987.

Patrick, J. Max. *The Prose of John Milton*. Garden City, N.Y.: Doubleday, 1967.

Patterson, Frank Allen, ed. *The Student's Milton*. Rev. ed. New York: Appleton, Century-Crofts, 1961.

Paul, William W. "Decision." *Baker's Dictionary of Christian Ethics*. Ed. Carl F. H. Henry. N.p.: Canon Press, 1973.

Peck, M. Scott, M.D. *The Different Drum: Community-Making and Peace*. New York: Simon & Schuster, 1987.

Perry, Donna. "Procne's Song: The Task of Feminist Literary Criticism." *Gender/Body/Knowledge: Feminist Reconstructions of Being and Knowing*. Ed. Alison M. Jaggar and Susan R. Bordo. New Brunswick, N.J.: Rutgers University Press, 1989.

Petchesky, Rosalind Pollack. *Abortion and Woman's Choice: The State, Sexuality, and Reproductive Freedom*. Boston: Northeastern University Press, 1984.

Phipps, William E. *Recovering Biblical Sensuousness*. Philadelphia: Westminster Press, 1975. Despite its profoundly heterosexist bias, I am heavily indebted to this work.

Radl, Shirley Rogers. *The Invisible Woman: Target of the Religious New Right*. New York: Dell, 1983.

Reports to the 203rd General Assembly (1991), Presbyterian Church (U.S.A.): Part I. Louisville: Office of the General Assembly, 1991.

Rich, Adrienne. *Compulsory Heterosexuality and Lesbian Experience*. Denver: Antelope Publications, 1980.

Robinson, Wayne Bradley. *The Transforming Power of the Bible*. New York: Pilgrim Press, 1984.

Rose, Mary Beth. *Women in the Middle Ages and the Renaissance*. Syracuse: Syracuse University Press, 1986.

Ruether, Rosemary Radford. "Brain Theory." *Christian Century* (March 8, 1989): 263–64.

————. "Women, Sexuality, Ecology, and the Church." *Conscience: A Newsjournal of Prochoice Catholic Opinion* 11 (July–August 1990): 1–11.

Ryrie, Charles C. *The Place of Women in the Church*. New York: Macmillan, 1958.

Scanzoni, Letha. *Sexuality: Choices–Guides for Today's Woman*. Philadelphia: Westminster Press, 1984.

Scanzoni, Letha, and Virginia Ramey Mollenkott. *Is the Homosexual My Neighbor?* San Francisco: Harper & Row, 1978.

Schaef, Anne Wilson, and Diane Fassel. *The Addictive Organization*. San Francisco: Harper & Row, 1988.

Schuller, Robert. *Self-Esteem: The New Reformation*. Waco, Tex.: Word Books, 1982.

Scroggs, Robin. *The New Testament and Homosexuality*. Philadelphia: Fortress, 1984.

Showalter, Elaine. *Speaking of Gender*. New York: Routledge, 1989.

Smedley, Lauren. "Further than F.A.R. [Feminists for Animal Rights]: In Search of a New Name." *Feminists for Animal Rights* 5 (Summer–Fall 1990).

Smith, Wallace Charles. *The Church in the Life of the Black Family*. Valley Forge, Pa.: Judson Press, 1985.

Soskice, Janet Martin. *Metaphor and Religious Language*. Oxford: Clarendon Press, 1985.

Sperry, Lin, M.D., Ph.D. "From Teddy Bear to God-Image: Object Relations Theory and Religious Development." *Psychologists Interested in Religious Issues Newsletter*, 14: 5–8.

Stagg, Evelyn and Frank. *Women in the World of Jesus*. Philadelphia: Westminster Press, 1978.

Stoltenberg, John. *Refusing to Be a Man: Essays on Sex and Justice*. New York: Penguin Books USA, 1990.

Swartley, Willard M. *Slavery, Sabbath, War, and Women: Case Issues in Biblical Interpretation*. Scottdale, Pa.: Herald Press, 1983.

Tannahill, Reay. *Sex in History*. New York: Stein and Day, 1982.

Taylor, Michael J., S.J. *Sex: Thoughts for Contemporary Christians*. Garden City, N.Y.: Doubleday, 1972.

Thistlethwaite, Susan. Conversation, April 9, 1991. Thistlethwaite, whose husband is a surgeon, was shown the warning by emergency room nurses.

Trawick, Buckner B. *The Bible as Literature: The Old Testament and the Apocrypha*. New York: Barnes and Noble, 1970.

Trible, Phyllis. *God and the Rhetoric of Sexuality*. Philadelphia: Fortress, 1978.

Tripp, Edward. *Crowell's Handbook of Classical Mythology*. New York: Thomas Y. Crowell, 1970.

Tuttle, Paul Norman. *Conversations with Raj Newsletter*. Available for $15.00 per year from Northwest Foundation for A Course in Miracles, Box 870, Hanalei, HI 96714.

———. *You Are the Answer: A Journey of Awakening*. Seattle, Wash.: Kairos, Inc., 1985.

Tyson, Patricia A. "The Force of Women of Color and Reproductive Rights: An Expanded Agenda beyond Abortion." *Common Ground, Different Planes: Religious Coalition for Abortion Rights Women of Color Partnership Program Newsletter* (Spring 1991).

Unger, Merrill F. *The New Unger's Bible Dictionary*. Ed. R. K. Harrison. Chicago: Moody Press, 1988.

Waetjen, Herman C. "Abortion and the New Testament." *Christian Reflections on the Issues of Abortion*. New York: Advisory Council of Church & Society, n.d.

Walker, Barbara G. *The Crone: Woman of Age, Wisdom, and Power*. San Francisco: Harper & Row, 1985.

Welch, Sharon. *Communities of Resistance and Solidarity*. Maryknoll, N.Y.: Orbis Books, 1985.

White, Zoe. Letter to Virginia Ramey Mollenkott from Brussells, Belgium, September 20, 1990. Used by permission.

Wren, Brian. *What Language Shall I Borrow? God-Talk in Worship: A Male Response to Feminist Theology*. New York: Crossroad, 1989.

Young, Robert. *Young's Analytical Concordance*. Grand Rapids, Mich.: Associated Publishers and Authors, n.d.